T0360587

The Role of Distributed Ledger Technology in Banking

Distributed Ledger Technology (DLT) is a way of managing, storing, and sharing information over a distributed network. The position of DLT in banking can be seen as controversial as it is a rapidly evolving technology with both potential benefits and challenges. *The Role of Distributed Ledger Technology in Banking* presents a balanced assessment of both the opportunities and risks behind such recent innovations. Combining theory and practice, it explores the impact of DLT in the banking sector and offers the opportunity to exploit different points of view from different disciplines. It presents topics from both a theoretical and practical point of view, highlighting concrete applications. Written by a team of experts from academia and the banking sector, this book looks at DLT not as a threat but as an exciting opportunity to bring the banking/financial system in the future.

SABRINA LEO is Tenure Track Assistant Professor at Sapienza University of Rome. She is a lecturer in Strategies, Performance, and Digital Innovation in banking. Her main research areas are DLT, digital payments, digital banking, and IT Governance in banks, and recently on the impact of technologies like AI/ML in the financial system.

IDA CLAUDIA PANETTA is Full Professor at the Sapienza University of Rome, where she teaches International Financial Markets and Institutions and Bank Economics and Management. Her more recent research interests (and publications) regard the impact of new technologies in reshaping the financial system, focusing in particular on Mobile Payment, DLTs, and Cybersecurity.

The Role of Distributed Ledger Technology in Banking

From Theory to Practice

Edited by

SABRINA LEO
Sapienza University of Rome

IDA CLAUDIA PANETTA
Sapienza University of Rome

CAMBRIDGE
UNIVERSITY PRESS

CAMBRIDGE
UNIVERSITY PRESS

Shaftesbury Road, Cambridge CB2 8EA, United Kingdom

One Liberty Plaza, 20th Floor, New York, NY 10006, USA

477 Williamstown Road, Port Melbourne, VIC 3207, Australia

314–321, 3rd Floor, Plot 3, Splendor Forum, Jasola District Centre, New Delhi – 110025, India

103 Penang Road, #05–06/07, Visioncrest Commercial, Singapore 238467

Cambridge University Press is part of Cambridge University Press & Assessment, a department of the University of Cambridge.

We share the University's mission to contribute to society through the pursuit of education, learning and research at the highest international levels of excellence.

www.cambridge.org
Information on this title: www.cambridge.org/9781009411745

DOI: 10.1017/9781009411783

First published 2024

A catalogue record for this publication is available from the British Library

A Cataloging-in-Publication data record for this book is available from the Library of Congress

ISBN 978-1-009-41174-5 Hardback

Pat, Pat

Contents

Figures

Tables

Boxes

Contributors

ANTONIO ADINOLFI is a lawyer and lecturer at Scuola di Polizia Tributaria (Guardia di Finanza). Since 2003, he was Head of Unit (within the Treasury Department, DG Prevention of Use of the Financial System for Illegal Purposes, now DG Banking and Finance, Ministry of Economy and Finance). In 2015, he became a member of the G7 Cyber Expert Group. In 2018, he was appointed the co-chair of International Co-operation Review Group (ICRG)- Financial Action Task Force (FATF). In 2022, he became FATF Head of Delegation of Italy. In 2020, he became a substitute member of Financial Security Committee. Until 2020, he served as Director of the Central Means of Payment Anti-Fraud Office.

ALESSANDRO AGNOLETTI is Head of Digital Currency & DLT at Nexi, with responsibility for positioning the company both in the field of digital currencies and in the application of DLT technologies to new inclusive and systemic payment solutions. He was previously Head of Innovation at SIA and has also held various roles in the areas of strategy and innovation at Bain & Company, H-Farm, and CDILabs, a startup he co-founded. Alessandro holds a degree in International Management from the Università Cattolica in Milan and an MBA from the Collège des Ingénieurs in Paris.

FILIPPO ANNUNZIATA is Associate Professor of Financial Markets and Banking Legislation at Bocconi University. He was Co-Director of the RULES Unit, Baffi-Carefin Centre, Bocconi University; Academic Board Member of European Banking Institute; Academic Member and Fellow of Jean Monnet Centre of Excellence EU Sustainable Finance and Law (EUSFIL); and Board Member of European Society for Banking and Financial Law (AEDBF) of Italy.

SILVIA ATTANASIO is Head of Innovation in Associazione Bancaria Italiana (ABI) since May 2019 and Member of the ECB Digital Euro Market Advisory Group. She graduated in Statistical Science and

Economics. She worked for more than 15 years starting from its foundation in ABI Lab Consortium. Since 2017, she has been project leader for the Spunta project, an initiative of implementation of DLT applied to the interbank reconciliation process.

BIAGIO BOSSONE is Economist and a financial advisor to international institutions, national governments, and private sector financial institutions. He is also a banker and former central banker. He is the (co-)author of several studies and publications on economics, finance, and economic development.

ANDREA CIVELLI is Associate Professor in Economics at the Walton College of Business (University of Arkansas) and former Senior Economist at Algorand Inc. Andrea's research interests focus on monetary policy transmission and inflation modelling, with a particular interest in the role of the banking sector and business loan supply in the propagation of macroeconomic shocks. His research has been published in numerous economics and financial journals. Andrea received a PhD in Economics from Princeton University in 2010 and also held visiting positions at UT Austin and NC State University.

ANDREA DALY is graduated in Law from 'Università degli Studi di Torino'. After working as a lawyer, Andrea entered the Sella Group Compliance in 2015, specialising in investment services and then in crypto-assets regulation. Currently, he is Head of 'Compliance Investment Services Research and Consulting & Digital Assets' at Banca Sella Holding.

PAOLA DEL VITTO has worked in the Innovation Office of ABI since January 2020 until March 2023 following the evolution of the ECB project on the digital euro and other subjects concerning digitalization of Financial Institutions.

ANDREA DELLE FOGLIE received a PhD in Banking and Finance (Sapienza University of Rome) and is currently Contract Professor at the Department of Law and Economics, University of Macerata and Postdoctoral Research Fellow in Banking and Financial Intermediaries at the Department of Management, Sapienza University of Rome. He focuses on the field of international financial systems, particularly the regulatory framework of the banking system, Islamic Banking and Finance, sustainable finance, and financial markets' technology application.

CLAUDIO DI CICCIO is an associate professor at the Department of Computer Science at Sapienza University of Rome (Italy). His research spans across the domains of process mining, formal logics in AI, and blockchain technologies. He is Member of the Steering Committee of the IEEE Task Force on Process Mining.

EMANUELA GIUSI GAETA received a PhD in Political Economy Sapienza University; she was Researcher in Political Economy Tor Vergata University and Supervisor of Research Projects in Criminal Economy. She teaches courses on Political Economy, Political Economics, Monetary Economics, International Economics, Applied Economics, Criminal Economy, and Endogenous Growth course at the Research Doctorate. Her research areas are Cryptocurrencies Market, Energy-Saving Technologies, Technological Transfer, and Criminal Economy.

CO-PIERRE GEORG is Associate Professor at EDHEC Business School. Previously, he held the South African Reserve Bank Research Chair at University of Cape Town. He is Director of the Algorand-UCT Financial Innovation Hub. Co-Pierre teaches courses on 'Fintech and Cryptocurrencies'. His research interests focus on the nexus of financial innovation and financial stability. He obtained his PhD from the University of Jena in 2011 and has published both in finance and interdisciplinary journals. Co-Pierre's research has received awards from the Algorand Foundation, the Ripple University Blockchain Research Initiative, the European Central Bank, and the Volkswagen Foundation. He has been a consultant at various central banks and held visiting positions at MIT, Oxford, Princeton, and Columbia University.

PIETRO GRASSANO is Business Consultant in the Asset Management and Fintech space. He has been Business Solutions Director – Europe at Algorand between 2019 and 2022. At J.P. Morgan Asset Management from 2002 until 2019, Pietro has been Head of Sales for Italy, responsible for business in Greece, and Country Head for France. Having previously worked in BNP Paribas and Accenture, he has more than 20 years of experience in the asset management sector. He holds a master's in economics and social sciences (DES) from Bocconi University in Milan.

JOHN HO is Global Head of Legal, Financial Markets for Standard Chartered Bank. He is a mentor for the UK FCA Digital Sandbox and is an active participant in the industry's Fintech events and is a public speaker on topics such as Blockchain, Digital Assets, Financial Markets, Sustainability, and Regulatory Reforms.

NAVEED IHSANULLAH is VP of Engineering Research at Algorand where he focuses on future technology and features for Algorand's blockchain platform. He is a senior engineering leader and technologist with more than 20 years of experience and continues to be fascinated by distributed systems and performance. Most recently of Mozilla, Naveed was instrumental in designing and leading the Quantum Flow program that focused 400 engineers to double Firefox's performance in just one year. He also led the adoption of new technologies across all the major browsers (Chrome, Safari, and Firefox) to close the performance gap with native applications. These technologies include WebAssembly, SIMD.js, and Shared Array Buffer. Naveed is also previously of Carbon Black (then Bit9) where his teams developed next-generation application security software and cloud-based software reputation services. Passionate about improving how enterprises use technology, he has consulted on large organisational-level projects for Fortune 500 companies including Boeing Jeppesen.

TAIJI INUI is proposing Asia Digital Common Currency (ADCC) with Professor Wataru Takahashi. He proposed a digital currency before Bitcoin. He is a JICA expert, an ADB consultant, and an ISO/TC68 member. He worked for BOJ and NTT Data developed payment infrastructures in Japan. He was also a member of BIS meetings.

SABRINA LEO, a PhD graduate in Banking and Finance, is Tenure Track Assistant Professor at Sapienza University of Rome. She is a lecturer in Strategies and Performance of bank accounts and Digital Banking. Her main research areas are DLT, Digital Payments, Digital Banking, and IT Governance in banks, and recently on the impact of technologies like AI/ML in the financial system.

HARISH NATARAJAN leads a global team working on payments and market infrastructures topics in the Finance, Competitiveness, and Innovation Global Practice at the World Bank. His work spans Payments and market infrastructures, Financial Inclusion, Digital ID, Digital Economy, and FinTech. He represents the World Bank in several international working groups on these topics.

IDA CLAUDIA PANETTA, a PhD graduate in Banking and Finance, is Full Professor at the Sapienza University of Rome, where she teaches International Financial Markets and Institutions and Bank Economics and Management. Ida's more recent research interests (and publications) regard the impact of new technologies in reshaping the financial system, focusing in particular on Mobile payment, DLTs, and Cybersecurity.

GIANCARLO SFOLCINI is a senior product manager within Digital Currency & DLT at Nexi, with focus on new business models enabled by emerging technologies. He has developed various experience leading innovation project in energy (ENI), telecommunications (BT), and managing consulting (EY).

WATARU TAKAHASHI received MPhil in Economics from Oxford University in 1984 (Tutor; Prof. John Muellbauer, Nuffield). Prior to the current position, he had worked at the Bank of Japan for 35 years, mostly in academic research sections. He also worked for international affairs as an advisor to the Governor from 2001 to 2006.

Acknowledgements

Dear Readers,

First of all, we want to express our sincere gratitude to you for expressing interest in our book and wanting to take the time to read it. Your interest means a lot to us, and we are honoured to have you as part of our audience.

We want to express our heartfelt gratitude to all the authors for their work. Your contributions have not gone unnoticed, and we truly appreciate the time and care you have taken to help bring our project to life. We thank you for believing in it as much as we do. Your insights and expertise have had a significant impact, and we are grateful for the opportunity to work with you.

We want to extend special thanks to Alicia Brewer and AcademicWord, whose tireless efforts and attention to detail significantly improved our chapters in this book.

We would also like to convey our appreciation to Vincenzo Contri and to the Editorial Team at Cambridge University Press for their expert guidance and recommendations throughout the publishing process. We appreciate their commitment to making this idea a reality and their conviction in it.

Finally, we would like to acknowledge our Families, whose encouragement and support made this book possible. Their love and belief in us have inspired us, and we are forever grateful for their unwavering support.

Introduction
The Banking in the Era
of Distributed Ledgers

SABRINA LEO AND IDA CLAUDIA PANETTA

Distributed ledger technology (DLT) refers to a decentralised and distributed digital system for recording and verifying transactions where multiple parties have access to the same database and can validate transactions without the need for intermediaries. A network of nodes maintains and updates the database, and transactions are secured through cryptography.

The conceptualisation of DLT can be traced back to the 1990s, but the first practical application of DLT was the creation of Bitcoin in 2009. Since then, DLT has evolved and expanded and is now being used in a wide range of industries. Among other sectors, the financial system as a whole, and banking in particular, have started to apply DLT to improve financial transactions and processes and to offer new products and services to their customers. In this sense, the financial system is going to be reshaped from the inside, in a process managed by the institutions that belong to it, exploiting the following main straights of DLTs:

- Security: DLT systems use cryptography to secure transactions and ensure that data cannot be altered retroactively.
- Transparency: They provide a shared ledger that is publicly accessible, making it easier to track transactions, and detect fraudulent activity.
- Efficiency: They can automate many manual processes, reducing errors and saving time.
- Decentralisation: They do not rely on a single central authority, reducing the risk of downtime and increasing the system's resilience.
- Cost savings: They can reduce the need for intermediaries, reducing the cost of financial transactions and improving accessibility.
- Traceability: They provide a clear and transparent record of transactions, making it easier to track the movement of assets and prevent money laundering.

By improving the efficiency, security, and transparency of financial transactions, this technology has the potential to (i) streamline payment processing: DLT is being used to automate and streamline payment processing, reducing the time and cost of transactions; (ii) reduce redundancy of roles: DLT is being used to eliminate intermediaries in financial transactions, reducing the cost and increasing the efficiency of these transactions; (iii) improve security: DLT is being used to improve the security of financial transactions, reducing the risk of fraud and hacking; and (iv) provide more access to financial services: DLT is being used to create new financial services and to provide access to financial services to those who previously lacked access, such as the unbanked and underbanked populations.

Due to the potential to provide significant benefits to the financial system, many traditional banks, stand-alone or joining a consortium, are exploring ways to use DLT to improve their services and remain competitive. At the same time, DLT has the potential to pose a threat to the traditional banking system for several reasons. First of all, by enabling decentralised and peer-to-peer transactions, DLT may reduce the need for intermediaries and disrupt the traditional business models of banks. Furthermore, being a decentralised technology, DLT takes away from banks the control they traditionally exert on the financial system. Moreover, DLT, equally to the other disruptive technologies that are reshaping banking models in recent years, has the potential to create new players in the financial services industry, increasing competition for traditional banks.

Security concerns are a key issue in evaluating the threats of DLT in the financial sector. While this technology can improve the security of financial transactions, there is still a risk of cyberattacks and other security breaches, which could threaten the financial system's stability. Finally, banking faces many regulatory challenges. Often, DLT operates outside of the traditional regulatory framework, and there are still questions about how this technology will be regulated and what impact this will have on traditional banks.

In light of the above, the position of DLT in banking can be seen as controversial as it is a rapidly evolving technology with both potential benefits and challenges. It is crucial for individuals and organisations to carefully evaluate the potential impact of DLT on the banking industry and to make informed decisions based on their risk tolerance and business objectives. Even current literature is unable to provide a definite answer. The academic literature on DLT in banking typically takes a multi-disciplinary approach, incorporating computer science, finance, economics, and law insights. Some of the key themes that the academic literature addresses include:

- Technical aspects of DLT: many studies focus on the technical aspects of DLT, exploring how this technology can improve the efficiency, security, and transparency of financial transactions.
- Economic implications of DLT: other studies focus on the economic implications of DLT, exploring how this technology is changing the financial landscape and what this means for traditional banks and other financial intermediaries.
- Regulatory challenges: the academic literature also addresses the regulatory challenges posed by DLT, exploring the need for new regulatory frameworks to ensure that this technology is used safely and responsibly.
- Social and ethical implications: some studies also focus on the social and ethical implications of DLT, exploring the impact this technology has on society, and considering the ethical and social issues that must be addressed.

To explore the impact of DLT in the banking sector (as of December 2022), we offer the reader the opportunity to exploit different points of view of contributors pertaining to different disciplines. In doing so, the book attempts to combine theory and practice in two ways: (i) by involving academic contributors of international relevance, authors from regional and international institutions, and practitioners active in the financial system and (ii) by trying as much as possible to represent the topic in each chapter from both a theoretical and practical point of view, also highlighting concrete applications with the help of boxes. Aiming to create a more effective and engaging experience for the reader, the book is divided into the following five parts:

(i) Why pay attention to Distributed Ledger Technology in the banking? (Chapters 1–2)
(ii) Opportunities and Challenges in Crypto-Asset Regulation (Chapters 3–5)
(iii) The Power of Distributed Ledgers in Payments (Chapters 6–9)

(iv) Enabling Financial Inclusion and ESG with Distributed Ledger Technology (Chapters 10–11)
(v) A Further Look at DLT in Banking: Lessons Learned, Current Applications, and Future Scenarios (Chapters 12–13).

Going deeper into the book's content, Chapter 1, authored by Di Ciccio, recalls the technical aspects of DLT and blockchain and their economic implications, which helps address and better understand the technical aspects addressed in the following chapters. Particular attention is paid to the technical features, essential procedures and guarantees, and implementation in a decentralised way. The advantages and disadvantages of this technology are also highlighted.

In Chapter 2, Leo and Delle Foglie, with a purely academic approach, conduct a thorough literature review to define the shape of research carried out by researchers on the topic, in the belief that scientific research can significantly contribute to finding solutions to address critical issues arising from banking, given its fundamental role in the growth of today's market economies.

Chapters 3 – authored by Annunziata – and 4 – edited by Daly – present two different views on regulatory issues, the former more academic, the latter from a banker's point of view. More in detail, Annunziata focuses on major concerns posed by the Markets in Crypto-assets Regulation (MiCA), and Daly underlines how regulatory uncertainty, stemming mainly from confusion regarding the legal classification of crypto-assets, hinders the provision of services by banks and increases risks for consumers and investors. Chapter 5, written by Adinolfi and Gaeta, discusses how the nature of Virtual Asset Service Providers (VASPs) can be used for criminal purposes; in this scenario, authors point out how regulation is necessary for the uncontrolled development of the illicit exploitation of a DLT as an upstream subject of VASPs, and the role of the Financial Action Task Force (FAFT) in orienting international actions to counteract cyber laundering phenomenon throughout VASPs.

DLT is largely used to transform the payment system. Chapter 6, co-authored by Agnoletti and Sfolcini, discusses how flexibility, transparency, and rapid scalability of DLT and cryptographic resources could revolutionise the finance and payments industry. The authors assert that the payments industry has an opportunity to innovate, particularly in cross-border, micro, and conditional payments.

Moreover, how, for this innovation to reach its full potential, existing high levels of risk and uncertainty must be addressed and a clear and shared regulatory framework developed between national and cross-border authorities. The authors post on the case of Nexi, which drives a safe and easy transition to a better society by promoting widespread inclusion, protecting all private and public stakeholders, and regulatory clarity.

The use of DLT allows for a decentralised and secure system for issuing and managing Central Bank Digital Currencies (CBDCs). Consequently, we devoted Chapters 7–9 to address the issue from several points of view.

Chapter 7, written by Civelli, Georg, Grassano, and Ihsanullah, covers three main themes. First, it identifies the difficulties a CBDC might respond to and reasons for understanding them better. Second, it examines ideal CBDC design concepts based on interviews with central banks, national and supranational authorities, market actors, and academics in different jurisdictions. Finally, it presents an Algorand-based retail CBDC system that fits these design standards. Chapter 8, written by Attanasio and Del Vitto, through an illustration of the Spunta DLT project, discusses how the Italian Banking Association has concretely brought licensed blockchain to the Italian banking sector through an infrastructure for banks operating in Italy that will be able to host other applications. Then, the chapter discusses the European Central Bank's (ECB) ability to issue a CBDC and the Associazione Bancaria Italiana's (ABI) position. This competition illustrates an experiment of the digital euro based on the DLT experience. While Chapter 9, by Taiji and Wataru, argues for introducing an Asian digital common currency (ADCC) as a multilateral synthetic currency that coexists with local currencies in the region. Using DLT, the issuance of ADCC is relatively simple, similar to how central banks today receive physical banknotes produced at the printing office. Each country's central bank would then issue ADCC as its liability secured by ADCC-denominated bonds because ADCC is not each central bank's legal tender and is distributed to national economies through commercial banks to be used for cross-border payments.

The book then focuses on the role of DLT in financial inclusion in Chapter 10, authored by Natarajan and Bossone. The authors analyse this potential, using the literature on the underlying reasons for financial exclusion and what has worked, juxtaposing them with the benefits of DLT and how they might be relevant in addressing the underlying causes. The chapter describes the challenges in realising DLT's potential and risks.

Ho, in Chapter 11, focuses instead on the fact that the popularity of digital assets and blockchain solutions is accelerating, exploring the environmental, social, and governance (ESG) impact of digital assets due to the growing participation of retail and institutional investors. For the author, blockchain technology can help financial institutions achieve favourable corporate ESG outcomes.

Chapter 12, co-authored by Panetta and Leo, looks into the metaverse's intermediaries. The authors investigate that the metaverse is receiving significant attention from the banking industry because of its endless possibilities for virtual consumer interactions. As a natural progression of their sector, banks are interested in seeking the metaverse to develop stronger ties with their customers as they increasingly use technology to deliver their services. However, the value added for banks needs to be thoroughly analysed, and the absence of precise regulation may create reluctance. In addition, the metaverse may increase concerns about cybercrime in the financial and banking sectors. In the chapter, the authors examine banks' approaches to the metaverse as a new method of using the promise of DLT and provide a framework summarising the development prospects (and risks) for financial intermediaries.

Finally, in Chapter 13, Leo and Panetta provide an overview of DLT in the banking sector, highlighting current problems and fundamental changes in the industry. To this aim, the chapter examines the major DLT projects and implementations in the banking sector, classifying them into two main categories based on the type of need being met-that is, products and services designed to meet the needs of customers of financial institutions and internal processes and operations aimed at meeting the needs of financial intermediaries. The authors, in the chapter, focus on the main characteristics of the prevalent use cases in the industry, highlighting strengths and weaknesses.

In light of the above, we hope the book could be a valuable source of knowledge and information on the role of DLT in the banking system. Unlike others in this contribution, we want to emphasise how DLT can be used to respond to new user needs and pressures from competitors. DLT can represent an opportunity and not a threat to the banking system.

In a nutshell, the book looks at DLT not as a threat (as it did for banks in the first instance), not as a panacea (as it does for cypherpunks and blockchain enthusiasts), but as an exciting opportunity to bring the banking/financial system in the future (as scholars and academics should see it).

PART I

Why Pay Attention to Distributed Ledger Technology in Banking?

1 | Blockchain and Distributed Ledger Technologies

CLAUDIO DI CICCIO

Introduction

Distributed ledger technologies (DLTs) have attracted significant attention in the last few years. They gained a noticeable momentum, particularly after the introduction of blockchains as a basic building block for the development of new cryptocurrencies and tokens. This opportunity opened up new research directions to support the modern economy with numerous possibilities to redesign and innovate the market in accordance with the digital revolution we are witnessing. However, these technologies are yet to prove in practice their capability to match all the dependability and security requirements imposed in the economic and banking sector. In this chapter, we will provide an overview of the technical features of DLTs (and of blockchains in particular), outlining their potential impact in the economic field (Box 1.1). We will first introduce the reader to their definition from a technical point of view, illustrate its core mechanisms and the guarantees they provide, and describe how these features are realised in a decentralised way. Finally, we will draw opportunities and challenges stemming from the adoption of this technology. We begin this journey with a synthetic definition.

As is typical of synthetic definitions, the one below can also be seen as simplistic yet complex to catch at first read. In an attempt to compensate for both issues, we will delve deeper into the fundamental notions and devices behind distributed ledger and blockchain technologies.

Transactions and Ledgers

The building block of blockchains is the **transaction**. A transaction is a digital record that registers the transfer of value (and data) between accounts. Once processed, the transaction triggers the movement of crypto-assets (also known as cryptocurrencies) such as Bitcoin (BTC)

Box 1.1   Distributed ledger and blockchain

A distributed ledger is a registry replicated over a network of nodes that records the sequence of transactions between senders and recipients. A blockchain is a distributed ledger that uses blocks to collate sections of the ledger. DLTs, such as those underneath the blockchain platforms, are designed to guarantee properties that preserve the storage, exchange, and update of data, such as verifiability, liveness, robustness, and permanence.

---

or Ether (ETH). A transaction involves at least a sender account for the input and a recipient account for the output. Every transaction is digitally signed by the sender to show evidence that the account owner – and nobody else! – issued it. To do so, the owner retains a **private key**, with which only they can sign data, and a **public key** associated with the account address. Everyone can verify that the digital signature belongs to the owner through an automatic procedure based on the public key. As the account address is derived from the public key, the fact that the signee owns the account is also automatically verifiable. Please note, thus, that transactions do not require the personal details of the account holder to be known. The link between the signature and the account number is cryptographically guaranteed. In fact, the owner of an account can remain completely unknown within the blockchain. Nevertheless, all transactions report the account address of recipients and the senders. Therefore, one can trace all the transfers from and to an account. This setting thus guarantees *pseudonymity* within the blockchain platform, instead of complete anonymity.

Figure 1.1 illustrates a simplified example of a transaction. In the figure, a transfer of 2,000,000,000 units of cryptocurrency to account 0x1472...160c is requested from the 0xca35...733c account's owner. Considering the Ethereum[1] blockchain platform (Buterin 2014), the transferred value is expressed in Wei, and the amount in the picture equates to two Gwei (i.e., 0.000000002 Ether). The transaction is cryptographically signed by the sender to attest that the transaction is authentic. Every transaction has a unique ID and can bear additional information in the payload.

---

[1] See *Ethereum*. Available online: www.ethereum.org/ (accessed: 20/01/2023).

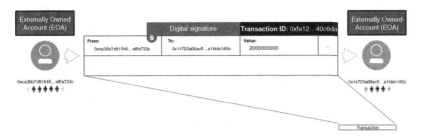

Figure 1.1 A simplified example of Ethereum transaction
Note: The sender account (to the left) sends 2,000,000,000 Wei (i.e., 2 Gwei)
to the recipient account (to the right)
Source: author's elaboration.

Ledger is a term that began being used in England during the fifteenth century to indicate a register of accounts. This term represents the collation of transactions. Notice the use of the word *collation* in place of *collection*: maintaining the order of transactions is crucial as it prevents the so-called double spending.

The following example, illustrated in Figure 1.2, aims to give an idea of what double spending is, and why the order of transactions is necessary to prevent it. Assume that the account 0xB belongs to a digital service provider, Bob. Accounts 0xA and 0xC belong to the same owner, Alice. Alice wants to purchase a digital package from 0xB at the price of 90 units of cryptocurrency (which we shall henceforth denote with ¢, so 90 ¢ here). Remember that the ownership of accounts (let alone the purposes of the owners) is a piece of information that is not recorded within the blockchain, that is it is *off-chain*. In the beginning, the balance of account 0xA amounts to 100 ¢, the balance of 0xB is 10 ¢, and the balance of 0xC is 50 ¢. Alice sends a transaction worth 90 ¢ to 0xB to purchase the digital product. Let us associate this transaction with the identifier 0xA90B. This operation reduces 0xA's balance from 100 to 10 ¢ and increases that of 0xB from 50 to 140 ¢. Bob, then, sends the digital product to Alice. Notice that the digital product is not shipped *on-chain* but *off-chain*. After receiving the package (which we assume is transmitted at very high speed), Alice tries to issue a new transaction from 0xA to 0xC, worth 50 ¢. Let us identify this transaction with 0xA50C. Since negative balances are typically not allowed in the blockchain, transaction 0xA50C is rejected – notice that 0xA's balance would drop to –30 ¢ otherwise.

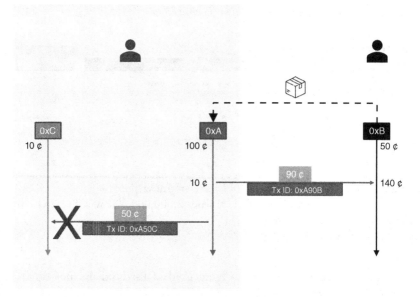

Figure 1.2a A double-spending scheme
Note: Account 0xA sends 90 units of cryptocurrency to buy a digital product, sent outside of the blockchain by the owner of the recipient account 0xB. Afterwards, a new transaction from the 0xA account of 50 units of cryptocurrency is rejected due to insufficient funds
Source: author's elaboration.

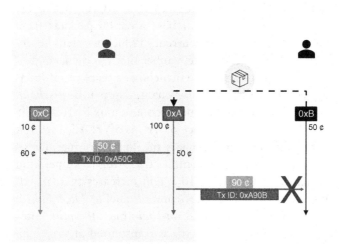

Figure 1.2b A double-spending scheme
Note: The effect of inverting the order of transactions reveals the double spending mechanism: the transaction paying 0xB is rejected, although the digital product has already been delivered
Source: author's elaboration.

Here we get to the double spending issue. Alice could try to argue, once she has received the digital package, that transaction 0xA50C took place *before* 0xA90B. In that case, the latter would be rejected. As a result, Bob would have already delivered the service without being paid, whereas the total balance of Alice's accounts would remain intact as if the 90 ¢ of transaction 0xA90B were spent twice. We conclude that not only keeping transactions unaltered but also preserving their order is vital in this context.

Distributing the Ledger

If the ledger were saved on only one computer system, however much it can be secured, it would impose a question of trust: it is assumed that those to whom the administration and safeguarding of this system are delegated do not let the content be lost or destroyed, made invalid or corrupt, truncated thus bearing incomplete information, or altered with forged transactions. In our setting, this problem is overcome by ensuring that multiple copies of the ledger are saved in separate locations through intercommunicating systems on a computer network (in jargon, these systems are called /nodes/), as illustrated in Figure 1.3. These nodes are entitled to the same rights on the data, so they are interchangeable. We name this paradigm peer-to-peer. In a peer-to-peer network, any node can crash, get offline or become unavailable for whatever reason: the other nodes will let the information safely stored. In theory, it is sufficient that just one node resists, and the whole history of transactions is preserved. The platform is resilient even to events such as nodes being under cyber threat or overtaken by malicious players. The ledger can still be considered safe

Figure 1.3 Centralised and distributed architectures
Note: The centralised architecture to the left illustrates a single system retaining the information and offering services to the other nodes in the network. The peer-to-peer network to the right shows a replica of information and services on all nodes. Notice, however, that replicas may not be identical
Source: author's elaboration.

if the majority is still correctly functioning and properly behaving. A deliberate attack or malfunction must propagate on a large scale to take effect: on one copy (or on a limited number of copies), it does not affect the system. These are the main arguments in favour of a distributed solution to handle the ledgers. Hence the name: *distributed ledger technology*.

To keep the local copies of the ledger synchronised, all nodes should receive updates from the network. This requirement entails that every node being informed about an update should register it and bounce it to the neighbouring nodes in the network. It is noteworthy to recall that the updates pertain to transactions. Therefore, every node is aware of every transmission of value among accounts. From this standpoint, we may agree that keeping *pseudonymity* is a good compromise between the need for nodes to update the status of accounts (if they did not know from and to what accounts the transactions were issued, how could they keep track of the balances?) and the preferably avoidable situation in which all nodes know every detail about personal belongings and exchanges. Notice that if full anonymity was kept, nodes would not be aware of the transactions' sender and recipient accounts nor would they be able to reconstruct this piece of information. They could keep on piling up new transactions from the network but then who could guarantee that transactions were legitimate? For instance, who could verify that there were enough cryptos in account 0xA to send 90 ¢ to 0xB? An authority should be invoked to solve this conundrum, in case – which would dismantle the whole idea of decentralisation and restore the risks of data loss, corruption, and crashes.

Transactions are thus collated in ledgers, one after the other. As a consequence, ledgers tend to grow. Thinking about the old, paper-based one, it would seem natural to write down the ledger onto separate books. Books would also be sorted to ensure that the order of transactions is preserved across the books. In blockchains, the notion of a book is replaced by that of a *block*. A block contains a segment of the ledger plus additional heading information – including the timestamp.

To keep the order among blocks, each block is linked to the previous one through a one-way function called *hashing*. In brief, hashing is a mathematical one-way function that produces a number (the digest, also commonly known as hash) that works as a digital fingerprint for any piece of input data. The hash characterises the input data (just like a fingerprint identifies a person) though being typically of a fixed size (normally, smaller), regardless of the input data size. More than the fingerprint metaphor, though, the hash is tightly bound to the input data. The hashing function returns the same hash out of two identical pieces of data. Altering a bit in the data, though, turns the associated hash into a completely different number to the extent that it is not feasible to reconstruct what the alteration was by solely looking at the digest.

Equipped with this notion, we can see what happens when every block stores the hash of the previous one in its header. This scenario serves as a good intuition of the approach underlying Bitcoin[2] and Ethereum, among others. The actual mechanism is a bit more refined to save computation efforts, but we can omit the details for the sake of understandability. Let us consider three blocks in a sequence now, which we shall refer to as previous, current, and next. If we try to remove, add, change, swap, or reorder transactions in the previous block, its content is altered and, thus, its hash turns into something that is completely different. Consequently, the previous block's hash does not match the copy stored in the current one anymore. To keep it consistent, the current block has to change its local copy of the previous hash accordingly. This update, in turn, changes the header and hence the hash of the current block. The next block, then, has to modify its copy of the current block hash accordingly. At this stage, we can quickly figure out what happens to the block following the next one. We conclude that this mechanism makes every change reverberate as a sort of domino effect along the whole sequence of blocks. The older the changed block, the longer the domino effect.

The sequence of hash-based links thus forms a chain, as depicted in Figure 1.4. Hence the name, *blockchain*. DLTs such as Bitcoin and Ethereum are blockchain platforms as they employ the slicing of ledgers into consecutive blocks that are backlinked from the current to the previous one. IOTA,[3] instead, is a DLT that does not implement this approach. Blockchain platforms use blocks as packets transmitted within the chain to update the ledger with a new segment.

Transactions are broadcast by all nodes in the network to all their neighbours, so that every node can be aware of the fact that the transaction was issued. In blockchain platforms, they remain in a temporary

---

[2] See *Bitcoin*. Available online: www.bitcoin.org/en/ (accessed: 21/01/2023).
[3] See *Iota*. Available online: www.iota.org/ (accessed: 20/01/2023).

Figure 1.4 A schematised view of the backward link–based chain of blocks
Note: Every block contains a segment of the sequence of the transactions issued
to that moment. The collation of transactions goes under the name of ledger
Source: author's elaboration.

storage named *transaction pool*, from which the publishing node collects the ones to include in the block. Until a block is published and accepted by the nodes in the network, indeed, the new transactions are not appended to the ledger.

The power in the hands of nodes publishing the blocks should not be overlooked: whether a transaction is included or not in a block depends on their choice. This is why *transaction fees* are usually included in the transactions by the senders: they are an economic incentive to motivate the miner to include the transaction in the next block.

Right to Publish and Consensus

We have already observed that decentralising the management and maintenance of a ledger strengthens the platform. However, this solution comes with a few infrastructural drawbacks. Firstly, the nodes must send digital messages through the network to keep the nodes updated with the latest transactions. These messages are prone to possible delays or complete loss. As a result, different nodes may have diverging views of the historical sequence of transactions. Secondly, the emission of the updates should be granted to nodes that give evidence of their reliability. Otherwise, malicious nodes could find it too easy to attack the network by flooding it with data reporting wrong or false information. Therefore, integrating at least two mechanisms appear fundamental to preserving safety and operational continuity. One should guarantee that the network eventually achieves a univocal view of the ledger (consensus). The other should cater for self-certification, ensuring that new messages are propagated only by nodes demonstrating their reliability. Terms like Proof of Work or Proof of Stake fall in the second category. Let us begin with the former, as it was historically introduced first and is still in use with platforms such as Bitcoin.

Proof of Work

The idea behind Proof of Work is that the nodes which aim to publish a new block should provide evidence of their will to keep the infrastructure in operation. To this end, those nodes show that they are ready to put computation time and resources at risk by attempting to solve a complex cryptographic puzzle. The solution to this puzzle is easily verifiable once it is given: finding it is the source of the difficulty. More specifically, Bitcoin's Proof of Work requires nodes to find a number (called a *nonce*) to be injected in the header of the block so that the hash of the block's header is a number that is lower than a given *target*. For example, the miner of the Bitcoin block number 769,424 inserted 2,927,826,006 as the nonce to make the whole block header's hash equal to 310,844,154,145,111,873,655,715,160, 191,695,224,044,144,394,078,051,380, which is less than the set target (762,342,638,057,996,256,581,733,267,702,136,683,580,848, 909,336,969,216).[4]

Recall that reverse-engineering the input of a hashing function given the output is nearly impossible. Therefore, the only way to find the nonce is adopting a brute-force approach: try all possible numbers until the hash of the whole block is right (i.e., less than the target). The challenge is already hard on its own but, to put more pressure on the nodes, it is an open race: if another node finds a suitable nonce first, the challenge for that block is over, and a new round starts with the next block. This approach is in line with the distributed computation scheme: any node in the network can concurrently run its own operations to be entitled to the right to publish the block. To make things worse, so to speak, we should consider that the previous computations do not lead to any advantage for the subsequent round. The new block is indeed different from the previous, so the nonce is to be inserted in a different data box. As a result, the new hash has to be recomputed from scratch for every possible candidate. Finally, notice that

---

[4] See *Blockchair*. Available online: www.blockchair.com/bitcoin/block/769424 (accessed: 20/01/2023).

the *difficulty* of the puzzle is set by the target: intuitively, the lower the target, the fewer the numbers that are below it. These numbers form the set of acceptable block-headers' hash values. Every such hash value roughly corresponds to a nonce. Therefore, fewer nonces are there to be guessed, and finding one becomes a tougher challenge. The difficulty is thus *tunable*. The need to keep the average time to publish a block stable and around 10 minutes determines how the knob is turned. If the average publication time is lower than that, the difficulty gets increased. Otherwise, it is lowered. Notice that this decision is not governed by any single actor: the protocol lets every node know how to autonomously determine the necessary change at regular intervals of 2,016 blocks (about 2 weeks).

At this stage, a doubt could legitimately arise: what moves the nodes to try and guess the nonce, given the required considerable efforts in spite of no guarantee to win the game? To pay the electricity bill and the hardware consumption back, the winners who manage to publish the block included in the blockchain are rewarded with freshly minted cryptocurrency (plus other non-negligible extras such as the transaction fees, discussed earlier). As such a prize is akin to finding gold behind a stone wall of a cave after extenuating excavations, we say that nodes publishing blocks (or trying to do it) are *mining* nodes. At the time of writing, the *mining reward* amounts to 6.25 BTC. Cryptocurrencies therefore perform the function of *cryptofuel*, which supplies monetary resources to the nodes that maintain the infrastructure using their own computational resources. Cryptofuel attracts miner nodes as cryptocurrencies are traded in fiat money on dedicated markets by investors around the world. At the time of writing, the mining reward equates to about 20,000 €.

Notice that the mining reward was established in May 2020 and is getting halved every 210,000 blocks (i.e., about four years: in 2009, it amounted to 50 BTC). Quoting the Bitcoin white paper: 'Once a predetermined number of coins have entered circulation, the incentive can transition entirely to transaction fees and be completely inflation free.' (Nakamoto, 2008) The incentive can help encourage knots to remain honest. Quoting the white paper again: 'A greedy attacker [...] ought to find it more profitable to play by the rules, [as] such rules [...] favour [them] with more new coins than everyone else combined' (Nakamoto 2008).

Verifying that the solution to the puzzle is correct has to be relatively easy because every node in the network should be capable of validating it: if the solution is incorrect, the block should be rejected. Other reasons for a proposed block to be discarded include incorrect transactions, wrong signatures, or excessively distant timestamps reported in the block header. We remark that these checking operations are carried out virtually by every node in the network.

Proof of Stake

Proof of Work has been subject to criticism due to the high consumption of electricity, heating, and ultimately pollution that mining nodes cause. With regular periodicity, new reports are published on the comparison between the power consumption of entire states and that due to mining. The trend has long been upward, that is comparable states increase in size at every update. Furthermore, in an attempt to win the puzzle, larger and larger mining rigs have been assembled. Mining rigs consist of a multitude of machines equipped with dedicated hardware that have the sole objective of running the mining processes in parallel to increase the chances to win. As a consequence, the risk of re-centralising the decision process becomes more and more tangible.

To overcome this issue, Ethereum transitioned to a different approach: the Proof of Stake, already applied natively in other blockchain platforms such as Algorand.[5] In Proof of Work, miners put capital at risk by expending energy. In Proof of Stake, *validators* explicitly stake capital in Ether, the Ethereum platform's cryptocurrency. More specifically, candidates propose themselves as validators by depositing a given amount (32 ETH, at the time of writing) from their balance: this amount is referred to as the *stake*, indeed. The stake cannot be used by the original owners as long as they remain in the role of validators. Validators are pseudo-randomly selected to become part of validator *committees* (currently) of 128 members each. Within the committee, one node is chosen as the *proposer*. The proposer replaces the role of the miner as block publisher. The members of a validation committee vote for (i.e., they broadcast their *attestation* to) the next block to be put at the head of the chain. For every published block that gets included in the blockchain, both the proposer and the validators get a *reward* that is topped up to the stake.

---

[5] See *Algorand Foundation*. Available online: www.algorand.foundation/ (accessed: 20/01/2023).

With Proof of Stake, the block time is fixed in Ethereum (set to 12 seconds at present). The block time is named /slot/. The first half of the slot is the time the proposer has to submit the new block. Every 32 slots (an /epoch/, i.e., 6 minutes and 24 seconds currently), committees are drawn from the set of members with sufficient ETH at stake, one per slot and so that no two committees share any members in the epoch.

The *finality* of blocks is handled explicitly by the protocol: the first block published in every /epoch/ requires an additional vote from the committees. The decision is two-staged. The committee votes for pairs of epoch-boundary blocks: an older one (source) and a newer descendant (target). Both source and target need to be attested by two-thirds of the votes to be bound by a so-called *supermajority link*. The target in the supermajority link becomes *justified*. The source is typically already justified (as it was the target in a previous voting round) and thus becomes *finalised*. Validators attesting to blocks that are included in a supermajority link receive specific extra rewards for justified and finalised blocks. A finalised block is nearly impossible to be removed from the net. Notice that not all attestations have the same weight. The weight depends on the quota left at stake – in particular, the so-called *effective balance*, which cannot amount to more than 32 ETH. Notice that the staked ETH can also decrease.

With this scheme, indeed, inactive members could hamper the process. This is why the protocol includes the so-called *inactivity penalties*. Penalties remove limited amounts of the capital at stake as errors, temporary disconnection from the network, or seldom malfunctions can happen, after all. What is treated with a more severe countermeasure is the occurrence of (allegedly malicious) misbehaviour: nodes that publish multiple blocks (/equivocation/) attest to different blocks (*double vote*) in the same round, or vote for a source and a target that occur in epochs surrounding an already voted pair, are subject to *slashing* of their staked funds. Notice that slashing leads to the removal of the member from the set of validators. Interestingly, conditions for slashing can only be verified if other nodes signal and report evidence of them. This is why a special reward is dedicated to *whistleblowers* (who notify the misbehaviour) and proposers who include the whistleblowing messages in the block. Also, notice that the slashed funds become higher if the misbehaving player operates in collusion with other players. The reason why finalised blocks are considered as such lies in the enormous slashing that their replacement in the blockchain would require: as two-thirds of the validators have voted for it, there cannot be another two-thirds of validators attesting to another block unless one-third of the total were double votes.

Choosing the Fork

As we said, the network is subject to delays and loss of blocks. It is perfectly reasonable that, at some stage, a node observes that more alternatives are coming as an update – different blocks that are valid but report on different transactions.

The temporary situation in which more branches are taken into account as possible evolutions of the chain is typically named **fork**. Forks can happen with the top, most recent blocks. The further we go down the chain, the less likely they become. However, notice that if a block is included in the chain, its transactions are appended to the ledger and thus remain in the collective memory of the network. If a block is initially considered part of the chain but then gets replaced by another sub-chain, its transactions become non-existing all of a sudden (unless, of course, the new chain still retains that very block). Owing to this, it is recommended to wait for six blocks to be appended in Bitcoin before considering the transaction as finalised.

How to determine the fork to include in the blockchain in a way that eventually all nodes opt for the same one? The mechanism under-neath this choice is the basis of consensus. With Proof of Work, the preference leans towards the block at the head of the sub-chain with the highest amount of work put in the mining – which translates with good approximation to the longest sub-chain. Every block received by a node brings with itself the hash-based link to the previous one. If the node observes that the new block does not appear to have the predecessor in the chain, it keeps the new block aside and waits until the predecessor is delivered from the network. Notice that the same process could occur with the predecessor's predecessors, and so on, until a convergence point is found. At that moment, the node can decide which branch to take as the main chain. In Ethereum, the sub-chain that accumulates the highest weight of attestations is chosen.

We remark that this choice is made by all nodes and recall that all nodes are in charge of individually verifying that the block they receive is correct, contains valid transactions, and is consistent with the remainder of the history of the blockchain. For practical reasons, though, some nodes may not store the whole ledger locally, but only a section of their interest. These nodes are named *light nodes*. A typical example of light node is a *wallet*, that is the software that account holders use to keep track of their funds in cryptocurrencies.

This aspect offers food for thought about the nature of blockchain as a platform (Voshmgir 2019). It is politically decentralised because no entity controls the network. It is architecturally distributed because the information is held and managed by all nodes in the system. However, it is logically centralised because each entity has its own copy of the ledger, in a state that tends to be unanimously agreed.

Transaction Model and Balance Model

Not only the consensus mechanisms distinguish Bitcoin and Ethereum. Another key specificity lies in the paradigm with which the two blockchain platforms handle the transfer of value among accounts. Ethereum adopts a *balance model*: accounts are associated with their current amounts of Wei's, which they can spend by adding a value to the transaction. If account 0xE owns, for example, three ETH, its owner can sign a transaction with which they send 1.5 ETH to account 0xF. Therefore, the nodes in the network should keep track of the current balance of every account to verify whether they can spend the declared amount in a transaction or not. A metaphor for the balance model used in Ethereum is that of the bank transfer: akin to Ethereum transactions, bank transfers typically report the account coordinates of the sender, the account coordinates of the redeemer, the transferred amount, the transaction fee, and a unique identifying number for the transaction. When executed, they determine the subtraction of the indicated amount and the fee from the sender's account and the addition of the amount in the recipient's account. The transaction fee goes to the issuing bank. Notice that in blockchain platforms, banks do not constitute the underlying organisation guaranteeing for the safety and security of the transfers and accounts. The whole network does, thus network nodes (specifically, the block proposers in Ethereum) are rewarded the transaction fees for their efforts.

Bitcoin, instead, uses a *transaction model*. Suppose that account 0xB had received a transaction worth 5 BTC, another one of 6 BTC, and a third one of 1 BTC in the past. The balance amounts to 12 BTC in total, which corresponds to the sum of the denominations of its Unspent Transaction Outputs (UTXOs). Imagine that the owner of account 0xB wants to send 11.5 BTC to 0xC. To do so, the owner should sign the three UTXOs we mentioned, setting 0xC as the redeemer, and wrap them into a new transaction. UTXOs cannot be split into sub-units. To get the difference in return, the new transaction should include a new transaction unit that transfers 0.5 BTC (or less) from 0xC back to 0xB. If the change amounts to less than 0.5 BTC (say, 0.4 BTC), the difference becomes the *transaction fee* to the benefit of the miner (0.1 BTC in this case). In this setting, the balance of every account is computable by summing up all the UTXOs that belong to it. Considering that account addresses mark every transaction in which they occur as sender or redeemer, UTXOs can be tracked for all their lifetime. As a good metaphor for UTXOs, we can consider transferable cheques that are not redeemed.

Smart Contracts

A second generation of blockchain arose when, from the intuition of Vitalik Buterin, the focus shifted from the concept of blockchain as a distributed system for the exchange of electronic money to the concept of blockchain as a */programmable distributed environment/* (Buterin 2014). The notion through which this conceptual leap became possible is the *smart contract.*

The smart contract is a program run by the blockchain platform. Programmers typically use a coding language such as Solidity,[6] which is later automatically turned into a set of low-level operations executable by computerised systems. Figure 1.5 shows the same smart contract written in Solidity (left) and turned into the so-called operation codes, or opcodes for short (top right in the figure), for execution. At the bottom-right corner of the figure, we can see the direct transposition of the instruction codes into binary codes that the delegated component of Ethereum named Ethereum Virtual Machine (EVM) executes. One of the crucial characteristics of smart contracts is that their code, and only their code, fully determines how their status evolves ('*The code is the law*').

Smart contracts, despite their name, are not necessarily linked to a binding contract between counterparts. Of course, they can *also* represent contracts in the most commonly adopted sense. However,

---

[6] See *Solidity*. Available online: www.solidity.readthedocs.io/ (accessed: 20/01/2023).

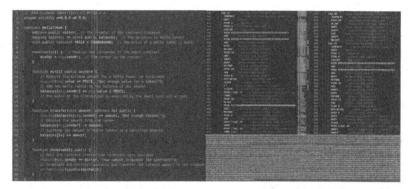

Figure 1.5 The Solidity code of a sample smart contract in Ethereum (Hello Token)
Source: author's elaboration.

the spectrum of possible usages is much larger as, in Ethereum, they can express anything a computer program could do. For example, smart contracts are typically used to manage the life cycle of tokens such as the Hello Token in Figure 1.5. The Hello Token contract offers four operations: (1) the constructor function to deploy new instances of the smart contract and record the account address of the creator; (2) the mint function to buy new tokens at the price of 2 Gwei each; (3) the transfer function to send tokens from the sender account to another account; and (4) the terminate function to cease the operations of the smart contract and transfer the funds from the account of the smart contract to the creator's account. Notice that the way in which the smart contracts are encoded fully and exclusively dictates the way in which they behave and manage the tokens they define. The challenge of creating smart contracts that precisely and consistently represent the intended requirements and purposes is among the core challenges posed by the research agenda of Magazzeni et al. (2017).

Next to the so-called *externally owned accounts* (EOAs), owned by human users or in any case from entities outside the ecosystem of the blockchain platform, we have the smart contract accounts (CAs), that is accounts entirely managed by the aforementioned programs. Notice that the status of a smart contract includes the

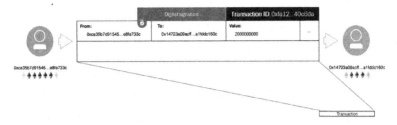

Figure 1.6 Invocation of a smart contract
Source: author's elaboration.

balance of its own account, then. The code, therefore, determines how the funds therein are to be transferred or kept. However, the smart contracts solely react to calls from other accounts: they do not independently trigger their operations. This entails that they cannot independently take action at some stage on their own free will, so to speak: there always is an invoker that is responsible for triggering the operations.

Smart contracts, in other words, offer functions. Functions are invoked by other accounts (let them be EOAs or CAs) to execute operations. Updating the bank-transfer metaphor we used earlier to support this new paradigm, imagine that the recipient of the transfer is the smart contract, and the message encoded the data necessary to perform the requested operation. When the recipient receives the bank transfer, it automatically starts executing the requested operations based on the payload of the message. Indeed, the means to invoke smart contracts from EOAs is using *transactions*, as illustrated in Figure 1.6 (Box 1.2). As a consequence, all operations are fully tracked, the signee is known, and the outcome too (because the smart contract's code determines it). Notice that the code, although at its low-level representation in terms of bytecode, is publicly known to every node in the network. The reason is, new instances of a smart contract are deployed (i.e., assigned an account and initialised) by means of transactions too. The recipient is a previously unoccupied account address (which will become their own) and the code is in the payload. The payload (i.e., the *code* of the new instance of smart contract just deployed) is part of the transaction, which is going to be stored in the ledger and, therefore, known to every node in the network and immutable.

Box 1.2   Smart contracts

If anything, *immutability*, *non-repudiability*, and *persistence* are good reasons to resort to smart contracts to coordinate the operations of *multi-party processes*, especially in the presence of partial trust among the participants (Mendling et al. 2018). All operations are tracked and cannot be erased, stored together with the smart contract that they testify the interactions with, in a permanent ledger that is replicated over all nodes. Therefore, the automated workflow is known to all participants, it is not going to change, and the ongoing evolution of the running processes can be monitored (Di Ciccio et al. 2022).

The outcome of every invocation is known to every node in the network because virtually every node will execute the triggered operations after they read the invoking transaction in the published block – hence, after the proposer node has actually pre-executed and validated them: since the proposer is responsible for grouping trans- actions into a block, it must be the first to verify their correctness. The operations of a smart contract function are thus going to be run multiple times across the whole network, with the same input and the same output, akin to a polygraph machine as metaphorically described by Dannen (2017). Therefore, their execution is associ- ated with a price for the invoking account. The paid units go under the name of gas. Every opcode low-level operation (see the listing in Figure 1.5 at the top-right corner) is bound to a specific price in gas. Typically, altering the state of the smart contract and deploying new smart contracts are the most expensive operations, whereas math- ematical and hashing operations have a lower cost. A full pricing list can be found in the Ethereum yellow paper (Wood 2014). Deploying a smart contract like the one in Figure 1.5 has a cost of 531,255 units of gas, invoking its mint operation to buy four Hello Tokens requires 43,821 units of gas. Also, the amount of data sent to the smart con- tract and treated therein are mirrored in additional costs: the more the data, the higher the overall price. Transaction fees in Ethereum are solely based on gas. Transactions with no smart contract invoca- tions require gas, too. Notice that the gas is independent of the value we send. Therefore, to buy four Hello Tokens, we should send eight Gwei to the smart contract backing the token, in addition to the gas expenditure (for further details on the difference between tokens and cryptocurrencies, see Box 1.3). To make sure that the invocation terminates and no harmful contract drains unlimited funds from the invoking account, the senders set a limit to the maximum amount of gas they are ready to pay (the gas limit).

The price of every unit of gas in units of cryptocurrency (Wei) oscillates depending on two factors, both to be multiplied by the units of gas consumed to run a smart contract's function code: a priority fee, which the invoking account can raise at their will to increase the chances that the proposer will include that transaction in the next block, and a base fee, decided by the protocol and used to counterbalance the use of the network (the more the traffic, the higher the base fee). Notice that the priority fee (times the units of gas) will end up in the account of the proposer, whereas the base fee (multiplied by the units of gas) is going to be burnt. Ethereum, thus, allows for a deflationary mechanism unlike Bitcoin and permits units of cryptocurrency to be not only issued but also removed from the network.

Box 1.3   Token versus cryptocurrency

Notice the difference between a token and a cryptocurrency. Cryptocurrencies like ETH or BTC propel the infrastructure. Their emission (or burning in the case of Ethereum) depends on the protocol and its policies. Cryptocurrencies can be minted or exchanged for fiat money and sold back. This trading will determine their price in the market. Aside from this, there is hardly any other operation that can let users influence the nature of cryptocurrencies. Tokens, instead, are digital entities whose existence is bound to smart contracts supporting them. Their lifecycle, emission, exchange, and deletion are fully controlled by the backing smart contracts. Unlike cryptocurrencies, the rules of the game governing every token are fully determined by the custom code of which the smart contract consists. The infrastructure keeping up smart contracts (and tokens) is propelled by cryptocurrencies, and tokens are acquired from them in exchange for cryptocurrencies. Thus, they lie at different levels of abstraction in what computer scientists call the protocol stack, so to speak: cryptocurrencies are on a layer below contracts. **Smart contracts and tokens** are thus the main instruments to creating new blockchain-based projects for the **automation of services and processes.**

To make an example from the real world, we can acquire points in the context of a fidelity program for customers when we buy a product or service from a given company. We buy products and services with money we can transfer with our credit card from our bank account, or withdraw at an Automated Teller Machine (ATM). The rules determining the market value of the currency of our bank account are not easily customisable by individuals. Also, we cannot typically deposit fidelity points in our bank account. Fidelity programs, however, are fully controlled and manageable by their company. Fidelity points, therefore, are akin to tokens.

The purpose of tokens is typically classified according to their *fungibility*. Tokens are fungible whenever individual units can be mutually substituted as they are indistinguishable. For instance, the Hello Token in Figure 1.5 is fungible. If a token represents an individual entity, with its own characteristics, different to another one and thus not interchangeable, it is *non-fungible*. Tokens representing the ownership of a physical or digital good, an artwork, or a digital identity, are all examples of non-fungible tokens. *Semi-fungible* tokens are fungible until a given expiry date or in case of a change of status like their redeeming, after which they become non-fungible (like tickets for concerts or vouchers).

Blockchain is often compared to the internet. The comparison concerns the current potential and the possible development that is obtained from it. In the beginning, the internet itself was an experimental project that required implementation effort by highly skilled software developers. However, its revolutionary nature has meant that its adoption has spread to the levels we know today. Blockchain and DLTs in general seem to follow this path. In fact, web services can integrate the blockchain. The effect has reduced visibility to the end user, through. Since its inception, the web has been based on a paradigm of clients and servers, with the former requesting services from the front-end (accessible by the user) to the latter, on the back end. In its first generation, the front end was delegated minor operations other than displaying and formatting the content provided by the servers. With the advent of Web 2.0, there has been a migration and outsourcing of operations from the back end to the front-end side, thanks to an increase in the capabilities of desktop PCs, laptops, handheld devices, etc. At the same time, although not evident on the user side, web servers have also delegated operations and data processing to specific management systems (e.g., on the cloud). The new *Web 3.0* paradigm integrates blockchain platforms on the back-end side, taking advantage of smart contracts for carrying out (part of the) operations though maintaining a front-end that does not impact the user interface. Applications that adopt the Web 3.0 paradigm are commonly known as *Decentralised Applications (DApps)*.

Thus far, we have observed characteristics and traits that are typical of blockchains that are publicly accessible and in which every node can potentially contribute to the validation and publishing of new blocks. However, there are other approaches to DLTs that restrict the aforementioned openness criteria. We briefly examine them next.

Public, Private, Permissioned, and Permissionless

Blockchains are often classified according to two criteria: *transactability* (or visibility) and *consensus* (Bellia et al. 2019). Table 1.1 displays the four categories that stem from these criteria. If a blockchain is *public*, every node can make transactions and view them. If only selected nodes are entitled to this right, it is *private*. If any node in the network can participate in the consensus decision-making process, the blockchain platform is *permissionless*. Instead, if only specific nodes can determine the next status of the blockchain, it is *permissioned*. Bitcoin, for example, is public and permissionless like Ethereum, natively. On the other side of the spectrum, Hyperledger Fabric[7] (Gaur et al. 2020) is an example of a private permissioned blockchain. The LTO network[8] offers a private though permissionless blockchain. EOSIO[9] is an example of a public blockchain platform with a permissioned consensus system.

Choosing the right combination (public or private? Permissioned or permissionless?) is a design choice that is up to the system architect based on the application context and foreseen use. Several decision models have been proposed to determine whether taking the blockchain as a building block is appropriate in the first place and, if so,

---

[7] See *Hyperledger*. Available online: www.hyperledger.org/use/fabric (accessed: 20/01/2023).
[8] See LTO network. Available online: www.ltonetwork.com/ (accessed: 20/01/2023).
[9] See EOSIO. Available online: www.eos.io/ (accessed: 20/01/2023).

Table 1.1 *Blockchain types according to their visibility and consensus mechanisms*

| | | Transactability/visibility | |
		Private	Public
Consensus	*Permissionless*	**Selected** nodes can transact and view, **every** nodes can participate in consensus	**Every** node can transact and view, participate in consensus
	Permissioned	**Selected** nodes can transact and view, or participate in consensus	**Every** node can transact and view, **selected** nodes participate in consensus

which type of blockchain should be adopted. A renowned example of such guidelines is provided by Wüst and Gervais (2018).

To sum up, blockchains are fit for purpose whenever storing the status of the system is necessary, multiple entities concur to provide information on the evolution of the system while not all of them are trustable, and no trusted third parties are fully available. Otherwise, other solutions, such as distributed or centralised databases, can be more appropriate.

If a blockchain is appropriate for the intents and purposes of the project, the policy on whether making the circle of information providers and validators open or restricted drives the decision on whether the blockchain should be public or private, and permissionless or permissioned, respectively.

Concluding Remarks

This chapter illustrated and discussed the key traits of DLTs and blockchain platforms, with a focus on the technical mechanisms underpinning their guarantees. Transactions, the fundamental building block, allow for the transfer of cryptocurrencies and invocation of smart contracts' functions. Digital signatures enable the authentication of transaction senders. The order of transactions is preserved by the sequential nature of ledgers. The distributed architecture ensures data persistence, as a replica of the ledger is saved virtually on every node. Hashing makes the blockchain robust, as it impedes changes in older transactions without altering the whole sequence of blocks that follow. Mechanisms such as proof-of-work and proof-of-stake ensure that the publishing rights of new blocks are given to nodes that prove their reliability. Consensus algorithms guarantee that the blockchain is eventually consistent in the replicas stored on the network nodes. Smart contracts make blockchain programmable and, among other things, able to support tokens.

Distributed ledger and blockchain technologies are not a panacea for all projects in information technologies and beyond. Their use is suitable for settings where multiple actors cooperate in a regime of partial (or lack of) mutual trust and in the absence of trusted third parties that can authoritatively exert control of the stored information. Entering the details of the core mechanisms and rationale thereof reportedly is a challenging task on its own, and their installation or integration requires the intervention of technically skilled experts. However, they offer a number of critical guarantees by design, including authentication, inviolability, full traceability of data, and robustness, availability, and customisability of service. Arguably, building a novel system that offers *ex novo* all that would be a highly challenging task, let alone in regimes of partial trust between the key actors. Notice that the observations made thus far refer to using distributed ledger and blockchain technologies as an information technology (IT) core infrastructure within larger projects integrated with business processes (Xu et al. 2019). Their potential is enormous and can be fully unleashed when their adoption goes beyond the mere exchange of cryptocurrencies. The next chapters of this book will document success case studies in which endeavours of this sort are carried out in the banking sector.

References

Bellia, M., Kounelis, I., Anderberg, A., Calès, L., Andonova, E., Sobolewski, M. 2019. *Blockchain now and tomorrow: Assessing multidimensional impacts of distributed ledger technologies.* Publications Office of the European Union, Luxembourg: European Commission, Joint Research Centre.

Buterin, V. 2014. Ethereum: 'A next-generation smart contract and decentralized application platform'. White paper. Available online: https://ethereum.org/669c9e2e2027310b6b3cdce6e1c52962/Ethereum_White paper_-_Buterin_2014.pdf

Dannen, C. 2017. *Introducing Ethereum and solidity*. Berkeley: Apress, Vol. 1, 159–160

Di Ciccio, C., Meroni, G., Plebani, P. 2022. 'On the adoption of blockchain for business process monitoring'. *Software and Systems Modeling*, 21(3), 915–937.

Gaur, N., O'Dowd, A., Novotny, P., Desrosiers, L., Ramakrishna, V., Baset, S. A. 2020. *Blockchain with hyperledger fabric: Build decentralized applications using hyperledger fabric 2*. Birmingham, UK: Packt Publishing Ltd.

Magazzeni, D., McBurney, P., Nash, W. 2017. 'Validation and verification of smart contracts: A research agenda'. *Computer*, 50(9), 50–57.

Mendling, J., Weber, et al. 2018. 'Blockchains for business process management-challenges and opportunities'. *ACM Transactions on Management Information Systems*, 9(1), 1–16.

Nakamoto, S. 2008. Bitcoin: 'A peer-to-peer electronic cash system'. Decentralized Business Review, 21260.

Voshmgir, S. 2019. *Token economy: How blockchains and smart contracts revolutionize the economy*. Berlin, Germany: Shermin Voshmgir-BlockchainHub.

Wood, G. (2014). 'Ethereum: A secure decentralised generalised transaction ledger'. *Ethereum project yellow paper*, 151(2014), 1–32.

Wüst, K., Gervais, A. 2018. 'Do you need a blockchain?'. *2018 Crypto Valley Conference on Blockchain Technology*, 45–54.

Xu, X., Weber, I., Staples, M. 2019. *Architecture for blockchain applications*. Berlin, Germany: Springer.

2 | The Integration of Distributed Ledger Technology in Banking
State of the Art in Literature

SABRINA LEO AND ANDREA DELLE FOGLIE

Introduction

The term *Distributed Ledger Technology* (DLT) explicitly refers to the technological framework and protocols that provide the concurrent access, verification, and modification of records that define distributed ledgers. DLT operates through computer networks that span several organisations or places. DLT employs cryptography to encrypt data and restrict access to only authorised users by means of cryptographic signatures and keys. Additionally, the technology generates an immutable database, meaning that information that has been stored cannot be removed and that any revisions are preserved forever.

DLT architecture marks a substantial change in how information is received and conveyed by shifting recordkeeping from a single authoritative place towards a decentralised system in which all pertinent entities may read and amend the ledger. All other entities can thus see who is accessing and making changes to the ledger. The high degree of trust fostered by DLT's openness almost entirely prevents any fraudulent activity from taking place in the ledger.

DLT eliminates the need for entities utilising the ledger to rely on a third-party provider to serve as a safeguard against manipulation or a reliable central authority to manage the ledger. Blockchain and DLT are frequently used in tandem and occasionally even interchangeably. Nevertheless, they are not substitutes because, although Blockchain is a type of DLT, not all DLTs use blockchain technology. This misconception is reasonable, given how interchangeable the technologies may be in practice. Both can be either permissioned (private), limiting access to authorised users who agree to specific standards of use, or permissionless (public), making them open to anyone, as is the case with Bitcoin. Both technologies are used to create decentralised ledgers using cryptography; both make immutable records that include time stamps; and both are considered nearly unhackable.

What, then, distinguishes them? The key distinction is that, as its name implies, Blockchain uses data blocks chained together to construct the distributed ledger. DLT also encompasses technologies that build a distributed ledger but use different design ideas. To be organised as a DLT, the distributed ledger does not need to divide its data into blocks. To ensure that everyone has access to the most recent version of the ledger and that its accuracy can be relied upon, DLT minimises or eliminates the sometimes lengthy and error-prone processes required to reconcile the various contributions to the ledger.

In what ways DLT will fundamentally alter the operations of businesses, organisations, and governments is still unknown. Industry experts marked DLT as a powerful technology that has the potential to significantly enhance current procedures and inspire creative new applications. Furthermore, they consider DLT a component of the Internet of Value, where transactions occur instantly across international networks. The Internet's widespread use makes DLT possible.

However, most analysts agree that the adoption of DLT will follow the standard technological curve, with a small number of leaders out front, followed by quick followers, and eventually laggards. Analysts also highlight that the scaling, operationalisation, and adoption of DLT are challenging for organisations. To accomplish these tasks, business executives, entrepreneurs, and visionaries must overcome the challenge of creating networks of organisations that can use DLT to drastically alter how records are shared and maintained and to innovate in areas where DLT can enable entirely new processes and business models.

Looking at the banking industry, DLT emerged as a promising answer for the potential advantages in banks' product and service offerings, customer relations, internal organisation, and interrelations with the other banks or financial intermediaries. However, this technology has not yet found full use in the banking industry, or, in other words, not many banks have oriented themselves towards the full use of this technology. Banks are still reluctant to adopt DLT, held back by doubts and what they perceive to be operational impediments, and some of their concerns are well founded. Banks with legacy technology stacks find it difficult to adopt DLT, since many fear being disintermediated by this technology, and some consider DLT just another expression of the difficulties of their legacy technology.

Operational experience shows that DLTs are widely used at the level of cryptocurrencies (in this case, the technologies used are blockchain-based), but little at the level of implementation in banking processes.

DLT therefore represents both a threat and an opportunity for banks. Banks should embrace DLT as a modern-day opportunity for the industry's many financial services, such as payments, clearance and settlement, loans and credit, Know Your Customer and fraud prevention, and trade finance.

Scientific research can significantly contribute to finding solutions to address the critical issues arising from banking, given its fundamental role in developing modern market economies. Its results could have policy implications and future project implementations given its role as a tool for efficient learning and knowledge building, understanding problems, and discovering, evaluating, and seizing opportunities.

So, what is the state of academic research in this field? This chapter's objective is therefore to provide a snapshot of the state of the art of the academic literature on implementing DLT in the banking sector.

To answer the research question of the state of academic research, this study conducts a systematic literature review (SLR) to synthesise information from multiple studies and to give an overall view of the topic. Specifically, it analyses and summarises current studies by classifying them along research lines. By providing a comprehensive overview of DLT adoption in the banking sector, this study aims to contribute to a better understanding of DLT and its potential to transform the banking industry. After explaining the research methodology, the chapter summarises the main results and provides the study's primary conclusions.

Methodology

The methodology consists of an SLR that observes a systematic and transparent approach to identify, evaluate, and synthesise all relevant studies on a specific research question (Paul and Criado 2020). A rigorous literature review can provide a more comprehensive understanding of the body of knowledge in the field and improve the quality of the review process and outcomes by employing a transparent and reproducible procedure.

To avoid selection bias and to consider only top-ranked international business journals and high-quality scientific papers, we gathered the data from the Web of Science database, one of the most comprehensive biblio-metric databases of peer-reviewed journals (Bahoo et al. 2020; Khan et al. 2022). The data selection process considers the longest period available in the Web of Science database, from 2017 (when the first data in the field were available) to 2022 (November), defining a keyword combina-tion that captures all contributions. The resulting keyword combination considers the ALL (searching all of the searchable fields using one query) and Boolean AND/OR operators, leading to the following query: **DLT** (All Fields) and **FINANC*** (All Fields) or **DLT** (All Fields) and **BANK*** (All Fields) or **BLOCKCHAIN** (All Fields) and **FINANC*** (All Fields) or **BLOCKCHAIN** (All Fields) and **BANK*** (All Fields) or **DISTRIBUTED LEDGER TECHNOLOG*** (All Fields) and **BANK*** (All Fields) or **DISTRIBUTED LEDGER TECHNOLOG*** (All Fields) and **FINANC*** (All Fields). Data cleaning filters are also applied, restricting the sample to articles published in English in the subject areas of business finance, management, and economics (to exclude more technical contributions related to other scientific fields, such as telecommunications and com-puter science). The database is then screened to ensure the relevance of the final sample by analysing each article's abstract (and, in case of disagree-ment, the entire article) to exclude from the sample all off-topic references (e.g., articles in computer science or mathematics), thus focusing only on papers in line with the scope of the research and whose full text was avail-able. Data cleaning ensures that the final dataset consists of only valid, complete entries. Finally, to summarise the discussion of the results and improve their readability, the SLR process identifies the main research stream concerning the application of DLT in the banking industry and several other research streams discussed in the following sections.

Results

Following the SLR process, the dataset includes an initial sample of 91 papers obtained from the Web of Science. After the sample screening process mentioned in the methodology, the removal of off-topic refer-ences, and the exclusion of papers whose full text was not available, the final dataset results in 57 articles. An examination of the dataset indicates that the most relevant sources or journals have yet to be identified, owing to the topic's relative newness and its limited litera-ture (the first paper available in the dataset dates back only to 2017). However, 2022 has been the most productive year for the topic, with

13 papers published, following a growing trend. Bibliometric data from the sample identify the *Technology Innovation Management Review* and the *Journal of Risk and Financial Management* as the most productive journals, with Chiu and Koeppl (2019), Yosino et al. (2021), and Oh and Shong (2017) as the three most globally cited documents (with, respectively, 66, 54, and 40 global citations). The analysis of local citations of authors and documents (co-authorship and co-citation analysis) reveals no findings, given the topic's novelty.

Although the outcomes of the sample confirm the increased research interest in the field of DLT in banking, they also highlight how limited the published literature on this topic is. Two main strands distinguish studies focusing explicitly on DLT in banking from those that analyse technological innovation, including Blockchain, in the banking industry and other financial environments.

DLT in the Banking Industry

As mentioned above, the literature review reveals limited research (only five studies; see Table 2.1 published on the topic of DLT applications in the banking industry) even though DLT has the potential to revolutionise the way financial transactions are recorded and processed in the banking industry.

Melnychenko et al. (2020) and Druhov et al. (2019) focus on new technologies used in digital banking in Ukraine and the European Union (EU), but do not emphasise DLT much. Regarding Ukraine, the authors highlight changes in regulatory frameworks, access to capital and investments, and the readiness of the domestic financial sector as factors influencing the use of financial technologies in digital banking. Regarding the EU, the authors study the impact of modern information technology on banking systems and expectations for their development. In particular, the authors highlight that blockchain applications in payment transactions are already narrow. One of the main challenges is the processing speed of Blockchain networks. Currently, most blockchain networks can process only a few transactions per second, which is significantly slower than traditional payment systems. This means that the use of Blockchain technology for high-volume transactions, such as those in retail environments, is not yet practical. Another challenge is the need for a solid power infrastructure to support Blockchain technology in the payment system. This includes the development of secure and scalable networks that can handle large numbers of transactions without slowing down, as well as the development of user-friendly interfaces and applications that make it easy for consumers to use Blockchain-based payment systems.

Jantoń-Drozdowska and Mikołajewicz-Woźniak (2017) investigate the potential impact that DLT transfers in the banking sector in Europe may have on the functioning of the Single Euro Payments Area (SEPA) instruments. Like modern payment systems, the SEPA system typically uses a master ledger to track transactions and a central counterparty to validate and process them. However, centralised payment systems also have limitations. They may be vulnerable to security breaches and are subject to a single point of failure, thus potentially disrupting the entire network if a system goes down.

One potential benefit of DLT systems is their ability to support multiple currencies. Because they are decentralised and do not rely on a central authority, DLT systems can potentially facilitate the exchange of different currencies without intermediaries. This could make it easier for individuals and businesses in the EU to make cross-border payments in various currencies, including national currencies and the euro. Another potential benefit of DLT systems is their transparency and security. Because all transactions are recorded on a public ledger that anyone can view, DLT systems can provide high levels of transparency and accountability. However, as previously mentioned, DLT solutions also have limitations that may make them less appealing to some users. They are often slower than traditional payment systems, requiring multiple parties to reach a consensus before a transaction can be completed. They may also be more complex to implement and use, requiring a new infrastructure and users to learn new technologies. According to the European Central Bank, the technology is not sufficiently mature for central banks' market infrastructure, precluding the operation of their settlement services in a DLT environment.

Nevertheless, it is possible that systems based on DLT, such as blockchain, could ultimately contribute to further financial integration in the EU and potentially extend the geographical scope of SEPA. However, it is important to note that DLT systems are still in the early stages of development and have not yet been widely adopted. Some challenges need to be addressed before they can be widely used in payment systems, including scalability, regulatory compliance, and user adoption. The coming years will likely see continued development and adoption of DLT systems, since they offer many potential benefits over traditional payment systems. Overall, DLT systems have the potential to contribute to further financial integration in the EU and enhance the capabilities of SEPA. It is important, however, to carefully consider these systems' potential risks and unintended consequences and regulate them appropriately to ensure they are used safely and responsibly.

Luo and Yan (2022) have developed a bank risk mitigation framework and find that decentralised digital identity and encryption technology are the most important factors for attaining market equilibrium between a decentralised consensus and information distribution by helping mitigate default risk. In these systems, a digital identity serves to establish the identity and reputation of an individual or entity, while encryption technology helps to protect sensitive information and ensure transaction security. In financial transactions, as in borrowing from a bank, a robust digital identity can reduce the risk of default by providing a record of an individual's financial history and reputation. This can be particularly important in decentralised systems, where there may be a lack of traditional intermediaries, such as credit agencies, to provide this information. In addition, the use of encryption technology can help protect sensitive information, such as financial records and personal data, from being accessed by unauthorised parties. This can help reduce the risk of fraud and abuse and contribute to the system's overall security and stability. Overall, the combination of decentralisation, digital identity, and encryption technology can help to create a more equitable and efficient market where all participants have access to the information, allowing them to make informed decisions and engage in fair and secure transactions.

Finally, the research stream related to financial innovation includes the work of Cheng et al. (2022), who investigate the impact of banks' strategic move to cloud computing on bank performance and risk taking. According to these authors, the banking industry's adoption of cloud computing can have a complex impact on cost efficiency, profit efficiency, and operational risk. Specifically, banks that adopt cloud computing tend to have lower cost efficiency but higher profit efficiency. This may be because cloud computing can help financial institutions reduce their information technology infrastructure costs, but it may also displace traditional business models, which could impact profitability. Cheng et al. also indicate that the adoption of cloud computing can impact operational risk, with state-owned banks experiencing

Table 2.1 *Literature on DLT in the banking industry*

Papers' aims	Main findings	References
• Define the dominant ideas/research areas of financial technologies in digital banking. • Determine the impact of modern information technology in the banking systems of EU countries and their prospects for development. • Determine the potential impact that the transfer of DLT to the banking sector may have on the future functioning of SEPA. • Propose a simple two-period model to consider consumers' borrowing behaviour in a decentralised consensus and information distribution platform.	• Demonstrate the effects of technologies such as artificial intelligence, biometrics, and big data on digital banking, which can improve data analysis, personalisation, decision making, and security. • Confirm that the digitalisation level of banking activity is directly related to countries' economic development level. • Group EU countries according to their different levels of digitalisation → countries with the most developed economies are found to have the highest levels of banking activity digitalisation. • Identify trends in the banking business over the next five years, such as changes in the format of banking service organisation and in the format of competition in the banking service market due to the emergence of new competitors such as technology companies, social networks, and online stores.	Jantoń-Drozdowska and Mikołajewicz-Woźniak (2017); Druhov et al. (2019); Melnychenko et al. (2020); Cheng et al. (2022); Luo and Yan (2022);

- The problems with current SEPA payment schemes could be solved by supplementing them with applications based on DLT.
- These systems will provide real-time processing and a global reach, as well as extend functionalities to transfer other currencies.
- Implementing this technology will lead to new financial products and business models. Existing SEPA schemes are likely to be modified and supplemented rather than quickly replaced.
- Decentralised digital identity and encryption technology are important for achieving market equilibrium between a decentralised consensus and information distribution in a consumer default model. A greater scope of digital identity construction and more blockchain consensus records reduce the likelihood of borrower default. Digital identity owners must bear greater costs if they want to collude with the recorder and default, resulting in a smaller default risk.

a reduction in operational risk and all other banks experiencing an increase. This could be due to various factors, including the banks' level of experience and expertise with cloud computing, their specific needs and capabilities, and regulatory and legal considerations. Finally, cloud computing can interact with other emerging technologies, such as blockchain, and jointly affect bank efficiency and operational risk.

Other Technology Innovations

This section contains contributions focusing on applying new technologies, primarily Blockchain, in the banking system and other financial environments. Regarding a focus on the banking sector, Yoo (2017) investigates the use of blockchain in the Korean financial sector, highlighting the principal applications and how they can respond to the Korean banking industry. The Korean market seems to have developed entirely since the country's 16 central banks joined the R3CEV Blockchain international consortium. Considering both international and Korean markets, Yoo finds settlement, remittances, securities, and smart contracts to be the most widespread applications. In addition, according to emerging trends in international remittance services, Korea is accelerating the introduction of a closed (private) distributed ledger operating without a central bank.

Similarly, Golubev et al. (2020) discuss the development of the Russian banking system, focusing on the introduction of new technologies such as Blockchain and artificial intelligence. The Russian banking sector has been exploring the use of Blockchain technology in various applications. For example, some banks have begun using Blockchain to streamline and secure financial transactions, such as cross-border payments and trade finance. This was necessary because the monopolisation of Russia's banking sector has necessitated new development paths for small and medium-sized banks, given their issues of progress and competition.

Moreover, Bataev et al. (2020) have designed a model to estimate the efficiency of the development and use of Blockchain-based information systems for customer identification by financial institutions. The economic efficiency of Blockchain can be a concern, and it might not always be the most cost-effective solution for small or medium-sized financial institutions. Several factors can impact the economic efficiency of Blockchain in customer identification solutions, such as the size of the customer base, the complexity of the system, and the resources required to maintain and update it. Generally, it may be more cost-effective for large financial institutions with a large customer base to implement Blockchain-based customer identification systems, since the costs can be spread across many users. The technology could become more efficient and cost-effective in the future as it continues to evolve and improve. It is important for organisations to carefully consider the benefits and costs of different identification solutions and choose the one that best meets their needs and capabilities. Finally, Blockchain information systems will likely continue to be developed and adopted by financial institutions of all sizes in the coming years. As the technology matures and becomes more widely understood, smaller banks will likely begin to explore the potential applications of Blockchain in their operations.

Seven literature reviews are included in this second research stream. Specifically, according to Paul and Criado's (2020) classification of literature reviews, it is possible to identify two SLRs (Daluwathumullagamage and Sims 2021; Anifa et al. 2022): a bibliometric analysis (Bhatt et al. 2022) and four mixed reviews that combine the systematic and bibliometric approaches (Grassi and Lanfranchi 2022) or apply a more narrative-oriented method (Becker et al. 2020; Rejeb et al. 2021a; Kumari and Devi 2022). Daluwathumullagamage and Sims (2021) have conducted a systematic review of blockchain adoption focused on banking and have developed a framework for banking-based blockchains, covering 407 articles from 2013 to 2020. The authors find that the contributions focus on common themes such as Blockchain and FinTech. However, there seems to be a gap in the focus of Blockchain applications in the banking industry, with industry reports often discussing banking use cases and the academic literature tending to focus on FinTech and cryptocurrencies. Additionally, several areas that have not been fully explored in the academic and industry literature, such as corporate voting, trading, and exchanges, could potentially benefit from the use of Blockchain technology. The adoption of Blockchain in the banking industry also faces several challenges, including reputation, culture, interoperability, scalability, latency, privacy and security, regulation, and energy consumption. While the potential for Blockchain-enabled banks is significant, it may take time before the technology is widely adopted and integrated into traditional banking systems.

Anifa et al. (2022) aim to enrich the understanding of FinTech innovations in payments and financing and investigate the correlation and significance of regulatory framework in maintaining a fair ecosystem, covering contributions in 2014–2022. Their literature review shows that FinTech has significantly impacted financial services by introducing innovative technologies focused on financing, payments, and regulation. These innovations have improved effectiveness and efficiency, leading to the systematic growth of the finance industry. FinTech has been driven by entrepreneurial innovations and received support from governments worldwide, contributing to its growth. Moreover, FinTech is expected to continue to grow and evolve, with numerous inventions in the pipeline from both businesses and consumers. The future of FinTech looks bright, with Internet finance predicted to see significant growth in the coming years. FinTech innovations have greatly benefited the financial services industry, and this trend is expected to continue for the next two decades. Similarly, Bhatt et al. (2022) have conducted a bibliometric analysis and a thematic literature review to identify the main areas and current dynamics of FinTech, digitalisation, and financial services. The authors examine 583 journal articles from 1984 to 2021, identifying four different thematics: the regulation of FinTech and digital financial services, the role of technology in the digital transformation of financial services, digital financial inclusion (enabled by mobile money, mobile banking, and digital finance), and technology adoption in digital financial services (a niche theme). Differently, Kumari and Devi (2022) provide a narrative review focusing on FinTech and Blockchain in the banking sector. Their study finds that FinTech, specifically Blockchain technology, will significantly change investment practices and offer improved customer information through decentralised, equitable systems. The authors also highlight the potential for FinTech, specifically Blockchain-based systems, to provide a more effective alternative to traditional banking through fast money transfers, enhanced security, and transparent financial tracking. Another relevant analysis is provided by the literature review of Rejeb et al. (2021a), who investigate the role of cryptocurrencies in modern finance. According to their findings, cryptocurrencies can offer numerous benefits to businesses and individuals, including lower transaction costs, increased efficiency, enhanced security and privacy, diversification opportunities, alternative financing solutions, and financial inclusion. However, there are also challenges to integrating cryptocurrencies into modern finance, including the lack of regulatory standards, the risk of criminal activity, high energy and environmental costs, regulatory bans and usage restrictions, security and privacy concerns, and the high volatility of cryptocurrencies.

Finally, two review works have analysed regulatory technology (RegTech). Becker et al. (2020) provide a comprehensive overview of the technologies used in RegTech as addressed in the scientific literature, examining 55 journal articles and discussing the most relevant topics, such as compliance management and risk management and most applied technologies, such as artificial intelligence and blockchain. Grassi and Lanfranchi (2022) present a comprehensive and multidimensional framework for organising and synthesising the existing body of knowledge on RegTech to shed light on underexplored areas and provide a holistic understanding of the field. Their findings indicate that RegTech applications often involve increased digitalisation in compliance processes, making it necessary to rely heavily on data and technological innovations. Proper management, storage, and data protection will likely become critical in RegTech. Additionally, supervision and regulation are likely to shift towards a more data-driven approach, leading to increased interactions between regulators and regulated entities and the possibility of more predictive, proactive, transparent, and responsive regulation (Grassi and Lanfranchi 2022). However, the current regulatory environment may also pose challenges, including higher compliance requirements and costs for regulated entities, which may limit innovation and restrict the entry of new players into the market. Finally, with many players offering RegTech solutions, there is the potential for conflicts of interest or disruptions in the competitive landscape. RegTech itself may eventually be regulated to address these issues. As mentioned, this research stream covers different topics, including DLT applications in central banking (Table 2.2), financial markets applications such as (i) financial institutions and business models (Table 2.3), (ii) fund industry (Table 2.4), (iii) insurance (Table 2.5), (iv) Sukuk (Islamic investing) (Table 2.6), (v) post-trading industry (Table 2.7), (vi) the regulatory framework of DLT (Table 2.8), (vii) cryptocurrencies (Table 2.9), and (viii) crypto-assets (Table 2.10). The constituents of this research stream cover heterogeneous topics, and, to improve readability, these papers' aims, and main findings are summarised in corresponding tables, as previously mentioned.

In addition, the contributions explore the regulatory framework of DLT, analyse the use of DLT in Qatar, and provide recommendations for improving blockchain transactions and regulating the technology. They also review the US Securities and Exchange Commission's stance on initial coin offerings (ICOs) and suggest increasing the number of market participants, adding the ability to conduct transactions in electronic fiat money or a digital currency pegged to fiat money, and establishing arbitration on the platform to resolve conflicts.

Conclusion

A few years ago, due to fierce competition from nonfinancial firms and fintech digital startups, analysts started to doubt the continued survival of banks. Banks have bright futures ahead of them, but only if they can rise to the revolutionary challenges posed by two key trends: the importance of the client and contemporary technology.

The academic literature has not focused much on theoretically and/or empirically demonstrating the implications of DLT on bank operations, either at the infrastructure or the business model level, according to an analysis of the sample publications. Only five publications address banks and specific features of clearly defined geographic settings or the payment system.

Despite concentrating on DLT, most studies heavily mention the use of the Blockchain. We have previously examined how the two differ and how DLT's features are better suited for application in the banking industry. DLT has the potential to revolutionise several financial industry segments, including central banking and financial markets, as has been previously indicated. DLT can be used in central banking to create and distribute digital currencies, which may increase financial inclusion and lower the costs of conventional payment systems. DLT can reduce the need for intermediaries and improve market efficiency by streamlining the settlement of securities and other financial instruments.

The literature also supports the widespread interest in blockchain technology, cryptocurrencies, and related applications. A novel hypothesis of the best exchange rate pegs, a detailed analysis of cryptocurrency owner data, and an explanation of cryptocurrencies and Blockchain technology are all included. The literature also looks at the prospects and threats of cryptocurrencies, the economic implications of the advent of cryptocurrencies, and the effects of Blockchain and cryptocurrency-related name changes on company and financial performance.

Appendix to Chapter 2. Summary of Other Research Strands

Sabrina Leo and Andrea Delle Foglie

Table 2.2 Other research strands: DLT in central banking

Papers' aims	Main findings	References
• DLT applications in the monetary system (R3 Corda). • Analyse the dynamics of central banks' views on virtual currencies. • Application of central bank digital currencies (CBDCs) to the supply chain.	• DLT is more likely to increase the role of central banks → competition and new alternatives to bank-based payment systems, which could lead to a more stable financial system (see the synthetic CBDCs – *sCBDS*, Adrian and Mancini-Griffoli 2019). • Existence of misunderstanding between virtual currencies and cryptocurrencies → more attention to central banks' analysis and warnings and disclosure about these different positions. • Companies that arrange their activities in low-volatility CBDC periods could generate vast benefits. • Possibility to develop an intelligentised supply chain based on Blockchain (smart contract integration), improve cybersecurity, etc.	Teresiene (2018); Huibers (2021); Ding et al. (2022)

Table 2.3 *Other research strands:* financial institutions and business models

Papers' aims	Main findings	References
• Blockchain applications in Korea	• Distributed characteristics of Blockchain cannot be applied when developing financial services → some issues to be resolved, but there is potential to improve the existing information handling process of financial institutions.	Yoo (2017); Oh and Shong (2017); Matsepe and Van der Lingen (2022); Golubev et al. (2020); Bataev et al. (2020); Schär (2021); Rejeb et al. (2021a); Rejeb et al. (2021b); Festa et al. (2022);
• Business model innovation related to Blockchain and financial institutions.	• Suggest the application of Blockchain for the automation of financial institutions' business processes.	
• Determinants influencing the adoption of emerging technologies in South African financial services firms.	• Adopter traits, technology usability, industry characteristics, and organisational leadership and characteristics are influential in technology adoption → complexity and user insecurity have inhibited adoption.	
• Opportunities and potential risks of the decentralised finance ecosystem.	• At the firm level, competitive pressure, regulatory support, customer demands, decision maker risk orientation, opinion leadership, effective communication mechanisms, and top management have supported the adoption.	
• Investigate the influence of FinTech determinants as potential facilitators in an entrepreneurial ecosystem in Tunisia.	• Decentralised finance still is a niche with certain risks and issues to be resolved → interesting properties in terms of efficiency, transparency, accessibility, and composability.	
• Role of centralised and decentralised ledgers in the money supply process.	• Knowledge, availability, and accessibility of crowdfunding and blockchain have an impact on young entrepreneurial intention.	
• Development of the Russian banking system, focusing on introducing new technologies	• A powerful contribution to a more general entrepreneurial ecosystem and to young Tunisian entrepreneurs → improving financing for startups and innovative projects.	
	• Mobile payment seems to generate no significant stimulus on entrepreneurial intention.	
	• Entrepreneurial education exerts a relevant influence.	

- Centralised ledgers are still critical in the recordkeeping of financial transactions → use of decentralised ledger systems expected to induce several disruptions in the future of money supply → likely to become a widely used tool in finance.
- The strengths and opportunities of decentralised ledgers outweigh those of centralised ledgers.
- The Russian banking sector has been exploring the use of blockchain technology in various applications (streamlining and securing financial transactions, such as cross-border payments and trade finance).
- This exploration has been necessary because the monopolisation of the banking sector has led to the need for new development paths for small and medium-sized banks, tackling their issues of progress and competition.
- The economic efficiency of Blockchain can be a concern, and it may not always be the most cost-effective solution for small or medium-sized financial institutions.
- Factors impacting the economic efficiency of Blockchain in customer identification solutions (size of the customer base, the complexity of the system, and the resources required to maintain and update it).
- Generally, it may be more cost-effective for large financial institutions with a large customer base to implement Blockchain-based customer identification systems, since the costs can be spread across many users.

Table 2.4 *Other research strands:* fund industry

Papers' aims	Main findings	References
• DLT applications in social financing schemes and small-scale real estate projects (hometown investment trust funds)	• Higher investments in funds due to increased risk mitigation (more transparency, security, and auditability) introduced by DLT. • DLTs have the potential to enhance social funding schemes for real estate projects such as the hometown investment trust fund. • Need to test regional differences.	Yoshino et al. (2021)

Table 2.5 Other research strands: insurance

Papers' aims	Main findings	References
• Yield-based insurance and index-based insurance comparison.	• DLT, in combination with index-based insurance, might not only resolve existing problems but also facilitate the development of innovative risk management tools. • DLT solutions in the cryptocurrency market demonstrate positive features. • Use insurance with index-based insurance in agriculture → DLT could improve real-time exposure assessments, facilitate accident and/or risk forecasting, and assist with reserve calculations for reinsurance.	Schwarze and Sushchenko (2022)

Table 2.6 *Other research strands:* Sukuk (Islamic investing)

Papers' aims	Main findings	References
• Review the literature on Blockchain sukuk and identify legal, regulatory and potential Shariah issues.	• Digitising the issuance of sukuk through Blockchain remedies certain inefficiencies associated with sukuk transactions. • Increase the transparency of underlying sukuk assets and cash flows → reducing costs and the number of intermediaries in sukuk transactions. • Technology cannot replace all the risk mitigation mechanisms in sukuk issuance → need to enhance the existing mechanisms using technology.	Kunhibava et al. (2021)

Table 2.7 *Other research strands:* post-trading industry

Papers' aims	Main findings	References
• Technological trends in post-trade securities • Feasibility of settling securities on a Blockchain	• Laws not yet found solutions to the risks and opportunities of post-trade DLT. • Gaps in the regulation of the post-trading of crypto-assets. • Any Blockchain-based settlement system – whether permissionless or permissioned – needs to ensure settlement → users are willing to pay transaction fees.	Chiu and Koeppl (2019); Droll and Minto (2022)

Table 2.8 *Other research strands:* DLT and regulatory frameworks

Papers' aims	Main findings	References
• Overview of the benefits and drawbacks of such applications of DLT from a legal and technical perspective in Qatar. • Review the US SEC's initial statements on ICOs and the evolving legal framework.	• Provide suggestions to improve Blockchain transactions: • Increase the number of participants. • Add to 'Blockchain the ability to conduct transactions in electronic fiat money or in a digital currency, which is pegged to fiat money'. (Ibrahim and Truby 2022, p. 432) • *'Establishment of arbitration on the platform itself, which allows resolving main conflict situations without court involvement.* (Ibrahim and Truby 2022, p. 432) • Provide a multi-layered governance approach to Blockchain regulation in Qatar (embrace international regulations and standards, replicate foreign regional and national rules that are appropriate and innovative, apply sandbox regulations to Blockchain products and services).	Ibrahim and Truby (2022); Cumming et al. (2019)

Table 2.9 *Other research strands: cryptocurrencies*

Papers' aims	Main findings	References
• Exploration of representative data on cryptocurrency owners and examine socioeconomic correlates. • Impact of blockchain and crypto-related name changes on corporate and financial performance. • Develop a new theory of optimal exchange rate pegs. • Present an overview of cryptocurrencies and Blockchain technologies and applications. • Facebook's and Meta Platform's digital currency projects • Best methods to process international transfers, considering overall metrics, and whether cryptocurrencies hold a bright future in the financial world.	• No evidence that cryptocurrencies are alternatives to fiat currencies or regulated. • No differences between the general population and US cryptocurrency investors in terms of security concerns with either cash or commercial banking services. • Crypto investors find traditional banking less convenient. • Men tend to invest more in cryptocurrencies than women. • A positive relation between higher levels of income, education, and digital financial experience and cryptocurrency ownership. • Positive correlation between income and education and the owners of ether and XRP → negative correlation for Litecoin. • Diem project is not yet ready for launch → need to adapt regulatory requirements. • Cryptocurrencies offer a wide range of features, such as faster, cheaper, and more secure cross-border money transfers → more beneficial options for users in cross-border transfers compared to traditional methods of fund transfer → potential to replace paper money and gain mainstream recognition throughout the world.	Hsieh et al. (2018); Stefan (2018); Zadorozhnyi et al. (2018); Kucheryavenko et al. (2019); Yatsyk and Shvets (2020); Alexander et al. (2020); Uyduran (2020); Fauzi et al. (2020); Dutta et al. (2020); Akyildirim et al. (2020); Rrustemi and Tuchschmid (2021); Pele et al. (2021); Routledge and Zetlin-Jones (2022); Andolfatto and Martin (2022); Lee et al. (2022); Brauneis et al. (2022); Ajouz et al. (2022); Auer and Tercero-Lucas (2022); Kang (2022);

Table 2.9 (*cont.*)

Papers' aims	Main findings	References
• Discuss opportunities in cryptocurrency.	• Crypto tokens are highly volatile due to their nature and various other factors.	
• Determine the economic aspects of the emergence of cryptocurrencies.	• Improvements and future work on cryptocurrency using the by-product of proof of work and applying the knowledge management system.	
• Develop a model to study a double-spending prevention mechanism without payment confirmations.	• Define cryptocurrency as a variety of e-money used as an additional alternative currency based on Blockchain technology.	
• Analyse Bitcoin as DAO.	• If the cryptocurrency system supports agents checking the history of double-spending attempts for any digital wallet used to trade cryptocurrency, then double spending can be prevented without precautionary confirmations.	
• Discuss the development of cryptocurrencies.		
• Examine whether and how online analysts help mitigate information asymmetry in fundraising campaigns that lack financial intermediation.	• If the loss of a good wallet that has a good reputation based on a history of double spending attempts outweighs the short-run gain from double spending, an agent will not commit double spending with a good wallet.	
• Analyse price discovery in the cryptocurrency Ethereum	• Double-spending incentives critically depend on the confirmation time that is determined by the level of difficulty of the mining work.	
• Study BTCUSD liquidity and determinants.	• Analysts' ratings predict potential fraud and token price volatility →both of which have received considerable attention from regulators and market participants.	

- Investigate the perceptions of Shariah scholars on the concepts and features of Shariah-compliant precious metal–backed cryptocurrency.
- Investigate a framework using machine learning forecasting methods to predict daily Bitcoin prices.
- Provides insights for the separation of cryptocurrencies from other assets.

- Ether perpetual swaps on BitMEX have a dominant trading volume and price discovery over the major spot exchanges.
- Identify interesting hour-of-day and day-of-week effects in trading volumes → more informed institutional players are trading ether spot and derivatives.
- BTCUSD liquidity is primarily explained by same exchange past liquidity, past cryptocurrency market wide liquidity and volatility, and fees charged on blockchain for bitcoin transfers.
- Respondents support and recommend Shariah-compliant precious metal–backed cryptocurrency, carefully investigating all perspectives → increasing transparency, etc.
- Most of the variation among cryptocurrencies and classical assets can be explained by three factors: the tail factor, the memory factor, and the moment factor.
- A random asset is likely to be a cryptocurrency if it has the following properties: very long log return distribution tails, high variance, and low values of the α-stable tail parameter, indicating a large departure from normality.

Table 2.10 *Other research strands:* crypto-assets

Papers' aims	Main findings	References
• Define the essence of crypto-assets in financial accounting, attributes for its taxonomy, and multipurpose overview of the crypto-assets market environment.	• US, Hong Kong, and Singapore are the countries with the largest numbers of registered crypto-asset exchanges → now reducing due to regulatory requirements.	Rrustemi and Tuchschmid (2020); Uyduran (2020); Olsen et al. (2018; Cong et al. (2022); Masiak et al. (2020); Ivashchenko et al. (2018); Howell et al. (2020); Duran and Griffin (2021);
• Digital economics and challenges that can be encountered during ICO including limits and alternative solutions.	• Types of crypto-assets are identified: cryptocurrency (payment tokens), security tokens, utility tokens, asset-backed tokens, and hybrid (or mixed) tokens.	
• Explain the architecture and design choices of the Lykke Wallet exchange.	• LakeDiamond, an ICO project did not succeed due to the confusing tokenisation procedure, not targeted group of investors and the absence of basic monitoring and proprietary right (lack of comprehensive white paper).	
• Develop a dynamic model of a platform economy where tokens serve as a means of payment.	• Need greater information and transparency for the success of ICO, security token offering (STO), and initial exchange offering (IEO) operations → good alternatives compared to ICOs?	
• Assess the risks associated with smart contracts.	• Design a global Internet exchange where all financial instruments can be traded.	
• Investigate the market cycles of ICOs	• Tokens are optimally rewarded to platform owners when the token supply is low and burnt to boost franchise value when the normalised supply is high.	

- Define proper ways to implement best European ICO practices.
- Examine which issuer and ICO characteristics predict real-world successful outcomes.

- Although the token price is determined in a liquid market, the platform's financial constraint generates an endogenous token issuance cost that causes underinvestment through the conflict of interest between insiders (owners) and outsiders (users).
- Blockchain technology mitigates underinvestment by addressing owners' time inconsistency problem →
  Extensive use of bilateral agreements, complexity and lack of standardisation, transparency, misuse, and speed of contagion contributed to the global financial crisis, which could also become material concerns for smart contract technology.
- Other contextual factors, such as the risk of defects in smart contracts and cyberattacks, could lead to potential destabilisation of the broader financial system.
- ICO market cycles exist and that shocks to the growth rates of ICO volumes are persistent → shocks in cryptocurrency returns have a substantial and positive effect on ICO volumes → the volatility of cryptocurrency returns does not significantly affect ICO volumes.
- Favourable ratings are associated with aggressive initial token subscriptions, ICO fundraising success, and long-run token returns.

Table 2.10 (*cont.*)

Papers' aims	Main findings	References
	• Of the 15 biggest ICOs, Switzerland leading in regulating relevant ICO activity →European Securities and Markets Authority regulations have great importance in terms of performing activities connected with capital raising, where ICO is not an exception and should be performed according to existing rules.	
	• Success is associated with disclosure, credible commitment to the project, and quality signals. Instrumental variables analysis finds that ICO token exchange listing causes higher future employment, indicating that access to token liquidity has significant real consequences for the enterprise.	

References

Adrian, T., Mancini-Griffoli, T. (2019). 'The Rise of Digital Money'. Fintech Notes, 2019/001, International Monetary Fund, pp. 1–15. Available online: www.imf.org/en/Publications/fintech-notes/Issues/2019/07/ 12/The-Rise-of-Digital-Money-47097?utm_campaign=BitDigest& utm_medium=email&utm_source=Revue%20newsletter

Ajouz, M., Abdullah, A., and Kassim, S. 2022. 'Shari'ah oriented precious metal backed cryptocurrency: From Shari'ah advisors' and financial experts' perceptions', *The Singapore Economic Review* 67(1): 439–58.

Akyildirim, E., Corbet, S., Sensoy, A., and Yarovaya, L. 2020. 'The impact of blockchain related name changes on corporate performance', *Journal of Corporate Finance* 65: 101759.

Alexander, C., Choi, J., Massie, H. R. A., and Sohn, S. 2020. 'Price discovery and microstructure in ether spot and derivative markets', *International Review of Financial Analysis* 71: 101506.

Andolfatto, D., and Martin, F. M. 2022. 'The blockchain revolution: Decoding digital currencies', *Review* 104(3): 149–65

Anifa, M., Ramakrishnan, S., Joghee, S., Kabiraj, S., and Bishnoi, M. M. 2022. 'FinTech innovations in the financial service industry', *Journal of Risk and Financial Management* 15(7): 287.

Auer, R., and Tercero-Lucas, D. 2022. 'Distrust or speculation? The socioeconomic drivers of U.S. cryptocurrency investments', *Journal of Financial Stability* 62: 101066.

Bahoo, S., Alon, I., and Paltrinieri, A. 2020. 'Corruption in international business: A review and research agenda', *International Business Review* 29(4): 101660.

Bataev, A., Plotnikova, E., Lukin, G., and Sviridenko, M. 2020. 'Evaluation of the economic efficiency of blockchain for customer identification by financial institutions', *IOP Conference Series: Materials Science and Engineering* 940('1): 012038.

Becker, M., Merz, K., and Buchkremer, R. 2020. 'RegTech – The application of modern information technology in regulatory affairs: Areas of interest in research and practice', *Intelligent Systems in Accounting, Finance and Management* 27(4): 161–7.

Bhatt, A., Joshipura, M., and Joshipura, N. 2022. 'Decoding the trinity of Fintech, digitalisation and financial services: An integrated bibliometric analysis and thematic literature review approach', *Cogent Economics and Finance* 10(1): 2114160.

Brauneis, A., Mestel, R., Riordan, R., and Theissen, E. 2022. 'Bitcoin unchained: Determinants of cryptocurrency exchange liquidity', *Journal of Empirical Finance* 69: 106–22.

Cheng, M., Qu, Y., Jiang, C., and Zhao, C. 2022. 'Is cloud computing the digital solution to the future of banking?', *Journal of Financial Stability* 63: 101073.

Chiu, J., and Koeppl, T. V. 2019. 'Blockchain-based settlement for asset trading', *The Review of Financial Studies* 32(5): 1716–53.

Cong, L. W., Li, Y., and Wang, N. 2022. 'Token-based platform finance', *Journal of Financial Economics* 144(3): 972–91.

Cumming, D. J., Johan, S., and Pant, A. 2019. 'Regulation of the crypto-economy: Managing risks, challenges, and regulatory uncertainty', *Journal of Risk and Financial Management* 12(3): 126.

Daluwathumullagamage, D. J., and Sims, A. 2021. 'Fantastic beasts: Blockchain based banking', *Journal of Risk and Financial Management* 14(4): 170.

Ding, S., Cui, T., Wu, X., and Du, M. 2022. 'Supply chain management based on volatility clustering: The effect of CBDC volatility', *Research in International Business and Finance* 62: 101690.

Droll, T., and Minto, A. 2022. 'Hare or hedgehog? The role of law in shaping current technological trends in the securities post-trading system', *Accounting, Economics, and Law: A Convivium*. 1–46.

Druhov, O., Druhova, V., and Pakhnenko, O. 2019. 'The influence of financial innovations on EU countries banking systems development', *Marketing and Management of Innovations* (3): 167–77.

Duran, R. E., and Griffin, P. 2021. 'Smart contracts: Will Fintech be the catalyst for the next global financial crisis?', *Journal of Financial Regulation and Compliance* 29(1): 104–22.

Dutta, A., Kumar, S., and Basu, M. 2020. 'A gated recurrent unit approach to bitcoin price prediction', *Journal of Risk and Financial Management* 13(2): 23.

Fauzi, M. A., Paiman, N., and Othman, Z. 2020. 'Bitcoin and cryptocurrency: Challenges, opportunities and future works', *The Journal of Asian Finance, Economics and Business* 7(8): 695–704.

Festa, G., Elbahri, S., Cuomo, M. T., Ossorio, M., and Rossi, M. 2022. 'FinTech ecosystem as influencer of young entrepreneurial intentions: Empirical findings from Tunisia', *Journal of Intellectual Capital*, 24(1): 205–6.

Golubev, A., Ryabov, O., and Zolotarev, A. 2020. 'Digital transformation of the banking system of Russia with the introduction of blockchain and artificial intelligence technologies', *IOP Conference Series: Materials Science and Engineering* 940(1): 012041.

Grassi, L., and Lanfranchi, D. 2022. 'RegTech in public and private sectors: The nexus between data, technology and regulation', *Journal of Industrial and Business Economics* 49(3): 441–79.

Howell, S. T., Niessner, M., and Yermack, D. 2020. 'Initial coin offerings: Financing growth with cryptocurrency token sales', *The Review of Financial Studies* 33(9): 3925–74.

Hsieh, Y.-Y., Vergne, J.-P., Anderson, P., Lakhani, K., and Reitzig, M. 2018. 'Bitcoin and the rise of decentralised autonomous organisations', *Journal of Organisation Design* 7(1): 14.

Huibers, F. 2021. 'Distributed ledger technology and the future of money and banking: Banking is necessary, banks are not. Bill Gates 1994', *Accounting, Economics, and Law: A Convivium* 20190095.

Ibrahim, I. A., and Truby, J. 2022. 'Governance in the era of blockchain technology in Qatar: A roadmap and a manual for trade finance', *Journal of Banking Regulation* 23(4): 419–38.

Ivashchenko, A., Polishchuk, Y., and Britchenko, I. 2018. 'Implementation of ICO European best practices by SMEs', *Economic Annals-XXI* 169(1–2): 67–71.

Jantoń-Drozdowska, E., and Mikołajewicz-Woźniak, A. 2017. 'The impact of the distributed ledger technology on the Single Euro Payments Area development', *Equilibrium* 12(3): 519–35.

Kang, K.-Y. 2022. 'Cryptocurrency and double spending history: Transactions with zero confirmation', *Economic Theory*,75(2): 453–91.

Khan, A., Goodell, J. W., Hassan, M. K., and Paltrinieri, A. 2022. 'A bibliometric review of finance bibliometric papers', *Finance Research Letters* 47: 102520.

Kucheryavenko, M. P., Dmytryk, O. O., and Golovashevych, O. O. 2019. 'Cryptocurrencies: Development, features and classification', *Financial and Credit Activity Problems of Theory and Practice* 3(30): 371–74.

Kumari, A., and Devi, N. C. 2022. 'The impact of FinTech and blockchain technologies on banking and financial services', *Technology Innovation Management Review* 12(1/2): 1–11.

Kunhibava, S., Mustapha, Z., Muneeza, A., Sa'ad, A. A., and Karim, M. E. 2021. 'Ṣukūk on blockchain: A legal, regulatory and Sharī'ah review', *ISRA International Journal of Islamic Finance* 13(1): 118–35.

Lee, J., Li, T., and Shin, D. 2022. 'The wisdom of crowds in FinTech: Evidence from initial coin offerings', *The Review of Corporate Finance Studies* 11(1): 1–46.

Luo, H., and Yan, D. 2022. 'Blockchain architecture and its applications in a bank risk mitigation framework', *Economic Research-Ekonomska Istraživanja* 35(1): 3119–37.

Masiak, C., Block, J. H., Masiak, T., Neuenkirch, M., and Pielen, K. N. 2020. 'Initial coin offerings (ICOs): Market cycles and relationship with bitcoin and ether', *Small Business Economics* 55(4): 1113–30.

Matsepe, N. T., and Van der Lingen, E. 2022. 'Determinants of emerging technologies adoption in the South African financial sector', *South African Journal of Business Management* 53(1): 1–12.

Melnychenko, S., Volosovych, S., and Baraniuk, Y. 2020. 'Dominant ideas of financial technologies in digital banking', *Baltic Journal of Economic Studies* 6(1): 92.

Oh, J., and Shong, I. 2017. 'A case study on business model innovations using blockchain: Focusing on financial institutions', *Asia Pacific Journal of Innovation and Entrepreneurship* 11(3): 335–44.

Olsen, R., Battiston, S., Caldarelli, G., Golub, A., Nikulin, M., and Ivliev, S. 2018. 'Case study of Lykke exchange: Architecture and outlook', *The Journal of Risk Finance* 19(1): 26–38.

Paul, J., and Criado, A. R. 2020. 'The art of writing literature review: What do we know and what do we need to know?', *International Business Review* 29(4): 101717.

Pele, D. T., Wesselhöfft, N., Härdle, W. K., Kolossiatis, M., and Yatracos, Y. G. 2021. 'Are cryptos becoming alternative assets?', *The European Journal of Finance* 1–43.

Rejeb, A., Rejeb, K., and Keogh, J. G. 2021a. 'Cryptocurrencies in modern finance: A literature review', *ETIKONOMI* 20(1): 93–118.

Rejeb, A., Rejeb, K., and Keogh, J. G. 2021b. 'Centralised vs. decentralised ledgers in the money supply process: A SWOT analysis', *Quantitative Finance and Economics*, 5(1): 40–66.

Routledge, B., and Zetlin-Jones, A. 2022. 'Currency stability using blockchain technology', *Journal of Economic Dynamics and Control* 142: 104155.

Rrustemi, J., and Tuchschmid, N. S. 2020. 'Fundraising campaigns in a digital economy: Lessons from a Swiss synthetic diamond venture's initial coin offering (ICO)', *Technology Innovation Management Review* 10(6): 53–63.

Rrustemi, J., and Tuchschmid, N. S. 2021. 'Facebook's digital currency venture "diem": The new frontier … or a galaxy far, far away?', *Technology Innovation Management Review* 10(12): 19–30.

Schär, F. 2021. 'Decentralised finance: On blockchain- and smart contract-based financial markets', *Review* 103(2):153–74.

Schwarze, R., and Sushchenko, O. 2022. 'Climate insurance for agriculture in Europe: On the merits of smart contracts and distributed ledger technologies', *Journal of Risk and Financial Management* 15(5): 211.

Stefan, C. 2018. 'Tales from the crypt: Might cryptocurrencies spell the death of traditional money? – A quantitative analysis', *Proceedings of the International Conference on Business Excellence* 12(1): 918–30.

Teresiene, D. 2018. 'Central banks' responses to virtual currencies: An overview', in International Conference on Economics, Finance and Statistics, Topics in Economics, Business and Management, pp. 60–65. Volkson Press.

Uyduran, B. 2020. 'The crypto effect on cross border transfers and future trends of cryptocurrencies', *Financial Internet Quarterly* 16(4): 12–23.

Yatsyk, T., and Shvets, V. 2020. 'Cryptoassets as an emerging class of digital assets in the financial accounting', *Economic Annals-XXI* 183(5–6): 106–15.

Yoo, S. 2017. 'Blockchain based financial case analysis and its implications', *Asia Pacific Journal of Innovation and Entrepreneurship* 11(3): 312–21.

Yoshino, N., Schloesser, T., and Taghizadeh-Hesary, F. 2021. 'Social funding of green financing: An application of distributed ledger technologies', *International Journal of Finance and Economics* 26(4): 6060–73.

Zadorozhnyi, Z.-M. V., Muravskyi, V. V., and Shevchuk, O. A. 2018. 'Management accounting of electronic transactions with the use of cryptocurrencies', *Financial and Credit Activity Problems of Theory and Practice* 3(26): 169–77.

PART II

Opportunities and Challenges in Crypto-Asset Regulation

3 | Some Reflections on the Proposed MiCA Regulation

FILIPPO ANNUNZIATA

Introduction

Within the European Commission's Digital Finance Package approved by the Commission on 24 September 2020 (the EU Digital Finance Package), the *Regulation on the Market for crypto-assets* (MiCA)[1] stands out for its brave and comprehensive approach to such a complex and innovative topic. The EU Digital Finance Package, comprising a Digital Finance[2] and Retail Payments strategy,[3] is aimed at enhancing consumer choices, while at the same time ensuring their protection and financial stability. By the EU Digital Finance Package, the Commission pursues a twofold objective: to boost 'responsible innovation in the EU's financial sector, especially for highly innovative digital start-ups, while mitigating any potential risks related to investor protection, money laundering and cyber-crime' as well as to foster 'Europe's competitiveness and innovation in the financial sector, paving the way for Europe to become a global standard-setter'.

In the context of the EU Digital Finance Package, the proposed new legislation on crypto-assets includes MiCA as well as the pilot regime for distributed ledger technology (DLT)-based market infrastructures[4]

---

[1] Proposal for a Regulation of the European Parliament and of the Council on Markets in Crypto-assets, and amending Directive (EU) 2019/1937, COM (2020) 593 final.
[2] Communication from the Commission to the European Parliament, the Council, the European economic and social committee and the Committee of the regions on a Digital Finance Strategy for the EU, COM (2020) 591 final.
[3] Communication from the Commission to the European Parliament, the Council, the European economic and social committee and the Committee of the regions on a Retail Payments Strategy for the EU, COM (2020) 592 final.
[4] Proposal for a Regulation of the European Parliament and of the Council on a Pilot Regime for market infrastructures based on distributed ledger technology, COM (2020) 594.

introducing a so-called 'sandbox' approach for certain crypto-asset services. Another proposed regulation (the Digital Operational Resilience Act – DORA) tackles the issues of operational resilience. The legislative tools that the Commission proposes – Regulations – are indicative of the serious intentions in pursuing this project. If, and when, the new legislation will be in place, the EU will be the first global market, composed of 27 countries, to have a uniform regulation for the markets in crypto-assets, with a ground-breaking combination of regulation, coupled with the EU passport. The EU will therefore become the largest integrated market for crypto-assets in the world, backed up by sufficiently clear rules and framework, well ahead of the case-by-case or sectoral approaches to be found, for instance, in the USA, where the debate is still open as to how the legislator should address these issues.

MiCA in itself builds extensively upon a comprehensive set of preliminary reports and analysis, many of which conducted under the direction of the European Supervisory Authorities (ESAs), including the truly fundamental opinion of European Security and Market Authority (ESMA), provided to the Commission in January 2019 (ESMA 2019). It also makes treasure of several, innovative national experiences, both in the EU and in non-EU systems, including, amongst others, Switzerland, Singapore, France, Germany, Malta, to cite only a few.

There is already extensive and comprehensive literature on the MiCA proposal, and the scope of these brief notes is not to examine the proposed regulation, in its different aspects. Our scope is, instead, to set out a few remarks on some – necessarily not all, and with no claim to completeness – of the issues that MiCA (as it stands in the original proposal) raises, and that might be considered in the next steps of the legislative process. A new piece of legislation such as MiCA, ambitious *per se*, but necessarily complex and at odds with a rapidly changing technological environment, is necessarily subject to tensions: this should not be considered as a defect of the proposal, but rather as a natural room for improvement.

MiCA Taxonomy: MiFID and Prospectus Regulation

Token pluralism, and fluidity of terminology, have contributed, since the beginning of the phenomenon, to the difficulties of categorising these assets. In the burgeoning academic literature, and also in the experiences as of today under National Law (Blandin et al. 2019), crypto-assets are almost always placed into three functional categories.[5] The first is that of *utility tokens*. Scholars, and also those legislators who have moved in the direction of providing some kind of framework for crypto-assets under National Law, generally converge on the characteristics of this type of token, as those that grant some sort of access or right(s) to the issuer's ecosystem, goods, or services (Bourveau et al. 2022; Howell et al. 2020). A token falling into these schemes is not usually considered a traditional security, or a financial product, as its functions and aims are not those that are typically attached to a financial investment (Hacker and Thomale 2018; Klöhn et al. 2018).[6]

The second token category is that of *asset* or *security/financial tokens*. These are assets of a financial nature; they are tied to an underlying asset and offer rights to future profits. Under existing securities law, they are generally considered (depending on the relevant applicable Law) as financial products, securities, financial instruments, etc.

Payment tokens are the third category that lately has seen interesting developments, including – obviously – stablecoins, and e-money tokens (within which the original Libra project, now Diem, should be included).[7] A pure payment token fulfils the economic criteria of a means of payment, thereby providing functions of exchange, storage of value, and unit of account (Geva 2019).

Looking at the draft of MiCA, the influence of the wide debate on the qualification of crypto-assets is evident: whereas (9) reproduces the tripartition among crypto-assets that is the result of what we have labelled in a previous study as the 'bottom up' approach (Annunziata, 2020). This goes together with: (i) a *broad, general* definition of crypto-assets, that MiCA sets out, in line with the suggestions of the Financial

---

[5] Hacker and Thomale (2018), Maume and Fromberger (2018), and Barsan (2017) who identify only two token categories ('currency like' and 'security like' tokens). See also the distinction between 'app tokens' and 'protocol tokens' made by Rohr and Wright (2019).

[6] Other authors take a different view, based on a wide interpretation of the notions of transferable securities and financial instruments, that tend to include in the notion of financial instruments practically most, if not all, Initial Coin Offerings (ICOs) tokens (Boreiko et al. 2019).

[7] On Libra, see Zetzsche et al. (2019). An extensive analysis of stablecoins' main characteristics is provided by Dell'Erba (2019).

Action Task Force (whereas 8 MiCA);[8] (ii) a *specific* definition of asset-referenced (ARTs) and e-money tokens (EMTs); and (iii) a *specific* definition of utility tokens.[9]

The general definition of crypto-assets, contained in Article 3, MiCA is instrumental to the objective of identifying the general scope of the proposed Regulation, whose rules are then structured along two different lines: on the one side, those applicable to 'asset-referenced' and 'e-money tokens'; on the other side, those applicable to all other tokens.

Looking at this second group, MiCA sets out quite articulated rules applicable to the offering and circulation of the tokens. Such rules have an origin that is not difficult to identify, since they are either: (i) the by-product of widespread, existing market practices or (ii) the adaptation to crypto-assets of existing rules contained in EU Capital Markets Legislation (basically, MiFID, Prospectus, and Market Abuse). As to the first, and limiting these notes to the most relevant topics contained in the draft regulation, MiCA clearly consolidates, and at the same time legitimises, the market practice resulting in the publication of a 'whitepaper' in the context of token offerings. Whereby the same concept of a whitepaper can be seen as a genetic transformation of the traditional prospectus, MiCA follows in this respect an ultra-liberal approach: the whitepaper is, in fact, not subject to any preliminary check or approval by Supervisors.[10] The latter retain, however,

---

[8] Art. 3, para. 1, lett. (b): '"crypto-asset" means a digital representation of value or rights, which may be transferred and stored electronically, using distributed ledger or similar technology'.

[9] Art. 3, para. 1, lett. (g): '"utility token" means a type of crypto-assets which are intended to provide access digitally to an application, services or resources available on a distributed ledger and that are accepted only by the issuer of that token to grant access to such application, services or resources available'.

[10] Mirroring the approach to be found in the area of prospectus regulation, there are also exemptions from the obligation to publish a whitepaper, when (see Art. 4, para. 2): the crypto-assets are offered for free; or the crypto-assets are automatically created through mining as a reward for the maintenance of or validation of transactions on a or similar technology; or the crypto-asset is unique and not fungible with other crypto-assets; or the offering of crypto-assets is addressed to fewer than 150 natural or legal persons per Member State acting on their own account; the total consideration of such an offering in the Union does not exceed EUR 1,000,000, or the corresponding equivalent in another currency or in crypto- assets, over a period of 12 months; the offering of crypto-assets is solely addressed to qualified investors and the crypto-assets can only be held by such qualified investors.

the power to intervene once the offer is carried on, and therefore are supposed to carry out their functions after the publication of the whitepaper. Whereby MiCA justifies this approach with the need to avoid placing an excessive burden upon Public Authorities – which, *per se*, seems a weak justification[11] – mere *ex-post* enforcement does not really seem sufficient to ensure adequate levels of integrity and confidence in the market.

If the requirements that MiCA applies to whitepapers are the result of market practice consolidating in the regulation, with a clear eye towards prospectus legislation,[12] those concerning service providers and trading platforms in crypto-assets are, instead, the result of the application to the crypto-assets of solutions deeply embedded in the core text of EU Capital Markets legislation. Without going too much into the details, MiCA requires that those who intend to operate as providers of services in the market of crypto-assets[13] should be licensed by a Public Authority, should possess

---

[11] Whereas (19): given the novelty of the crypto-asset sector and to avoid an undue administrative burden on financial supervisors, competent authorities should not have the duty to review a *whitepaper* for approval before its publication. However, once published, competent authorities should have the power to suspend or prohibit an offering of crypto-assets that would not comply with the provisions of this Regulation. Competent authorities should also have the power to request further information to be included in the whitepaper and to publish a warning that the issuer fails in meeting the requirements set out in the Regulation.

[12] In Whereas (17), the *vis attractiva* of the prospectus results in an improper citation, that confuses whitepaper and prospectuses: 'Beyond the obligation to draw up a prospectus, issuers of crypto-assets should be subject to other requirements.'

[13] Whereas (15): 'This Regulation should also aim at regulating entities which provide services and activities related to crypto-assets. These main "crypto-asset services" consist in ensuring the operation of a trading platform for crypto-assets, in exchanging crypto-assets against fiat currencies or other crypto-assets by dealing on own account, and finally the activity consisting in ensuring the custody and administration of crypto-assets or the control of means to access such crypto-assets, on behalf of third parties. Other services related to crypto-assets, such as the placement of crypto-assets, the reception or transmission of orders for crypto-assets, the execution of orders for crypto-assets, and the advice on crypto-assets and the payment transactions in asset-referenced tokens, should also be in the scope of this Regulation. Any person which provides any crypto-asset service, on a professional basis, should be considered as a "crypto-asset service provider" and should be subject to this Regulation.'

requirements that mirror those required upon financial entities, and should have in place proper internal arrangements and measures to ensure adequate levels of investors' protection.[14] In this respect, MiCA is once again – after the Insurance Distribution Directive, and other pieces of legislation – a clear example of how strong the influence of regulatory standards taken from MiFID is, and of their ability to influence the structure of rules applicable in different sectors: MiCA does extend to providers of services in crypto-assets the typical, fundamental, and long-standing MiFID conduct rules, such as those on information, conflicts of interests, and suitability. Also, issuers of crypto-assets are captured by some of these provisions. Another area in MiCA where one clearly sees a transplant of rules designed for and applicable to other areas of EU Financial legislation is that of market abuse: the draft regulation contains specific provisions aimed at prohibiting and preventing insider trading and market manipulation, modelled directly upon the provision of the Market Abuse Regulation (Regulation no. 596/2014), including those that apply to particular types of financial instruments (such as emissions allowances) where the focus of the disclosure regime is not on the events or on the information concerning the issuer, but rather on market participants' positions.[15]

Having said that, and considering the significant effort that can clearly be seen in the attempt by MiCA to cover all of these aspects, it does seem odd that the draft does not take a clear position as to the

[14] Whereas (17): 'Beyond the obligation to draw up a prospectus, issuers of crypto-assets should be subject to other requirements, such as the obligation to act honestly, fairly and professionally, to communicate with the holders of crypto-assets in a fair, clear, and not misleading manner, to identify, prevent, manage, and disclose conflicts of interest, to have effective administrative arrangements and to ensure that their systems and security protocols meet appropriate EU standards. In order to assist competent authorities, the European Banking Authority (EBA) should be mandated to publish guidelines in order to further specify these EU standards'.

[15] See, for example, Whereas (35): 'Beyond information included in the *whitepaper*, issuers should also provide holders of asset-referenced tokens with information on a continuous basis. In particular, they should disclose the number of asset-referenced tokens and the value and the composition of the reserve assets, at least on a monthly basis. They should also be required to disclose any event that is likely to have a significant impact on the value of the asset-referenced tokens or on the reserve assets, irrespectively of whether such crypto-assets are admitted to trading on a trading platform for crypto-assets or not'.

scope of the new proposed regulation, with specific regard to tokens *other than* asset-referenced and e-money tokens. Tokens that do not fall within the definition that MiCA provides for the latter remain, therefore, controversial as to their qualification, and as to the regime that they are subject to. Three provisions of MiCA are sufficient in order to clarify this statement:

- According to Article 2, para. 2 shall apply to tokens that do not fall within the scope of existing EU Financial Legislation.[16]
- According to Article 6, the whitepaper's summary shall include a warning that the whitepaper *does not* constitute a prospectus under Regulation (EU) 2017/1129 of the European Parliament and of the Council of 14 June 2017 or another offering document pursuant to Union or National Laws.
- According to Article 30, issuers of asset-referenced tokens in the EU, or that seek admission of the token to trading on a trading platform for crypto-assets must apply for a specific authorisation and provide to the Supervisor 'a legal opinion that the proposed activity does not fall within the scope of other financial services legislation, such as those specified in Article 2(2)'.

These three provisions read in combination clearly indicate that MiCA expressly, and willingly, falls short of the task of providing a clear definition of crypto-assets. This problem, therefore – that we would call the *central* problem in all the recent debate over crypto-assets – remains unresolved. In its current wording, MiCA would actually leave things almost in the same uncertainty as they have been until now, thus contradicting its own declared intentions.[17] Save for

---

[16] According to Whereas (69): 'This Regulation should exclude from its scope crypto-assets that qualify as financial instruments. The EU financial service legislation should not give a particular technology an advantage over another. Crypto-assets that qualify as "financial instruments" or "electronic money" should remain regulated under existing EU legislation, such as the Markets in Financial Instruments Directive ((Directive 2014/65/EU) and the Electronic Money Directive (Directive 2009/110/EC), regardless of the technology used for their issuance or their transfer.'

[17] See para. 1, Contents of the Proposal: 'This proposal, which covers crypto-assets outside existing EU financial services legislation, as well as e-money tokens, has four general and related objectives. The first objective is one of legal certainty. For crypto-asset markets to develop within the EU, there is a need for a sound legal framework, clearly defining the regulatory treatment of all crypto-assets that are not covered by existing financial services legislation.'

the specific definition of asset-backed and e-money tokens, the rest of the tokens would continue to pose issues of qualification, and would be placed on the market with the risk of ex-post requalification.

Under the current version of MiCA, unless a crypto-asset clearly falls in the definition of asset-backed or e-money tokens provided by the latter, one would still have to struggle in order to understand whether the asset falls in the definition, at least, of transferable securities, units of collective investment undertakings, or, eventually derivatives. Considering that, as already discussed, the precise identification of the traits of each of these categories raises in and of itself interpretative issues, MiCA is far from being conclusive, and effectively capable of providing legal certainty.

Even looking at asset-backed and e-money tokens, the proposed solution is not entirely satisfactory: the qualification of the asset is, in fact, basically left to the support provided by a legal opinion, setting out and confirming that the proposed activity does not fall within the scope of existing EU financial legislation. While the requirements of the legal opinion, and of the entity providing it, should be better specified, in order to tackle, for example, issues of conflicts of interest, the legal opinion should not exonerate Supervisors to effectively carry out their investigation as to the nature of the token, in order to ascertain whether the intended activity should be otherwise licensed. In its current wording, reference to the legal opinion may ultimately result in an improper transfer of competences to the private sector, which increases the risk of re-qualification, particularly high in areas where crossing the boundaries of reserved activities might result in criminal offences under National law. Also, one wonders why no similar legal opinion is required in relation to the issue of tokens other than asset-backed tokens: the latter, in fact, can be placed on the market with no previous verification or authorisation by Supervisors.

If MiCA is a very interesting first experiment by the EU Institutions to imagine a comprehensive regulation of crypto-assets, it should be considered that any such attempt must inevitably come at grips with the problem of clearly setting crypto-assets within, or outside, the framework of existing EU financial legislation (especially, for assets different from asset-backed or e-money tokens, MiFID, and Prospectus rules). This issue is not solved by simply providing a negative scope for the application of the intended legislation, as MiCA does in Article 2, para. 2. Negative definitions, or the identification of the scope of legislation by referring simply to what 'does not fall' in other areas of existing rules is not sufficient. A clear example of how complex and confusing this approach may be is provided by the AIFM Directive of 2011, that identifies its scope by referring broadly to all collective investment schemes that fall outside the scope of the pre-existing UCITS Directive: a solution that, apparently, had the benefit of simplicity, but that has sparked a number of complex interpretative issues that, lately, have also been signalled in the Final Report provided by the High Level Forum on the Capital Markets Union.[18] In addition, the task of enforcing proper market discipline and transparency cannot be left almost entirely to *ex-post* interventions: Supervisors are essential watchdogs, and should try to prevent market disruptions, and protect investors/consumers *beforehand*.

It is quite interesting to note that the shortcomings of MiCA in terms of taxonomy do not really depend on the text of the Regulation as such but are more due to the uncertainties that still exist in framing the scope of existing EU Financial Legislation. There are different ways through which the approach of MiCA might be improved. Without claim to completeness, there might be room for granting the Commission the task of establishing (and updating regularly) technical standards that could include additional definitions and criteria useful for the taxonomy. Another solution might be that of setting up a permanent Committee, composed of representative of the three ESAs, that could serve as a preliminary 'entry point' for the market, and that could provide continuous guidance to the industry and to Supervisors as the qualification of tokens, including clarification in relation to a specific new asset to be placed on the market. This would ease the burden on the shoulders of National Supervisors, and also reduce the inevitable differences in national approaches and interpretation that would, otherwise, be inevitable. A further solution might be that of elaborating further on the measures, already suggested by the Commission, aimed at coordinating MiCA with existing EU Financial legislation, by including, in the current core texts (such as MiFID, Prospectus regulation, and AIFMD-UCITS), new provisions aimed at clarifying their respective scope vis-à-vis MiCA.

---

[18] The Report is available at: www.ec.europa.eu/info/files/200610-cmu-high-level-forum-final-report_en.

MiCAR's Scope of Application: Decentralised Finance

A second point of uncertainty that arises from the current version of MiCA is its approach vis-à-vis decentralisation. Decentralisation is, indeed, at the core of the technological developments leading to the issue of crypto-assets themselves even though, at times, one has the impression that the expression 'decentralised finance' is used in an imprecise way, without clearly distinguishing between different shades of grey and phenomenon.[19] However, one thing is clear: looking at the subjective and objective scope of the draft, it is doubtful whether its approach would ultimately be capable of capturing truly decentralised phenomena, such as bitcoin itself. The approach that MiCA takes is, actually, quite traditional: considering the primary market, for instance, MiCA requires the issuer of the asset to (amongst other) publish a white paper. For ARTs and EMTs, the duty to publish a white paper is coupled with a comprehensive licensing and supervisory regime for issuers of these tokens, largely mirrored and tailored upon the existing EU provisions on financial services providers, such as the Payment Services Directive and the Electronic Money Directive. Considering secondary markets, MiCA regulates, with an approach largely taken from MiFID, service providers in the crypto-environment: custodians, wallet providers, exchanges, advisors, etc. Again, and due to the inspiration that MiCA takes from existing core EU Financial legislation, the approach looks familiar, and is easily recognisable. MiCA, however, falls short of addressing truly decentralised crypto-finance, amongst which, naturally, and foremost Bitcoin and, likely, other major crypto-assets. Since, in case of a full and true decentralisation, one cannot identify a single entity, or a sufficiently precise group of entities, towards which rules would be targeted, this a clear shortcoming, even more relevant if one looks at the relevance on the market of assets like, for instance, Bitcoin. The same holds true for truly decentralised service providers like, for instance, exchange venues. Decentralised digital assets are, however, not entirely outside the scope of MiCA, as service providers in relation to those assets are, clearly, included.

It must be said, ultimately, that addressing truly decentralised finance is not an easy task, and that National experiences in regulating

---

[19] Lately, in this debate, see Martino and Spikkerman (2021).

crypto-assets had to face, and are still facing, this shortcoming. A new model for regulating crypto-assets and activities in a decentralised environment still needs to be found, and one thing is for sure: that model could not rest upon the solutions that, insofar, have supported financial regulation, particularly in the EU.

Assets' Tokenisation

MiCA clearly stands out for its comprehensive approach in regulating the crypto-assets industry. It addresses issues of consumer protection, financial stability, transparency, and enforcement. In doing so, as anticipated, it follows the approach that is typical of EU Financial legislation and pursues objectives that are similar to the latter. While this is understandable for some tokens that fall within its scope, in particular ARTs and EMTs, due to their functions and nature, and the risks that they raise for the market and also for (potentially) global stability, one may question whether this approach is proportionate and efficient in relation to 'pure' utility tokens, not performing any financial function, neither as an investment, nor as a means of payment. There are two aspects of this issue to be considered: the first is, naturally, the risk that the upcoming legislation results in an excessive overshooting, targeting risks and objectives that are truly not relevant for the market and the industry. Supporting competition and fostering innovation in the EU financial sector might there become more challenging, in a regulatory environment that might be overcharged. The other side of the problem is, however, the fact that some, if not most, crypto-assets might show the tendency to transform, and mutate, their functions and nature overtime, or even be hybrid right from the moment when they are placed on the market. Bitcoin itself is a clear example of hybridisation: originally imagined as a means of payment, it is now (also) employed as a means for investments, performing (in the eyes of its users) functions similar to those of a financial product. Another striking example is the recent development of non-fungible tokens in the art industry, originally (probably) conceived as a means of authentication and certification, but almost instantaneously transformed into a form of investment.

All of this complicates the issues at stake, and may possibly justify what might seem like a tendency of the MiCA proposal to go beyond its rationale. However, more proportionalities could be inserted in the regulation to take into account these aspects.

Always considering the regulatory approach of MiCA, a specific point concerns ARTs and EMTs.

ARTs are crypto-assets that purport to maintain a stable value by referring to the value of several fiat currencies that are legal tender, one or several commodities or one or several crypto-assets, or a combination of such assets. In short, these are tokens referencing a currency basket similar to Libra, now Diem. EMTs in turn are crypto-assets the main purpose of which is to be used as a means of exchange and that purports to maintain a stable value by referring to the value of a fiat currency that is legal tender. Examples include a 1:1 tokenised currency like *EURS* – the Euro Stablecoin. While addressed in similar titles of MiCA, the substantive rules, with the exception of the treatment of foreign exchange risk, exhibited many similarities which justify the joint discussion herein.

Title III and IV MiCA set authorisation requirements and the operating conditions for ARTs and EMTs issuers. While a bespoke authorisation requirement is set for ARTs issuers, EMTs issuers must be credit institutions or e-money institutions under the Capital Requirements Directive (CRD) or the E-money-Directive (EMD). The regulation further foresees some modifications to the minimum whitepaper content and ongoing disclosure rules (Articles 17, 21, 22, 24–26, 46 MiCA) and some standard conduct of business, including conflict of interest (Articles 23, 28 MiCA) as well as governance requirements (Articles 30 MiCA) and rules on acquisitions (Articles 37, 38 MiCA). These are all known from other pieces of EU financial law, for instance, Prospectus Regulation, MiFID, the Financial Holding Directive, and CRD and shall not be discussed here in detail.

Apart from the details of the various provisions, this approach is not fully in line with the alleged principles of technological neutrality that, since its inception, have been invoked for the regulation of Fintech services, products at activities. More specifically, issuers of EMT would be subject to a double level of standards: on the one side, those arising from the CRD package or the EMD (as amended overtime); on the other side, MiCA requirements, including provisions on enforcements and sanctions that are particularly severe. The use of a DLT for the issuance of e-money would therefore trigger the application of new sets of rules, thus impairing the 'same-business-same rules' model.

In relation to ARTs, the project that triggered MiCA was Libra, at the time of its announcement imagined as a *global* stablecoin. A closer look at MiCA reveals that the text only provides a legislative framework for a regional stablecoin, thus setting legal limits to innovation that could provide a solution to the many issues faced in cross-border payments. In particular, MiCA requires the legal entity to be established in the EU/EEA[20] and vests jurisdiction over any significant ARTs or EMTs issuer upon the European Banking Authority (EBA): Article 99 (2), 101 (2) MiCA defines EBA as chair of the supervisory college for issuers of significant ARTs and EMTs (that is global stablecoins). Relevant supervisory authorities of third countries with which the EBA has concluded an administrative agreement in accordance with Article 108 MiCA may participate in the supervisory college, but, according to Article 100(4), 102(4) they will have no voting rights on non-binding opinions that form the basis of many college decisions. Under these conditions no competent authority of a third country currency can accept the EBA lead. Further, MiCA does not foresee cooperation rules where the EBA or national competent authorities sit in supervisory colleges set up by authorities of third countries. Given that MiCA applies whenever there is an issuance in the EU, even a small amount of stablecoin issued in the EU would require the EBA to demand the lead in the college since the EBA lead is the sole way to allow for any cooperation with third countries. This is at odds with the concept of a 'global' stablecoin.

Further modes of cooperation need therefore to be explored with third countries. As suggested in a recent paper, mutual recognition has little appeal on this critical field, at least in stablecoins where currencies of EU/EEA countries are of minor importance and EU intermediaries not involved, or where the reserve function relating to European currencies is vested solely in European central banks (Zetzsche et al. 2021).

Corporate and Civil Law Aspects

At the core of the EU Digital Finance Package – 'a package of measures to further enable and support the potential of digital finance in

---

[20] Articles 15(2) MiCA. The same follows from Art. 43 (1) MiCAR where EMT issuers must be credit institutions or e-money institutions under the CRD or EMD since both pieces of legislation require the legal entity to be located in the EU/EEA.

terms of innovation and competition while mitigating the risks'[21] –
lies, as anticipated, MiCA[22] as well as a new Proposal for a Regulation
on a pilot regime on DLT market infrastructures (DLT Proposal).[23]
The latter represents the focus of this Section.

The DLT Proposal lays down appropriate provisions for the issuing, recording, transfer, and storing of financial instruments based
on DLT. Although MiCA and the DLT Proposal are closely related
under many circumstances,[24] their respective scope of application
differs. Specifically, securities covered by the DLT Proposal are
just a subset of crypto-assets subject to MiCA: the DLT Proposal
applies only to crypto-assets qualifying as financial instruments under
Directive 2014/65/EU (MiFID II) (*security* or *investment tokens*),[25]
which are exempted from MiCA's scope by virtue of Article 2(2)(a)
MiCA (Zetzsche et al. 2021).[26]

The tokenisation of financial instruments – that is to say their transformation into crypto-assets to enable them to be issued, stored, and
transferred through DLT – has required the European legislator to
assess the compatibility and the suitability of the existing European

---

[21] Proposal for a Directive of the European Parliament and of the Council
amending Directives 2006/43/EC, 2009/65/EC, 2009/138/EU, 2011/61/EU,
EU/2013/36, 2014/65/EU, (EU) 2015/2366 and EU/2016/2341, COM(2020)
596 final.

[22] Proposal for a Regulation of the European Parliament and of the Council
on Markets in Crypto-assets, and amending Directive (EU) 2019/1937,
COM(2020)593 final; The EU Digital Finance package includes also a
Proposal for a Regulation of the European Parliament and of the Council on
digital operational resilience for the financial sector and amending Regulations
(EC) No 1060/2009, (EU) No 648/2012, (EU) No 600/2014 and (EU) No
909/2014, COM(2020)595 final ('DORA').

[23] Proposal for a Regulation of the European Parliament and of the Council
on a Pilot Regime for market infrastructures based on distributed ledger
technology, COM (2020) 594.

[24] Article 3(2) MiCAR defines crypto-assets as 'A digital representation of values
or rights that can be stored and traded electronically, using distributed ledger
technology or similar technology'. See Zetzsche and Woxholth (2022).

[25] The European Commission proposed to amend the definition of 'financial
instrument' contained in MiFID II, in order to include financial instruments
based on DLT.

[26] On 19 November 2021, the Council adopted its position on MiCAR and
DORA, clarifying, among others, that MiCAR does not apply to crypto-
assets that are unique and not fungible with other crypto-assets. The
position is available at www.data.consilium.europa.eu/doc/document/
ST-14067-2021-INIT/en/pdf.

Union legislation (such as the Prospectus Regulation and the Central Securities Depositories Regulation) with the new framework introduced by the DLT Proposal. In fact, the EU Financial legislation was not designed with DLT and crypto-assets in mind, and there are provisions in existing legislation that may preclude or limit the use of DLT in the issuance, trading, and settlement of crypto-assets qualifying as financial instruments.[27]

After having considered three different options, the DLT Proposal opted for a so-called *sandbox* approach, creating a controlled space with temporary derogations from existing rules to facilitate the issuance of financial instruments through DLT (Zetzsche and Woxholt 2022).

However, it should be noted that crypto-assets have so far been considered by the European legislator mainly under a regulatory perspective leaving aside the related corporate and civil law implications. In fact, the DLT Proposal is not intended to establish a harmonised set of civil and corporate law rules for crypto-assets qualifying financial instruments. This view is supported by the European Commission, which raised the question whether harmonisation of national civil laws should also be considered in order to 'provide clarity on the legal validity of token transfers and the tokenisation of tangible (material) assets'.[28]

In the current scenario, the civil and corporate treatment of crypto-assets is therefore left to National Law. Pending the entry into force of the new regime, some European countries, such as Switzerland and Germany, have implemented dedicated regimes for issuing financial instruments using DLT.

In particular, in September 2020, the Swiss Parliament approved the Federal Act on the Adaptation of Federal Law to Developments in Distributed Ledger Technology (DLT Law), amending, among others, the Swiss Code of Obligation.[29] The DLT Law entered into force in two stages.[30] The new law provides for the introduction of a new

---

[27] Cf. Recital 3 DLT Proposal.

[28] European Commission 2019. *Consultation document on an EU framework for markets in crypto-assets.* Available online: www.ec.europa.eu/info/sites/default/files/business_economy_euro/banking_and_finance/documents/2019 crypto-assets-consultation-document_en.pdf.

[29] Federal Act on the Amendment of the Swiss Civil Code (Part Five: The Code of Obligations) of 30 March 1911.

[30] On 1 February 2021, the parts of the DLT Law that amend the Swiss Code of Obligations, the Federal Intermediated Securities Act and the Federal Act on International Private Law have entered into force. On 1 August 2021, the

category of securities according to the Swiss Code of Obligation, namely the 'uncertificated register securities' (Ledger-based Securities or *Registerwertrechte*)[31] defined as 'a right which, in accordance with an agreement between the parties: 1. is registered in a securities ledger; and 2. may be exercised and transferred to others only via this securities ledger'.

Uncertificated register securities come into existence by way of book-entry into an electronic register (*Wertrechteregister*) that meets certain conditions concerning safety and integrity, as well as transparency of information for parties involved.[32] The legal positions that qualify as admissible underlying rights of uncertificated register securities include rights against counterparties or issuers, such as contractual claims and membership rights (e.g., shares in a corporation) (Kramer and Meier 2020).

On 6 May 2021, the German Parliament adopted the Electronic Securities Act (*Gesetz über elektronische Wertpapiere, eWpG*) which came into force on 10 June 2021 (Heise 2021). The new law introduces the possibility to issue electronic securities (including crypto-securities), with the abandonment of the requirement of the physical securitisation, henceforth replaced by an entry in an electronic securities register. The scope of application of the Electronic Securities Law is restricted to bearer bonds, mortgage bonds, and certain fund units in purely electronic format.[33]

Unlike Switzerland and Germany, at present, no specific measures about DLT-based financial instruments have been adopted in Italy. However, Consob in different occasions[34] has stressed the need for a re-assessment of the existing civil and corporate provisions – in particular, Legislative Decree No. 58 of 24 February 1998 (the

---

second part of the DLT Law entered into force, clarifying, among other things, the treatment of crypto-assets according to insolvency law and introducing a licence for DLT trading facilities.

[31] Cf. Art. 973c Swiss Code of Obligation.

[32] Cf. Art. 973c (2) Swiss Code of Obligation.   [33] Ibid.

[34] Consob. Press Release. 12 February 2021. Available online: www.consob .it/documents/46180/46181/press_20210212.pdf/716c7750-3768-47bc-bb39-52cdd5607552; Chamber of Deputies, VI Financial Commission, Digital Finance Package CONSOB Hearing, Commissioner Paolo Ciocca, Rome, 8 June 2021. Available online: www.consob.it/ documents/46180/46181/Audizione_Ciocca_20210608_scheda.pdf/ b95ce6b1-650d-4b89-ad07-ad894fc1bf27

Consolidate Law on Finance) and Italian Civil Code – to allow and regulate the adoption of DLT in Italy. The amendment to the existing legislation is necessary to ensure that crypto-assets may actually qualify as *traditional security* (*security* or *investment tokens*), as in the intention of the DLT Proposal, and not only as derivatives of underlying traditional securities, the latter being more properly *tokenised securities.*[35]

In conclusion, it seems indisputable that the regulation of civil and corporate treatments of crypto-assets will rest with national legislators. However, there is a strong risk that divergent legislative approaches could lead to diverging results and cause legal fragmentation. Some authors suggest, as a remedy, that the private law of crypto-assets be harmonised to the highest degree possible, in line with the a-national nature of technology (Lehmann 2021).

References

Annunziata, F. 2020. 'Speak, If you Can: What are You? An Alternative Approach to The Qualification of Tokens and Initial Coin Offerings'. *ECFR*, Vol. 17, Issue 2

Barsan, Iris M. 2017. 'Legal Challenges of Initial Coin Offerings (ICO)'. *Revue Trimestrielle de Droit Financier (RTDF)*, vol. 3, 54–65.

Blandin, A., Cloots, A. S., Hussain, H., Rauchs, M., Saleuddin, R., Allen, J. G., Zhang, B. Z., and Cloud, K. 2019. 'Global Cryptoasset Regulatory Landscape Study'. *University of Cambridge Faculty of Law Research Paper*, n. 23.

---

[35] See Carrière (2020). '[...] as a matter of fact, in the light of a thorough understanding of the peculiar functioning model of the technological infrastructure necessarily underlying «security tokens» and «utility tokens» (i.e., blockchain technology or DLT) it is more difficult for such tokens to be qualified or even be described –*per se*, ontologically – in terms of traditional «securities», in the absence of specific provisions of corporate law that regulate and allow for the issuance and placement thereof, through the use of the said crypto-technology, then directly, simultaneously and without intermediaries. Looking at the market experience to date, many such tokens may be described, at most, as derivatives of underlying traditional securities, and therefore more properly «tokenised securities»; in order to conceive true «security tokens» it is necessary to refer to a primary legislation of civil-corporate law that will allow and regulate the adoption of DLT as a legal method of issuance/placement/trading/custody/entitlement alongside the «paper-based» and the «dematerialised» methods.'

Boreiko, D., Ferrarini, G., and Giudici, P. 2019. 'Blockchain Startups and Prospectus Regulation'. *European Business Organisation Law Review*, vol. 20, no. 4, 665–694.

Bourveau, T., De George, E.T., Ellahie, A., and Macciocchi, D. 2022. 'Initial Coin Offerings: Early Evidence on the Role of Disclosure in the Unregulated Crypto Market'. *Journal of Accounting Research*, vol. 60, no. 1, 129–167.

Carrière, P. 2020. 'The Phenomenon of Crypto-Assets from a Corporate Perspective'. *Banca Impresa Società*, 2020, III.

Dell'Erba, M. 2019. 'Stablecoins in Cryptoeconomics. From Initial Coin Offerings (ICOs) to Central Bank Digital Currencies (CBDCs)'. *New York University Journal of Legislation and Public Policy (Forthcoming)*. Available online at www.ssrn.com/abstract=3385840.

ESMA 2019. 'Advice on Initial Coin Offerings and Crypto-Assets'. Available online: www.esma.europa.eu/sites/default/files/library/esma50-157-1391_crypto_advice.pdf.

Geva, B. 2019. 'Cryptocurrencies and the Evolution of Banking. Money, and Payments', in C. Brummer (eds.), *Cryptoassets*, 11–38. Oxford University Press.

Hacker, P. and Thomale, C. 2018. 'Crypto-Securities Regulation: ICOs, Token Sales and Cryptocurrencies under EU Financial Law'. *European Company and Financial Law Review*, vol. 15, no. 4, 645–696.

Heise, C. 2021 – BaFin Division for Legislative Process and Policy Issues WA 11. Available online: www.bafin.de/SharedDocs/Veroeffentlichungen/EN/Fachartikel/2021/fa_bj_2107_eWpG en.html.

Howell, S. T., Niessner, M., and Yermack, D. 2020. 'Initial Coin Offerings: Financing Growth with Cryptocurrency Token Sales'. *The Review of Financial Studies*, vol. 33, no. 9, 3925–3974.

Klöhn, L., Parhofer, N., and Resas, D. 2018. 'Initial Coin Offerings (ICOs)'. *Zeitschrift für Bankrecht und Bankwirtschaft*, vol. 30, no. 2, 89–106.

Kramer, S., and Meier, U. 2020. 'DLT Draft Law – Civil Law Aspects. CapLaw'. *Available online*: www.caplaw.ch/2020/dlt-draft-law-civil-law-aspects/.

Lehmann, M. 2021. 'National Blockchain Laws as a Threat to Capital Markets Integration'. *Uniform Law Review*, vol. 26, no. 1, 148–179.

Martino, E., and Spikkerman, S. 2021. 'How Decentralises Are 'Decentralised' Autonomous Organisation' (DAOs)'. Oxford Blog, 5 November 2021. Available online: www.blogs.law.ox.ac.uk/business-law-blog/blog/2021/11/how-decentralised-are-decentralised-autonomous-organisations-daos.

Maume, P. and Fromberger, M. 2018. 'Regulation of Initial Coin Offerings: Reconciling US and EU Securities Laws'. *Chicago Journal of International Law*, vol. 19, 548–558.

Rohr, J. and Wright A. 2019. 'Blockchain-Based Token Sales, Initial Coin Offerings, and the Democratization of Public Capital Markets'. 70 Hastings L.J., 463. Available online: www.repository.uchastings.edu/hastings_law_journal/vol70/iss2/5.

Zetzsche, D. A. and Woxholth, J. 2022. 'The DLT Sandbox under the Pilot-Regulation'. *Capital Markets Law Journal*, vol. 17, no. 2, 212–236.

Zetzsche, D. A., Annunziata, F., Arner, D. W., and Buckley, R. P. 2021. 'The Markets in Crypto-Assets Regulation (MiCA) and the EU Digital Finance Strategy'. *Capital Markets Law Journal*, vol. 16, no. 2, 203–225.

Zetzsche, D. A., Buckley, R. P., and Arner, D. W. 2019. 'Regulating LIBRA: The Transformative Potential of Facebook's Cryptocurrency and Possible Regulatory Responses'. *European Banking Institute Working Paper Series*, vol. 44. 3–28. Available online: www.ssrn.com/abstract=341440.

4 | Crypto-Assets in Banks
Between Opportunities and Legal Uncertainties

ANDREA DALY

Introduction

Crypto-assets are a complex and diversified phenomenon, in which payment and investment services are often merged.

Tokenisation levels the products, makes negotiation and exchange easier, and removes inefficiencies and costs caused by unnecessary intermediation. In most cases, however, disintermediation does not mean reducing the role of banks, but transforming it, adapting it to a context in which the ever-increasing complexity of products and services raises exponentially the importance of consulting services with high added value. The financial system can benefit from the entry into the DLT ecosystem of banks, which can confirm themselves as an essential point of reference to meet the needs of investors, consumers, issuers, and for the productive system as a whole. At the same time, because of their essential role, banks are extremely exposed to compliance and reputational risks, which can only be managed in a context of regulatory clarity. Legal certainty is an essential condition for all market operators to compete on equal terms. Uncertainty, on the other hand, makes the playing field exclusive to non-supervised entities, less exposed to reputational risks.

The regulatory uncertainty that hinders the provision of services by banks derives mainly from the confusion regarding the legal classification of crypto-assets. After all, it is difficult for a new product to enter a hyper-regulated system such as the financial one without finding itself – at least – on the border of some existing regulation. As soon as the innovative and diffusion potential of the phenomenon became evident, the first objective of the regulators was to identify which crypto-assets were already regulated,[1] in order to build

---

[1] See European Commission. *Public consultation: an EU framework for markets in crypto-assets.* www.ec.europa.eu/info/law/better-regulation/have-your-say

a dedicated framework for those products which are not subject to any specific legislation.

On 24 September 2020, the European Commission published the first crypto-assets regulation proposal (MiCAR), with the aim of regulating all types of existing crypto-assets.[2] In accordance with the principle of technological neutrality, the applicability of the current legislation to tokens attributable to specific regulatory classes was confirmed, limiting the scope of the new regulation to all the others.[3]

The legislative choice was therefore to combine some new specific regulatory classes (utility token, asset-referenced token, and electronic money token) with a residual and potentially catch-all one (the so-called 'other than (…) token'), with the aim of attracting to the MiCAR perimeter any crypto-assets not clearly attributable to specific classes.

However, the regulatory proposal partially fails to ensure legal certainty and does not contribute to solving the majority of the regulatory classification issues that prevent banks and supervised entities from providing crypto-assets services protecting themselves from potential sanctioning and reputational risks deriving from the incorrect qualification of the offered tokens.

One of the fundamental still open issues concerns the boundary between the class of financial instruments, subject to the regulatory framework on investment services (MiFID II/MiFIR, Central Securities Depository Re [CSDR], etc.) and the residual one, which is the object of the MiCA Regulation itself (the 'other-than' tokens). Not a meaningless issue considering that the most significant interpretative doubts concern the classification of the most capitalised tokens, starting with Bitcoin, whose diffusion among the public was indeed the source of the attention reserved to crypto-assets by the legislators. It is therefore clear that the objective to guarantee legal certainty cannot be achieved without resolving the question of the legal classification of Bitcoins and the other the improperly named 'cryptocurrencies'.

/initiatives/12089-Directive-regulation-establishing-a-European-framework-for-markets-in-crypto-assets/public-consultation_en.

[2] MiCAR (Regulation (EU) 2023/1114) was published on June 6th 2023.

[3] The MiCA Regulation, therefore, does not apply to non-fungible tokens and to tokens that can be classified, among others as: financial instruments, funds, deposits, structured deposits, and securitisations (see MiCAR proposal, Art. 2).

The Classification of Bitcoins and 'Cryptocurrencies'

According to the classification criteria adopted by the crypto ecosystem, Bitcoins are 'cryptocurrency'. The use of this term is improper but consistent with the purpose for which Bitcoin was designed and, therefore, with the instances of financial inclusion and disintermediation of payment systems. At a theoretical level, for the public, Bitcoin is a private payment-token purchased on 'exchanges'; on a practical level, that same public often approaches Bitcoin as a speculative asset, traded on the market with a return expectation. Therefore, the high volatility of the asset led regulators and – in general – the financial ecosystem to wonder if Bitcoin could really have the same function as currency, being a suitable payment instrument, or if, instead, it should be considered a financial instrument.

The definition of financial instrument is provided by Directive (EU) no. 65/2014 (so-called MiFID II), which, in art. 4 para. 1 n. 15, refers to the list reported in Section C of Annex I. The list of instruments could therefore lead us to believe that the definition of financial instruments is based on a mandatory and closed nature and that only the products included in the list are such. However, the list of instruments referred to in Section C of Annex I includes 'transferable securities', defined as '*classes of securities which are negotiable on the capital market, with the exception of instruments of payment, such as: shares in companies and other securities equivalent to shares in companies (...)*' (Art. 4 para. 1 no. 44). Transferable securities are an open class, in which specific instruments (see letters (a), (b), and (c) of art. 4, para. 1, no. 44) have been mentioned purely by way of example, without any claim to be mandatory. Accordingly, even the mandatory nature of the list of financial instruments is only apparent, and each national Supervisory Authority could include a new product within the MiFID II scope as long as it presents specific features in common with the securities explicitly mentioned.

The proposal to specify in the MiFID II definition of financial instruments that it applies 'also' to financial instruments issued on DLT seems a merely formal addition, as on the one hand the MiCA Regulation expressly recognises the existence of security-tokens, and, on the other, the MiFID II definition remains not only 'technologically neutral', but also 'open'. In other words: given that security-tokens and tokenised-securities are already financial instruments, there is a risk that other crypto-assets (and in particular *cryptocurrencies*) will also be considered as such. Moreover, the classification of cryptocurrencies as financial instruments is debated in various legal systems: the Securities and Exchange Commission (SEC) position is well known, as it identifies an expectation of return in the purchase of cryptocurrencies associated with staking, considering Ether and thus proof stakes-based crypto financial instruments. If these considerations seem distant to us, we must reconsider it: the parameters on which the so-called 'Howey Test' is based to identify financial instruments are common to EU regulators and the SEC's classificatory interpretations could well cross the Atlantic Ocean.

The identification of financial instruments, in Italy, falls within the scope of Consob, which has identified their distinctive feature in 'negotiability', '*with this meaning the transferability and the ability to be subject to transactions*' (Sciarrone Alibrandi et al. 2019). Negotiability is then the qualifying element that marks the line between investment products and financial instruments, sharing both of them the additional features constituted by the use of capital, the promise/expectation of financial returns, and the assumption of a risk directly connected and correlated to the use of capital.[4]

In the case of Bitcoin, often purchased with speculative purposes, and for which negotiability is undeniable, it is understandable that the market wonders whether it should be considered a financial instrument; at the same time it is not clear whether a product with the above characteristics can be considered a security only if it has clear an specific similarities with the instruments listed in art. 4 para. 1 n. 44).

The issue is a boulder on the market if we consider that the provision of services relating to financial instruments is subject to a

---

[4] See most recently Consob 2019. *Document for discussion: Initial offers and exchanges of crypto-assets.* 19 March 2019. Available online: www.consob .it/documents/1912911/1972122/doc_disc_20190319_en.pdf/b79d2c93-1238-f632-23de-66032da83688. Moreover, in the same document, Consob highlights that a token is an investment product if it represents rights connected to investments in entrepreneurial projects. Therefore Bitcoin, not only does not fall within the definition of 'financial instrument', but not even that of an investment product. It is however necessary to keep in mind the judgement of Italian Corte di Cassazione no. 26807 of September 17 2020 regarding the classification as a public offering the communications addressed to the public that explicitly appeal for investment purposes.

complex and consolidated regulatory framework, which concerns both the provision of investment services (MiFID II Directive), the markets functioning (MiFIR) and subsequent post-trading, registration, and custody activities (again MiFID II/MiFIR, but also CSDR). Therefore, a bank providing Bitcoin services would find itself with the doubt of being faced with a hyper-regulated or – on the contrary – a deregulated – or soon to be regulated – product, and should determine whether not to apply the legislation on financial instruments, potentially exposing itself to different interpretations of the supervisory authorities, or, whether to adopt the more precautionary approach, finding itself faced with burdensome requirements, in some cases inapplicable in a DLT context. In both cases, the bank would be exposed to compliance and reputational risks. As can be understood, legal uncertainty is an obstacle to the evolution of a market, as well as a factor of disparity within an ecosystem, as it inevitably ends up conditioning and inhibiting the entities most sensitive to sanction and reputational risks.

In this context, up to now there has been a lack of explicit interpretations provided by European and National Supervisory Authorities, which have not clarified whether the most capitalised crypto-asset(s) should be considered financial instrument(s) or not.

In any case, the succession of publications in recent years allows, at least, to perceive a consistent interpretative path and the position of the regulators, starting with the European ones, is beginning to be more evident.

European Securities and Markets Authority (ESMA) in particular, proved to be aware of the difficulty of considering Bitcoin as financial instruments. In 2019, the European Authority published the results of a survey addressed to National Supervisory Authorities in order to understand the different opinions about the possibility of considering some crypto-assets as financial instruments. It is crucial to point out that Bitcoin was not included in the survey, as it was considered 'pure payment-type crypto-assets': '*Pure payment-type crypto-assets, like the Bitcoin which accounts for around half of the total market value of crypto- assets, are not represented in the survey sample*' (ESMA 2019a). The same interpretation can be found in the writings of the European Banking Authority, which soon included Bitcoin among the 'Payment/exchange/currency tokens' (EBA 2019). It can therefore be assumed that European Supervisory

Authorities agree on the difficulty of considering Bitcoin a financial instrument, stating, however, that *'the actual classification of a crypto-asset as a financial instrument is the responsibility of an individual NCA and will depend on the specific national implementation of EU law and the information and evidence provided to that NCA'*(ESMA 2019b).

The main doubts, therefore, remain at the national level, with the potential consequence that interpretative divergences lead to unequal treatment within the EU and to a violation of the 'level playing field' principle. It is also evident that the lack of a clear national statement on the nature of Bitcoin contributes keeping the compliance risk on a very high level for banks that wish to provide crypto-assets services. The interpretative issue then finds foundation and force if we consider that in some countries – European and non-European – there have been a succession of orientations aimed at considering Bitcoin as a financial instrument. For example, in Germany in 2013 the BaFin determined that Bitcoins are *'financial instruments in the form of units of account pursuant to* Section 1 *(11) sentence 1 of the Germany Banking Act'*.

In Italy, a somewhat strong position was expressed in a sentence provided by the Corte di Cassazione, which rejected the conclusion that 'virtual currencies' were not 'investment products, but means of payment', and, as such, 'removed from the legislation on financial instruments' (see Corte di Cassazione, Seconda Sezione Penale, Sentence no. 26807 of 17 September 2020); even if from a more in-depth analysis it would seem that the Supreme Court does not express on the legal classification of cryptocurrencies, limiting itself to consider a public offering of financial products the marketing communication that explicitly appeals for the purpose of investment, the use of the term 'financial instrument' reinforced doubts regarding the legal qualification of Bitcoins.

Coming to the positions of the Italian Supervisory Authorities, for a long time there was no clarification allowing to exclude Bitcoin from the perimeter of financial instruments. A first step in this direction, however, can be found in a study published by the Bank of Italy in 2019, which, analysing *'the economic, accounting and prudential profiles of bitcoin-like' 'crypto-assets'*, concluded: *'The literature examined shows that this particular class of 'crypto-assets' does not fall within the categories of money and financial instrument'* (Caponera and Gola 2019).

On the other hand, Consob did not express itself in such a clear way in any publication concerning crypto-assets, but hinted at a similar position in publication about 'marketplace lending', in which, with reference to the qualification of Bitcoin as a financial instrument, it highlighted the *'difficulties associated with the decentralised production system and therefore the absence of a subject that can be qualified as an issuer and the significant differences existing with respect to the most widespread categories of financial instruments'*.[5] If we add that a few months later, Consob itself specified that in order to be classified as a financial instrument, a token must have features of strict analogy with the categories of financial instruments detailed by MiFID II, it implicitly derives the exclusion of Bitcoins from the perimeter of financial instruments.[6]

The confirmation of this interpretation was finally provided by Consob itself – and by the Bank of Italy, warned the public about the risks inherent in crypto-assets, clarifying, after mentioning Bitcoins as an example, that *'the purchase of crypto-assets is not subject to the rules on (…) investment services and continues to lack specific forms of protection'*.[7]

Based on the analysis above, it can therefore be assumed that Bitcoins are not considered, at least in Italy, financial instruments; the applicable regulatory framework in not MiFID II/MiFIR (nor the CSDR Regulation), but the MiCA Regulation, falling cryptocurrencies within the residual class of tokens other than asset-referenced tokens, e-money tokens, and utility tokens.

In any case, this conclusion is the result of an interpretative effort to be repeated for each type of crypto-asset not clearly attributable to one of the classifications made explicit by the MiCA Regulation. At the same time, the lack of a closed definition of 'financial instrument' in Directive (EU) no. 65/2014 leads to potential interpretative divergences in Member States. At the same time, the interpretative doubt continues to exist for all those crypto-assets that present

[5] Consob - Market Place Lending – toward new forms of intermediation?, Quaderni Fintech, 5 July 2019.

[6] Consob - *"Initial offers and exchanges of crypto-assets: Final report"*, 2 January 2020.

[7] Consob-Bank of Italy 2021. *Consob and the Bank of Italy warn against the risks inherent in crypto-assets*. Press Release of 28 April 2021. Available online: www.consob.it/web/consob-and-its-activities/press-releases

similarities with some of the securities referred to in art. 4 para. 1 n. 44) of the MiFID II Directive. For example, we can consider a token that is not a digital representation of a share or a debt instrument mentioned in the MiFID II list, but which gives the holder the right to a share of revenues. In this case, being the product negotiable, it would appear to be a financial instrument. Most of the European Supervisory Authorities have the same opinion, stating that *'the existence of attached profit rights, without having necessarily ownership or governance rights attached (...) was considered sufficient (...) to qualify crypto-assets as transferable securities'*.[8] At the same time, however, differences in interpretation were found: '*NCAs that disagreed with this view may do so on the basis of a more restrictive transposition of MiFID, e.g. a restrictive list of examples of transferable securities*'. Again, this is not a purely theoretical exercise, but one with profound repercussions on DeFI and the possibility for banks to take advantage of it and build high value-added services. We can take as an example the importance that Decentralized autonomous organizations (DAOs) are acquiring, which are based precisely on governance rights attributed to the various token-holders. Not solving the problem of the legal-regulatory qualification of the governance tokens of DAOs could, in some countries, slow down the evolution of an entire ecosystem, or expose to unjustified risks those who decide to participate in it to exploit its potential for innovation and efficiency; or both.

It is therefore easy to understand how the crypto-assets service providers (including banks) would be facilitated in countries with a more closed/exclusive vision of the definition of financial instrument.

The European Authorities are well aware of this risk, as highlighted by ESMA at the beginning of 2019 in the context of the Advice on Initial Coin Offerings and Crypto-Assets.[9]

It can therefore be concluded that crypto-assets are showing all the limits of the defining technique adopted by the MiFID II Directive, in addition to the existence of a formally tech-neutral legislation, but which, in fact, presents requirements that are difficult to apply in a DLT context.

---

[8] ESMA "*Legal qualification of crypto-assets - survey to NCA*", January 9, 2019.
[9] ESMA 2019. "*Initial Coin Offering and Crypto Assets*". Advice.

It is therefore useful to briefly review, from a practical point of view, what are the consequences of the classification of some crypto-assets as financial instruments for banks and market infrastructures.

The Issuance and Registration of Security-Token

The issuance and circulation of financial instruments are regulated by national legislation, which protects investors and guarantees legal certainty. In Italy, the source of reference is 'Testo Unico della Finanza' (in addition to the discipline referred to in the civil code), and new D.L. 25/2023 which now regulates pure digital issuance.

Having said that, considering that the regulatory constraint only concerns traditional financial instruments (i.e., those included by way of example in art.4 para.1 n.44) of the MiFID II Directive), digital issuance can be considered possible for other security-tokens, not representing traditional financial instruments.

In any case, before D.L. 25/2023 and DLT Pilot Regime the transferable securities regulated by Italian law admitted to trading or traded on a trading venue may exist only in book-entry form (Article 83-bis of Testo Unico della Finanza). The rule is consistent with the provision referred to in art. 3 para. 1 of Regulation (EU) no. 909/2014 (so-called CSDR), pursuant to which '*any issuer established in the Union that issues or has issued transferable securities which are admitted to trading or traded on trading venues, shall arrange for such securities to be represented in book-entry form as immobilisation or subsequent to a direct issuance in dematerialised form*'.

The classification of a token as a financial instrument makes it impossible for it to be admitted to be traded on a trading venue, avoiding the breach of Regulation (EU) no. 909/2014, as the registration on DLT is not considered a 'book-entry form' pursuant to the same Regulation. At the same time, however, the nature of the token as a financial instrument determines that any trading platform or system that allows its exchange on a multilateral basis should be inevitably qualified as a 'trading venue' and, in particular, as a multilateral trading facility. It is therefore clear that a security-token could be only traded on multilateral systems managed by regulated entities and classified as 'trading venues' and, therefore, could not be issued without violating the CSDR legislation. This regulatory paradox leads to the conclusion that a security-token could be traded exclusively Over

The Counter (OTC), outside any organised system, or on its own account by authorised investment firms.[10]

This allows us to understand the reason why a security-token market has not yet developed; the potential of crypto-assets as a fundraising source is in fact frustrated, as is the role of investment firms and banks as advisors for raising capital through the issuance of tokens. Waiting for regulatory changes making the legislation applicable – in practice – in a DLT context, the financial and production ecosystem cannot therefore fully benefit from the potential of tokenisation.

For this reason, on June 2 2022, the Regulation (EU) n. 858/2022 of the European Parliament and of the Council '*on a pilot regime for market infrastructures based on distributed ledger technology*' was published in the Official Journal of the EU; an experimental legislative project aimed at making the regulatory framework suitable with the adoption of DLT by market infrastructures. The merit of the project lies in the awareness of the European legislator to make the regulation technologically neutral not only in a formal sense, but also from a substantial and effective standpoint. It is, therefore, crucial to provide regulatory requirements that can in fact be applied to different technological contexts, as inapplicability necessarily results in non-compliance and, therefore, in prohibition.

Among the most obvious examples, we can consider the mentioned art. 3 of Regulation (EU) no. 909/2014, which de facto excludes the management of multilateral trading venues based on DLT. We can therefore explain the provision referred to in art. 5 para. 2 of the Pilot Regulation of an exemption from article 3 of Regulation (EU) n. 909/2014 if the DLT SS '*demonstrates that the use of a "securities account" as defined in Article 2(1), point (28), of that Regulation or the use of the book-entry form as provided for in Article 3 of that Regulation is incompatible with the use of the particular distributed ledger technology*'. In this case, the aim of the European Commission seems not only to allow the exclusion of a requirement made obsolete by the use of a technology that finds its primary value in disintermediation, but also to experiment with the removal of an unnecessary regulatory obstacle.

---

[10] At the same time, considering – not only security-tokens – but also cryptocurrencies financial instruments would mean that all the trading platforms (and in general all the CASPs) should have a licence as investment firm under MiFID II.

Another example is the legitimation of direct access to the trading venue by the investor,[11] demonstrating the regulator's intention to verify that DLT-based systems can guarantee market protection without forcing them to adhere to regulatory schemes that are incompatible with the specific nature and features of the technology used.

While on the one hand the proposed legislation legitimises a disintermediation process, making the activity of Central securities depositories (CSDs) and brokers unnecessary, at the same time, by removing obstacles to the development of the security-token market, it opens up countless other possibilities for the provision of consultancy services. Consider, for example, the opportunities to advise SMEs and start-ups in the issuance of tokens for fundraising purposes, or, again, the possibility for banks to exploit their professional experience through the provision of investment services based on financial instruments issued and traded on DLT.

It would therefore be desirable to extend the experimental regime to other instruments in addition to those referred to in art. 3 para. 1 of the Regulation, making it potentially applicable to any type of security-token. Otherwise, the pilot regime would have the merit of favouring the experimentation of alternative regulatory regimes suitable in a DLT context, but would be limited to an absolutely residual perimeter, without actually removing the obstacles that prevent the exploitation of the potential of the tokenisation as a means of fundraising, leading to potential regulatory arbitrage in favour of countries with legal-regulatory systems ready to accept the issuance and circulation of security-tokens.

Crypto-Assets Services from a Regulatory Perspective

As clarified in the previous paragraphs, crypto-assets that can be classified as financial instruments are subject to the legislation on the provision of investment services and will continue to be so even

---

[11] Regulation (UE) n. 858/2022 'on a pilot regime for market infrastructures based on distributed ledger technology', Recital (26): 'At the request of an operator of a DLT MTF, the competent authority should therefore be allowed to grant a temporary exemption from that obligation of intermediation in order to provide direct access for retail investors and to enable them to deal on their own account, provided that adequate safeguards regarding investor protection are in place, that such retail investors fulfil certain conditions and that the operator complies with any possible additional investor protection measures that the competent authority requires.'

after the application of the MiCA Regulation, whose application will be limited to tokens that are not already subject to specific regulation. The difference is crucial if we consider that classifying a token as a financial instrument means moving from an unregulated context to a hyper-regulated one. It is true that the MiCA Regulation will introduce specific regulatory requirements for the issuance and offer of all crypto-assets, but this is a compliance effort that is absolutely not comparable to the one required by the MiFID II framework.

Crypto-assets service providers – including banks and investment firms – therefore, due to the different classification of the tokens used, could find themselves to manage different processes for the same service. In fact, it is clear that a bank that intends to provide, for example, custodial services will have to comply with different requirements for security-tokens compared to the others, with a consequent increase in costs and management complexity. It should not be noted that, as in the case of issuance and registration, also the legislation on the provision of investment services is in some cases inapplicable using DLT, having been conceived in relation to a context – and, therefore, to products and services – completely different.

Returning to the case of the custody of security-tokens, the legislation on the safekeeping of financial instruments is given by Directive (EU) no. 65/2014 (so-called MiFID II), by the Delegated Directive (EU) no. 593/2017 and, in Italy, by the Bank of Italy Regulation of December 5 2019. Pursuant to Article 3 of the Delegated Directive (EU) no. 593/2017 investment firms can '*deposit financial instruments held by them on behalf of their clients into an account or accounts opened with a third party provided that the firms exercise all due skill, care and diligence in the selection, appointment and periodic review of the third party and of the arrangements for the holding and safekeeping of those financial instruments*'. In Italy, financial instruments can only be sub-deposited with central securities depositories or authorised depositories such as banks. Also in this case the custody is brought back to an intermediation scheme which does not fit with the nature of crypto-assets. Similarly, the reference 'accounts' and, therefore, into an 'account-based' system makes the legislation on custody in itself inapplicable to security-tokens, except for extensive interpretations by intermediaries accepting a compliance risk.

The picture is also complicated for security-tokens traded on multi-lateral systems, which will necessarily be sub-deposited with CSDs if not exempted under Regulation (EU) n. 858/2022.

A partially similar issue concerns the investor protection requirements envisaged by the MiFID II regulatory framework for the provision of investment services. In this case, the differences between MiFID II and the MiCA regulation are considerable, with a consequent need for banks to adopt extremely differentiated processes for comparable activities. The analogy is evident if we analyse the services regulated by MiCAR, which are mainly the same as those referred to in Annex I Section A of Directive (EU) no. 65/2014. This determines, on the one hand, the paradoxical application to payment-tokens (e.g., e-money tokens) of a regulation inspired by MiFID II; on the other hand, it confirms the risk that an interpretative exercise – complex in itself and made even more uncertain by the open nature of the definition of financial instrument – leads to the application of different regimes not only within the EU, but also at the national level and, potentially, within each individual bank.

The differences are not meaningless. A token not classified as a financial instrument will be subject to the MiCA Regulation, while, to date, it is unregulated; a security-token, on the contrary, is part of a regulatory framework which – only at the European level – is made by 1 Directive (MiFID II), 1 Regulation (MiFIR), 1 Delegated Directive and 28 Delegated Regulations. In order to comply with such a complex regulatory framework, banks have equipped themselves with equally complex processes and service models, and the insertion of crypto-assets certainly requires an effort not comparable to that required for the other tokens.

In Italy, the 'portfolio' advice model is particularly widespread, which requires that the suitability of an investment is assessed in relation not to the individual transaction, but to the customer's overall portfolio, ensuring greater protection for the latter. To this end, Italian banks have equipped themselves with complex suitability assessment algorithms, based on parameters not always applicable to crypto-assets. Furthermore, in a 'portfolio' approach, banks assess the suitability not only of the recommended transactions, but also of those arranged by customers on their own initiative.

If it may be deemed necessary to extend the same rules applied to securities to tokens representing traditional financial instruments, the obligation could become excessively burdensome for tokens whose classification as financial instruments is doubtful and, perhaps, limited to a particularly restrictive interpretation of National Supervisory Authority. Even in this case, banks would find themselves arranging – perhaps as a precautionary measure – more restrictive rules than those adopted by unsupervised intermediaries. It is in fact necessary to highlight that under MiCA Regulation is not even required an assessment of appropriateness for executive services.

The application of the MiFID II investor protection requirements to crypto-assets is burdensome – in addition to being a source of potential interpretative discrepancies determined by the uncertainty regarding the definition of security-tokens, but they are de facto applicable. The analysis of the requirements provided by Regulation (EU) no. 600/2014 (so-called MiFIR) leads to opposite conclusions. As we have seen, a token cannot be traded on a trading venue, without the inevitable violation of specific CSDR obligation; at the same time, we have highlighted that a multilateral security-token trading system should be qualified as a trading venue, with the consequence that the secondary market of these instruments is relegated to bilateral trading in a context that can be defined as 'OTC'. At present, therefore, a security-token secondary market on a trading venue is not conceivable. Nevertheless, we must point out that, even a legitimation of market infrastructures and multilateral trading systems based on DLT (see the aforementioned Regulation establishing a Pilot Regime), would lead to obligations that are difficult to apply in a DLT context. This is the case, for example, of transaction reporting. Pursuant to art. 26 of Regulation (EU) no. 600/2014, the investment firm that executes a transaction on financial instruments traded or admitted to trading on trading venues, must report it to the competent authority, complying with the detailed requirements provided by the Delegated Regulation (EU) no. 590/2017. The necessary prerequisites in order to comply with the transaction reporting obligation are: the correct and complete identification of the trading platforms that must be classified as trading venues, that the latter have reported to ESMA the reference data of the instruments traded on their systems, and that the investment firm executing the transaction finds all the data required by the Delegated Regulation (EU) no. 590/2017. In the case of security-tokens, all the three aforementioned assumptions are lacking: the first two due to the uncertainty regarding the classification of security-tokens and the notion of trading venue applied to DLT-based trading systems, the third one as the information required from art. 26 MiFIR are in fact based on taxonomic criteria inapplicable to security-tokens.[12]

The same considerations can then be extended to post-trade transparency obligations, based on classes of instruments that refer to the traditional taxonomy.

The analysis therefore confirms the difficulty of applying the current regulatory framework to security-tokens and therefore explains the reasons why banks and market infrastructures are delaying their entry into the security-token market.

Further Regulatory Profiles: The Issuance of Electronic Money Tokens

Up to now, the discussion has been mainly focused on investment tokens, their potential as a means of fundraising, and the obstacles presented by the legislation on financial instruments; but the original purpose and value of crypto-assets are based on disintermediation and their potential as a means of exchange and payment. Cryptocurrencies and Stablecoins can change the face of the financial industry, reducing costs of cross-border payments, allowing funds to be transferred all over the world under the same conditions, guaranteeing financial inclusion. In particular, stablecoins, not being excessively exposed to market volatility, could constitute – together with Central Bank Digital Currencies (CBDCs)– the near future of payments. Therefore, banks find themselves having to rethink their services and exploring how crypto-assets could fit into their payment processes in order to fully exploit the potential deriving from the use of smart contracts and programmability.

The question is therefore whether current and future legislation is capable of regulating stablecoins without creating disproportionate and unjustified obstacles. It is interesting to note that the MiCA regulation reserves two of the three specifically regulated token classes for stablecoins (thus excluding the residual class of 'other-than' tokens)

---

[12] For example, we can consider field 43 of Table 2 of Annex I of the Delegated Regulation (EU) no. 590/2017, in which the indication of the classification of the instrument is requested.

confirming the attention of regulators for what is seen as a phenomenon with potential of exponential spread. Among these, e-money tokens are already subject to regulation on electronic money and, in particular, to Directive (EU) no. 110/2009 (so-called EMD2). Electronic money tokens are therefore the only asset for which MiCAR provides exceptions from the existing legislation, which leads, on the one hand, to wonder whether this solution is the most appropriate also for security-tokens and, on the other, to analyse which are the most significant differences between the two regulatory regimes (MiCAR and EMD2) and their impact on banking services and processes.

The MiCA Regulation therefore defines electronic-money tokens as 'a type of crypto-asset that purports to maintain a stable value by referencing the value of one official currency'. The definition of electronic money is provided in art. 2 para. 2 of Directive (EU) no. 110/2009: *'electronically, including magnetically, stored monetary value as represented by a claim on the issuer which is issued on receipt of funds for the purpose of making payment transactions (...), and which is accepted by a natural or legal person other than the electronic money issuer'*. A token that aims to maintain a stable value by anchoring it to a fiat currency and which constitutes a claim against the issuer is therefore currently subject to the EMD2 regulation and, in the future, to the MiCA Regulation. Both regulatory regimes reserve the issuance to banks and electronic money institutions.

As in the case of security-tokens, the interest of banks is dampened by the provision of regulatory requirements that are difficult to apply to a DLT context. Reference is made to the obligation provided for by art. 11 para. 3 of the EMD2 Directive, implemented by the Bank of Italy with articles 114-ter and 126-movies of the 'Testo Unico Bancario', which is de facto inapplicable to a naturally 'bearer instrument' such as a token. Once the electronic money token has been issued, it is used in various payment transactions with a chain of transfers that makes the obligation for the issuer to have a contract with each individual holder unsustainable. A bank that intends to issue an e-money token would find itself faced with a regulatory obstacle that is difficult to overcome, especially in jurisdictions in which the regulator gives a restrictive and formal interpretation of the obligation pursuant to art. 11 para. 3 EMD2.

Even the EMD2 regulation, like the CSDR one, is technologically neutral in a formal but not substantial sense.

Moreover, the mentioned requirement is not even justified by the need to fulfil the AML obligations, considering that each Virtual Asset Service Provider participating in the payment system is subject to the same AML/CFT requirements. The obligation to contractualise the relationship could therefore be limited to the phases of the direct distribution of the tokens by the issuer and to that of the customer's redemption request.

The impossibility of issuing electronic money tokens without incurring unacceptable compliance risks could lead some institutions not to guarantee a redemption right, thus subtracting the token from the scope of application of art. 2 para. 2 of the EMD2.

In this sense, the intervention of the MiCA Regulation is resolutive, since, on the one hand, it excludes the obligation to contractualise the relationship with the token-holder, recognising dignity to the nature of the tokens as bearer instruments and, on the other, it makes the redemption right a specific requirement deriving from the classification of the crypto-assets as electronic money (better: electronic money -token) and not a defining element. Until then, even the issuance of electronic money tokens by banks, as well as the provision of services relating to security-tokens, is delayed, with consequent and undeniable competitive disadvantages.

Which Crypto-Assets in Banks?

As outlined in the introduction, there are many advantages for banks in providing crypto-assets services. Programmability is the future of payments and is inherent in smart-contracts. Stablecoins (and in particular e-money tokens) are therefore one of the natural areas of interest for banks, which, through experimentation, could investigate many of the needs and applications of the Digital Euro, bringing value to the latter.

However, as we tried to argue in the previous paragraph, even stablecoins are not free from risks due to the opacity of regulation and interpretative positions on the matter.

To give an idea about the legal classification risk inherent in the provision of services relating to stablecoins and the consequent difficulties for banks wishing to enter this market, we have taken three different stablecoins, all of which can be classified as electronic money tokens pursuant to MiCAR Regulations and all with similar features (at least according to their white-papers and terms and conditions).

These features are:

– the issue of the token following the receipt of funds;
– the management of a reserve in order to guarantee that for each token issued the peg with the equivalent of fiat currency; and
– the provision of a conditional redemption right for the token holder.

We will mention them as Stablecoin A, Stablecoin B, and Stablecoin C. The purpose of the analysis is to argue that despite of similar conditions, the respective issuers have adopted three different legal-regulatory qualifications, assuming different compliance risks, without ever being able to exclude all of them at once.

In the case of Stablecoin A, the token holder has a redemption right. However, according to the terms and conditions, the mentioned right is recognised only to certain users who have opened an account with the issuer. Other token holders have no redemption right but can only exchange the Stablecoin A with fiat currency by trading it on crypto-exchanges, until the opening of the account is required at least. Since the opening of an account is allowed only to certain individuals, it can be considered that the mere possession of the token does not itself give rise to any redemption right (or rather: it gives rise to a conditional right).

As we have seen, this is a valid argument for excluding the classification of stablecoin as electronic money for Stablecoin A which will not be subject to EMD2 and, consequently, to PSD2 (since it is not 'electronic money', it does not even fall within the definition of 'funds' Pursuant to art. 4 no. 25) of Directive (EU) no. 2366/2015).

The same argument seems to apply to Stablecoin B, the terms and conditions of which require that in order to redeem the token, the holder must be a verified customer of the issuer.

However, it is necessary to highlight how this thesis could clash in future with different interpretations provided by the regulators; perhaps for this reason, the issuer of Stablecoin A appears to have obtained a specific licence for its services. At the same time, an equivalent licence was not requested by the issuer of Stablecoin B, making it clear that two similar stablecoins correspond to two different interpretations by the respective issuers.

Finally, Stablecoin C is a token with characteristics similar to A and B, which, on the contrary, has been classified by the issuer as electronic money, preventing the risk of requalification by the regulator, but clashing with the need to also apply the legislation on the provision of payment services. This could be the reason why it then decided not to provide the custody and transfer services of the token issued by itself, which would – probably – be considered PSD2 payment services.

A dilemma for banks: in the face of crypto-assets with the same characteristics, not only the issuers, but also the service providers (e.g., custody, transfer, etc.) are faced with the doubt whether:

– classify the token as electronic money, making it also fit within the PSD2 'funds' classification, so that a Crypto Asset Services Provider (CASP) that provides transfer or custody services would be providing payment services, with the consequent application of PSD2 authorisation and conduct requirements provided;
– the issue in this case is clear: how many exchanges and custody provider do have payments institution licence currently?;
– at the same time, the negotiability of the token makes the contractual obligation pursuant to art. 11 EMD2 – as well as to verify transactions and token transfers on the market – hard to comply with;
– exclude the classification of the token as electronic money, by leveraging the exclusion of the redemption right or the provision of a conditional redemption right. In this case, it is quite obvious that the above arguments could clash with a requalification of the token as electronic money, which would give rise to provision of financial services without the necessary licences by the CASPs that provide custody and transfer of the same token; and
– even outside of stablecoins, all the resistance and interpretative obstacles described in the previous paragraphs are in force. This is especially true, as we have seen, for the mistakenly called 'crypto-currencies' (or 'other-than (…) token' under MiCAR).

Regulatory uncertainty and a necessarily greater sensitivity concerning the compliance and reputational risks compared to other market operators may be among the reasons why the list of banks providing services is so short and, in most cases, the model adopted is that of the mere distribution of services provided by third-party CASPs and, therefore, already offered on the market. Even the adoption of this solution – which does not even allow for direct experimentation with innovative solutions and services – is an uphill road, since, in any case, the exposure of the distributed CASP to regulatory uncertainty in turn entails reputational risks for the distributing banks. If we add to this the fact that a new distinction between *backed* and *unbacked* crypto-assets is gaining strength in the regulators' positions, in which the latter tend to be labelled as bad crypto-assets with little chance of appeal, then even the distribution of third-party services is effectively limited to stablecoins.

For instance, in June 2022, the Bank of Italy published a communication in which it strongly discouraged financial intermediaries from making available and/or facilitating access for their clients to trading platforms on which unbacked crypto-assets are exchanged (Bank of Italy 2022).

The distinction between backed and unbacked crypto-assets – for which the former would be those 'crypto-assets lacking a stabilisation mechanism that anchors their value to a reference asset' (Bank of Italy 2022) – is perhaps excessively aprioristic; while not refusing to acknowledge its importance from a theoretical and general approach profile, in some cases a rigid division could be belied by the specifics of the concrete case. It is based on the assumption that unbacked crypto-assets are 'crypto-assets without any intrinsic value, not related to any activity in the real or financial economy'.

However, some crypto-assets, even if unbacked, may well have intrinsic value.[13]

That said, it could be argued that some crypto-assets derive their value from being in turn the building block of complex decentralised ecosystems. For instance, we have to acknowledge that services built

---

[13] The International Monetary Fund implicitly acknowledged that some unbacked crypto-assets have 'intrinsic value': 'Many unbacked crypto assets tend to have high price volatility (which makes them a poor store of value and unit of account) with little intrinsic value' ('Fintech Notes – Regulating the Crypto Ecosystem: the case of unbacked crypto-assets', IMF, September 2022); Bank of America argued that DLT and the crypto-asset industry have value beyond market speculation (July edition of report 'Global Cryptocurrencies and Digital Assets': 'We do not agree that blockchains and the applications that run on them have no intrinsic value – a comment we hear regularly').

and enabled by Ethereum layers lead to an increase in the value of the reference crypto-asset (Ether).

From this specific angle, some crypto-assets such as Ether, are not so different from shares in companies or other financial instruments, representing the value of what they bring to the system. This would also seem to be confirmed by the SEC's positions, which, while not entirely agreeable insofar as they lead to crypto-assets based on proof of stake being considered as financial instruments, are significant in their premises: some crypto-assets may give rise to an expectation of return that goes beyond mere negotiability on the market but is derived from their value and use.

Moreover, there are several projects conducted by the supervisory authorities themselves to exploit the potential offered by DLT for supervision and surveillance purposes. There is the recent news of a pilot project promoted by DG FISMA (European Commission) 'to develop, deploy, and test a technological solution for embedded supervision of decentralised finance (DeFi) activity. The project will seek to benefit from the open nature of transaction data on the Ethereum blockchain, which is the biggest settlement platform of DeFi protocols. Its focus will be on automated supervisory data gathering directly from the blockchain to test the technological capabilities for supervisory monitoring of real-time DeFi activity'.

In Italy, projects are being conducted on the use of public DLT applied in the contractual, compliance, and audit activities too.

That said, if the public and supervisory authorities themselves recognise the usefulness and importance of testing the use of DLT, one could argue that the (unbacked) crypto-assets of those DLTs have intrinsic value. Based on these considerations, crypto-assets such as Ether could not be placed on the same level as crypto-assets (whether backed or unbacked) that do not add any value to the ecosystem, indeed, we could argue that some unbacked crypto-assets not only have value but are destined to increase in that same value the greater their adoption (and thus demand), including by public authorities.

It is therefore acknowledged that some unbacked crypto-assets may also have 'intrinsic value', which could be defined by their scarcity, use cases, and technological application. To equate these assets with those that do not enable any services (and some 'stablecoins'), would be ungenerous and perhaps not entirely fair.

For this reason, to protect customers from mere speculation in assets with no intrinsic value – and themselves from the consequent legal and reputational risks – the banks could equip themselves with an evaluation process to which each individual crypto-asset would be subjected, in which not only the market-cap, legal-regulatory framework, etc., would be examined in depth but in which the market-cap, legal-regulatory framework, etc., would also be defined and verified. As the June Communication itself points out, it is not only a matter of market-cap, legal-regulatory framework, etc. but also one in which the requirements for a crypto-asset to be recognised as having intrinsic value and meeting society's needs are defined and verified in detail.

As pointed out in the June Communication itself: *'the phenomenon of crypto-assets (…) requires the ability to distinguish between different categories of products and uses based on the various levels of risk that characterise them, also depending on the existence or otherwise of intrinsic value'.*[14]

Moreover, as clearly expressed by the Deputy Director General of the Bank of Italy Cipollone, *'this is the approach taken by the Communication (…), which highlights, among other things, the importance of initiatives aimed at outlining a system of principles and good practices that, although not binding, mitigate the risks associated with the use of decentralised technologies (…) also through the definition of standards for the development of shared benchmarks, which can be formulated through forms of public-private collaboration, according to a co-regulation perspective that, as stated in the Communication, is inspired by a common vision of the Bank of Italy (…) also through the definition of standards for the development of shared benchmarks, which could be formulated through forms of public-private collaboration, according to a co-regulation perspective that, as stated in the Communication, is inspired by a constant dialogue between the Authority and the technological operators'* (Cipollone 2022).

The key is therefore not a more or less implicit ban on providing services involving unbacked crypto-assets, but the constant dialogue (that 'public-private collaboration') between the various players in the system.

---

[14] Bank of Italy - Communication on decentralised technologies in finance and crypto-assets"; June 2022.

Conclusions

As we have tried to argue, the current regulatory regime is, in some cases, an obstacle to the provision of crypto-assets services. Regulatory uncertainty primarily damages banks and supervised entities, which, as they are particularly exposed to sanction and reputational risks, continue to delay their entry into a market with significant development potential and which will constitute the future of the financial ecosystem. Furthermore, the risks for consumers and investors increase, given the lack of a reliable reference point for professional consultancy support. Finally, the production ecosystem as a whole cannot benefit from the advantages deriving from technology, with particular reference to the fundraising potential of Security Token Offerings (STOs) and to the efficiency of payment systems deriving from the use of electronic money tokens.

Therefore, crypto-assets can be fertile ground for the experimentation of regulatory solutions that are as innovative as the technology they aim to regulate. MiCAR and the Regulation '*on a pilot regime for market infrastructures based on distributed ledger technology*' are a laudable starting point, but it is the entire regulatory framework that should be revised in an effective and technology-neutral sense.

References

Bank of Italy 2022. 'Bank of Italy communication on decentralised technologies in finance and crypto-assets'. Available online: www .bancaditalia.it/media/approfondimenti/2022/cripto/Comunicazioni-della-Banca-d-Italia-DLT-cripto.pdf.

Caponera, A., Gola, C. 2019. 'Economic and regulatory aspects of crypto-assets'. Economic and Financial Issues (Occasional Papers) 484. *Bank of Italy, Economic Research and International Relations Area.*

Cipollone, P. – Deputy Director Bank of Italy 2022. 'Crypto-assets e questioni legate alla digitalizzazione della finanza'. Available online: www.bancaditalia.it/pubblicazioni/interventi-direttorio/int-dir-2022/Cipollone_crypto_assets_21102022.pdf.

EBA 2019. 'Report with advice for the European Commission on crypto-assets'. Available online: www.eba.europa.eu/sites/default/documents/files/documents/10180/2545547/67493daa-85a8-4429-aa91-e9a5ed880684/EBA%20Report%20on%20crypto%20assets.pdf?retry=1.

ESMA 2019a. 'Legal qualification of crypto-assets: survey to NCAs'. Available online: www.esma.europa.eu/document/annex-legal-qualifica tion-crypto-assets-%E2%80%93-survey-ncas.

ESMA 2019b. 'Initial coin offerings and crypto-assets, advice'. Available online: www.esma.europa.eu/sites/default/files/library/esma50-157-1391_crypto_advice.pdf.

Sciarrone Alibrandi, A., Borello, G., Ferretti, R., Lenoci, F., Macchiavello, E., Mattassoglio, F., Panisi, F. 2019. 'Fintech notebooks: Marketplace lending – towards new forms of financial intermediation?'. *CONSOB*. Available online: www.consob.it/web/area-pubblica/ft5

5 | Cyberlaundering, VASPs' Regulation, and AML Policy Response

ANTONIO ADINOLFI AND EMANUELA GIUSI
GAETA*

Introduction

Since digitisation has become one of the primary objectives for the growth of each country (the EU-Next Generation plan is just one example), there has been much discussion, even in the literature, about the phenomena that have a negative impact on growth itself, generated by the technology that has given the start of the digital age. The main antagonists of the digital age can be summarised below:

- Cyberlaundering;
- cybercrime;
- transaction monitoring; and
- fraud impacting the asset management and insurance industries.

In this paragraph, we focus on the first two phenomena: cyberlaundering and cybercrime, analysing the need for cybersecurity.

Since 2019, money launderers have taken advantage of the economic upheaval and useful developments for more financial crime opportunities. Digital payments and blockchain technology have helped create new avenues for criminals to launder funds to unprecedented levels.

With particular reference to money laundering (ML), criminals could launder money using the Internet. This happens through a multitude of ways (FATF 2020a).

1. Placement: the placement phase involves the physical disposal of cash/funds. An example of this placement phase could be the deposit of cash through an unregulated financial institution or at an Automated Teller Machine (ATM) by certain individuals who

* This work reflects the authors' opinions, without engaging the Ministry's responsibility. The views expressed in the chapter are those of the authors and do not involve the responsibility of the institutions to which they belong.

receive a commission for this 'service' rendered (these individuals are often referred to as 'smurfs').

2. Stratification layering: the stratification phase involved overall finances to maximise conceal the true origin of the funds (this is the phase in which criminals derive financial services online), opening various online accounts, so-called collection accounts to exchange the traces.

3. Integration: the integration phase is the final step in the ML process which involves the creation of a 'front' online service company. The company offers services that result in profits that are reflected in their deeds. The problem is that these services may never have been rendered and the 'profits' are laundered money.

In terms of the technicalities behind cyberlaundering, there are two different types.

1. Digital instrumental recycling
2. Full digital recycling

Instrumental digital recycling will use two of these steps (layering and integration), while full recycling will be the complete three-step process, as mentioned in the paragraphs.

The alarming fact is that ML nowadays is basically conducted through cyber domain, and money launders could operates through: social media, identity theft, gambling, online documents, wire transfers via money mules, lottery scams, all aspects already examined in the emerging trends for the Asia/Pacific Group on Money Laundering (APG).

In this scenario, anonymity on the internet becomes a guarantee of falsifying the position or using types of methods specific to a procedure. The police forces are therefore deceived by various techniques, this entails a continuous updating of the same and an increasingly fundamental international cooperation (Coelho et al. 2021).

It is difficult to unhinge cyberlaundering from cybercrime, however it can be said that the latter is more of a meaning than the former, seen as the tool to hide the proceeds deriving from crimes carried out on the Internet or in any case through computer systems, therefore from cybercrime, which could be a predicate offence. Cybercrime and its dangers existed long before the COVID-19 pandemic. With more and more people confined to their homes, this has led to increased use of the internet (for both work and leisure). The increase in the percentage of the world's population connected to the Internet has further opportunities for cybercriminals to use the most vulnerable segments of the population and has resulted in increased revenue for criminals and increased spending for targeted Internet users (Aldasoro et al. 2021).

Cybercrime can take place in many forms, which are the same ones analysed so far (for cyberlaundering) that generate illicit proceeds through the use of computer systems. In summary, it often happens, but not exclusively, that without cybercrime there cannot be cyberlaundering: cybercrime represents the predicate crime that gives rise to illicit funds, cyberlaundering can be seen as a set of techniques and tools to conceal such illicit proceeds. The main computer crimes include the following phenomena: phishing, disclosure of personal information, ransomware, computer fraud, misuse of social media for ML, identity theft, gambling, false documents, wire transfers via money mules, lottery scams, all aspects already examined in the emerging trends for the APG. The alarming aspect is that these crimes are also used for would-be terrorists, who can also launder the proceeds from cybercrime through cyberlaundering.

As the intensity and scale of cybercrime increased, the numerous new Internet users (due to increased use during the pandemic) were not prepared for the rise in cyber threats. By this way, the concept of cybersecurity has become one of the most important challenges we face in the emergency of digitisation from reach (Lallie et al. 2021).

Cybersecurity has always been on the radar of regulators, but with recent cyber-attacks being unprecedented, cybersecurity has become a priority for many regulators around the world. In some trends, we're seeing more legislative activity and the following measures:

- Cybersecurity training to establish and ensure formal policies, standards, and practices, as well as properly and test how to respond to a security incident.
- Development of cybersecurity regulation needs to be increased in the banking and insurance sector (to name a few of the financial services sectors).
- Formation of specific working groups, task forces, councils, or commissions with the aim of government research on cybercrime trends and providing advice on cybersecurity issues.

- Support or incentive programs for information security training and education.
- Responsibility in applying the regulation to all the Authorities most exposed to the risk of cybercrime.
- Redefinition and updating of the concept of cybercrime risk during the pandemic.

These aspects represent the main concepts of cybersecurity, also in the light of the latest developments during the pandemic and the conflict between Russia and Ukraine.

VASPs and Recent Phenomena

A consistent definition of virtual assets (VAs) and virtual currencies, with the 5th AML directives (5AMLDs) definition of VAs and The Financial Action Task Force (FATF) guidance on VAs and Virtual Assets Service Providers (VASPs) can be found in article 1 (20a) and (20b) of the 2004 AML/CFT Law by the amendments of the Laws of 25 March 2020: '"Virtual currency"' shall, in accordance with this law, mean a digital representation of value that is not issued or guaranteed by a central bank or a public authority, is not necessarily attached to a legally established currency and does not possess a legal status of currency or money, but is accepted by persons as a means of exchange and which can be transferred, stored and traded digitally.'

While for VA we have the following:

"Virtual asset" shall, in accordance with this law, mean a digital representation of value, including a virtual currency, that can be digitally traded, or transferred, and can be used for payment or investment purposes, except for virtual assets that fulfil the conditions of electronic money within the meaning of point (29) of Article 1 of the Law of 10 November 2009 on payment services, as amended, and the virtual assets that fulfil the conditions of financial instruments within the meaning of point (19) of Article 1 of the Law of 5 April 1993 on the financial sector, as amended.

FATF defines a VASP as a business that performs one or more of the following actions on behalf of its customers:

- Exchange between VAs and fiat currencies;
- an exchange between one or more forms of VAs;

- VAs' transfer;
- storage and/or management of VAs or equipment that enables management of VAs; and
- participating in and providing financial services related to the offering and/or sale of VAs by the Issuer.

This definition includes various cryptocurrency companies such as exchanges, ATM operators, wallet administrators, and hedge funds, so by this definition, it can be argued that VAs and VASPs are technological products, that include aspects of IT, legal, and economic engineering, but at the same time the fact that the virtual currency is beyond the control of central banks or public authorities except for the central bank digital currencies (CBDCs) exposes VAs and VASPs to the risk of being used also for illicit purposes. Transactions made with virtual currency are transcribed in a special register, which is part of the so-called block chain, that is, a set of Internet Protocol (IP) addresses linked together, which can slow down the inspection and investigation activity to trace the names of the authors of the transactions. This is possible through DLT, that is, systems based on a distributed ledger, where all the nodes of a blockchain network have the same copy of a database that can be consulted and modified by each node individually. In other words, the actors of the transaction through a virtual currency or more generally through a VASP are linked by the block chain, whose architecture is variable and depends on the technology. The more the latter borders on anonymity, the more the risk of illicit use of VAs is high. Now we are going to show some examples of illicit use of VAs and VASPs, since they are linked to cyberlaundering and cybercrime.

ML schemes and techniques have evolved over time, although, in essence, its characteristics have remained unchanged. Placement, layering, and integration represent the three phases of ML, but it remains arduous to trace back all money transfers, by discovering the identity of the transactions' holders, their intentions, and purposes.

The effects of cyberlaundering are not distributed in a homogeneous way in the world. Therefore, we go through the review of some international critical situations, which provide an idea of the heterogeneity of the phenomenon, in terms of objectives, techniques, risks, and vulnerabilities.

One of the regions where cyberlaundering is an emerging trend is the Asia-Pacific (APAC) region.

According to FATF studies, while cyberlaundering is nothing new to the western world, it gets a new attention in the APAC region. The APG, which is the anti-money laundering/combating the financing of terrorism (AML/CFT) regional body for APAC, has recently observed data on cyber fraud, that is a prevalent threat in APAC with a 35 per cent year-on-year growth, according to a 2017 survey.

APG says that Internet-facilitated ML and terrorist financing can be broadly understood as 'the use of the internet to conduct predicate offences (cybercrime) and the use of the internet to launder proceeds of crime or fund terrorist acts (cyber laundering)'. According to APG, there is also a growing number of ways by which cyberlaundering is happening in the region (FATF 2021b).

Identity Theft

Personal identification data, as well as banking data, are stolen through various methods such as phishing, electronic media, voice phone, or instant messaging platforms. Income is obtained and used to commit crimes, including ML, through credit or debit cards and unauthorised transfers via internet banking.

Use of Social Media

According to the cases mentioned by APG in the report, fraudsters use social media platforms like Facebook to generate illicit funds, which are used for recycling. There are at least two ways to get money from the public. The first one takes place through persuasion, leveraging radical ideals, a source of inspiration to donate money; the other one through deception, pretending to be a government authority that forces the withdrawal of money. In both cases, money is used for illegal purposes such as ML.

Business Email Compromise

Even in the private market, criminals can get money by declaring to belong to proven companies with which it is possible to carry out commercial exchanges. Criminals try to obtain false identities through which the trust of the managers of a company can be credited in order to have an amount of money and to use for ML purposes.

International Wire Transfer Fraud (Money Mules)

In the field of cybercrime, 2012 is the year of money mules. In 2012, email accounts were hacked, so the criminals were able to befriend the fraudulent email holders, to the point of pretending to be partners and to receive money. The amount is credited to bank current accounts belonging to nominees (money mules), who then pass the proceeds on to criminal organisations. The 'money mules' usually receive a commission for their role in the transfer of the funds.

Online Gambling

Online platforms facilitate gambling by means including poker, casinos, and sports betting which represent an alternative way in many Asian jurisdictions for illicit funds, even if the same jurisdictions ban or restrict online gambling. However, criminals transfer the ill-gotten proceeds to bank accounts to make them legitimate.

Online Lottery Scam

According to this fraudulent scheme, criminals pretend to be governmental authorities that require the crediting of certain amounts to unlock the winner lottery.

These are examples of illegal use of VA and VASP, but ransomware represents one of the last emerging trends.

Cyberterrorism activities may include activities such as terrorist propaganda for recruitment purposes thanks to social media, private or encrypted messaging channels, used to organise criminal and terrorist actions. Further cyberterrorism activity is financing of terrorism, that is, when illicit money is collected online for the purchase to send money, to buy weapons, drugs, and supplies for carrying out a terrorist action (this can also include ML or cyberlaundering).

There are two types of damage caused by computer crime, which differ in the effects: immediate/direct or indirect/delayed. In the first case, a cyber-attack implies direct damage to operation system and is comparable to a terrorist event: for example, hijacking of an aircraft at a distance; in the second case, the effects are produced over time and occur when there is an intrusion into a public system (hospitals, companies, public administration offices, health care) which causes the blocking or illegal export of data, causing inefficiencies, time wasters economic and reputational damage. Ransomware is an example of this type. Cyberterrorism producing indirect/delayed effects catches the attention of the main international authorities in the fight against ML and Terrorism financing (TF).

The proceeds of the ransomware constitute dirty money, so they are laundered for different purposes and can be one of the weak points of the phenomenon. In fact, a recent study by the European Cyber-Security Agency (ENISA 2021) shows an international interest in the topic. The study reveals one of the key aspects, which concerned the ML services used by ransomware actors, identifying that only a small number of money launderers controlled the process to clean up ransom payments across multiple ransomware groups. According to the report, 199 cryptographic addresses received 80 per cent of all funds sent by ransomware addresses in 2020, and an even smaller group of 25 addresses accounted for around 46 per cent (Paşca and Simion 2018).

However, there are several ways to circumvent ML compliance checks: 'non-compliant centralised exchanges are likely a key step in the stratification and obfuscation process of Convertible Virtual Currency (CVC) to fiat currency money laundering', according to the report.

Furthermore, ransomware actors increasingly diversify their activities to immunise themselves against the risk of being discovered, through the use of a plurality of wallet addresses gradually increasing after receiving funds from victims, then accumulating funds across multiple wallet addresses, and recycling the payments for each ransomware event separately.

According to the report, one of the ransomware's latest strategies is to rely on a well-known method called 'chain hopping', to obfuscate the origin of their funds, by jumping between different cryptocurrencies multiple times, before moving the funds to another service or platform. Threat actors can then pass the converted funds to large CVC and money services business (MSB) with lax compliance programs.

Hence it becomes a priority to control the ransomware phenomenon and to enhance international coordination, as well as preventive measures and investing in cyber resilience.

The concept of cyber resilience includes the strengthening the cyber expertise of the law enforcement agencies (LEAs), which are in the crosshairs of the ransomware actors. The best option for law enforcement in 2022 appears to be targeting the money launderers and financiers of this pernicious activity. When combined with advances in policy making and international cooperation, this is likely to produce the greatest results in the future.

There are several issues that still need to be addressed, that involve international cooperation but also private sector and LEAs. Some examples to tackle new-age ML schemes are given below:

- Improve domestic coordination between LEAs responsible for investigating cybercrime and ML/TF;
- address the lack of legislation to combat cybercrime or elements of related technology changes;
- strengthen cooperation with the private sector and LEAs as a priority.
- encourage cooperative rather than punitive approaches to gaining assistance from private companies, such as social media and telecommunications companies; and
- promote new-generation anti-ML software with multi-dimensional detection approach within financial institutions.

Behind these manifestations of illicit use of VA and VASP are recent contextual aspects that may have accelerated the illegal trend of the digital age. The pandemic has certainly accentuated the illicit use of VA, having imposed digitisation even on those most resistant to it. The COVID-19 pandemic is estimated to have cost the world $12.5 trillion so far, and there is no indication as to when the World Health Organisation (WHO) might declare the end of the pandemic. The impact of the pandemic on business and lifestyle produced various types of fraud and cybercrime will continue to be at high risk in the future. We can expect an increase in the following types of cybercrime:

- phishing scams and ransomware attacks stimulated by continuous remote work;
- cryptocurrency exchanges will be exposed to increased attacks;
- fraudulent payments following the increase in e-commerce activity;
- identity theft following government assistance programs implemented due to pandemic impacts;
- Internet Of Things (IoT) and 5G traffic between application programming interface (API) services and apps that could become targets; and
- skills shortage when it comes to hiring cybersecurity personnel.

The regulation of cyber data laundering has become critical and has forced countries to focus on creating legal frameworks to combat fraudulent practices. Just as ML has maintained the same set of characteristics, the regulatory and legislative reform of cyberlaundering should be based on the same founding principles or pillars. The pillars that are part of the AML legal regime can be summarised as follows:

1. Prevention;
2. application; and
3. compliance.

A key aspect of the COVID-19 pandemic is that change is inevitable, and we must continually learn, adapt, and evolve to make sure we come out stronger. However, the crackdown on ML and corruption is the common responsibility of all countries around the world, as well as the key with which the phenomenon can be contained. Several studies demonstrate how corruption plays a crucial role in determining ML phenomenon, by compromising the institutional control of National Authorities.

As well as COVID-19, Russia's special operation in Ukraine, through the sanctions imposed on the occupying country, has also accelerated the illicit use of VA and VASPs.

The sanction regime is one of the main tools that European countries, along with other jurisdictions, have in order to push other jurisdictions to terminate an unlawful conduct. As an example, the United States, by imposing sanctions, has the dual effect of both an economic collapse of the nation affected by the sanctions and a sharp reduction in the reserves of dollars (Flitter and Yaffe-Bellany 2022). Therefore sanctions circumvention cases may arise, by the concerned jurisdictions, by accessing systems that are not regulated and/or with poor regulation.

Cryptocurrencies fit into this context with a specific function, which can be illustrated within the conflict between Russia and Ukraine, which began in 2014. Since that period, sanctions have been applied to Russia amounting to 50 billion per year, which didn't produce the desired effects on Russia's behaviour towards Ukraine, according to several economists (Åslund 2019; Hunter Christie 2015). This aspect is clearly confirmed in the war between Russia and Ukraine that broke out on 24 February 2022.

However, following the sanctions applied in 2014, Russia has recorded serious losses in terms of dollar reserves, which is why in recent years it has been thinking about how to counter this phenomenon in the event of a new conflict with Ukraine, through various countermeasures. The first Russian strategy, announced by the DUMA (the Russian parliament) in April 2022, involves the development of its own digital currency of the central bank, a so-called digital ruble that is used by countries allied to Russia, as if it were a dollar and without converting it into dollars by actually accepting this virtual currency for transactions.

Iran and North Korea are two countries that have used digital currencies with the purpose to diminish the effects of Western sanctions. This is a trend that the United States and the United Nations have recently observed. For example, North Korea has chosen ransomware as a strategy to steal cryptocurrency in order to finance its nuclear program, the United Nations reported. Furthermore, Russia could continue to transact with exactly those countries that have been hit by US sanctions in the past, including Iran, which is developing government-backed digital currency.

Policy Response: FATF Role on VASPs' Regulation

Some jurisdictions have adjusted their regulatory perimeter to include crypto-assets, related activities, and providers under the scope of the AML/CFT framework (see Box 5.1). By doing so, they have aligned their regulatory frameworks with the recommendation adopted by the FATF in 2018 and in 2019, although the relevant standard has yet to be fully implemented by countries. In some jurisdictions, the AML/CFT legal framework was considered sufficiently flexible to accommodate Crypto-asset Service Providers (CSPs) without requiring any specific changes. As the FATF pointed out, however, the vast majority of jurisdictions in the world have not implemented the standard or done so fully.

The FATF is an inter-governmental, founded by the members of the G7. Today it has 39 members, including 37 independent states and two regional bodies (European Commission and Gulf Cooperation Council). The main task of the FATF is to draw up international standards for the fight against ML and the financing of terrorism. In the context of mutual checks of individual countries (mutual evaluation), the FATF also checks the actual implementation through legislative,

---

Box 5.1   The UAE policy on cryptocurrencies

The United Arab Emirates (UAE), with its strategic geographical position and the abundant reserves of fossil fuels that have driven its economic growth, has become a modern state in the span of half a century whose citizens enjoy a high standard of living.

The UAE has an established infrastructure, a stable political system, and one of the most liberal trading regimes in the Gulf region.

The Emirates have enjoyed favourable economic growth also thanks to the creation of free zones. These areas, first of all, the Jebel Ali Free Zone in Dubai, were created with the aim of facilitating foreign investment. Consequently, the procedures for settling in free zones are relatively simple and quick. In these areas, there is no restriction on the transfer of profits or repatriation of capital. Given the importance of the cryptocurrencies and the favourable financial condition in the UAE, the country has suddenly become one of the most attractive currency trading agencies or blockchain technology companies. Since the beginning of 2021, many policies have been introduced in Dubai to increase investment by blockchain technology companies. In July 2021, the Central Bank of the UAE announced the launch of its first digital currency by 2026. This announcement was part of the '2023–2026 strategy' which aims to 'place it among the top 10 central banks in the world'. So, the UAE has devised a course of action to turn into a worldwide crypto centre where the world's biggest crypto organisations will be attracted to settle in the country. The Middle Eastern nation is purportedly intending to give licences for cryptographic money-related firms, and bureaucratic crypto licences to virtual resource specialist organisations (VASP) in a bid to permit driving organisations working in the crypto area to work in the nation unreservedly.

The UAE Securities and Commodities Authority (SCA) has launched a series of regulatory activities, inspired by the policies of the USA, UK, Singapore, and by the FATF standards. Moreover, through a close collaboration with the national bank of the Emirates, the authority administered the authorisation system, also in a capillary manner through the offices territorial monetary policies, which follow their own authorisation rules. In doing so, the UAE could present itself as a good contender to global fintech centres, such as Singapore and Hong Kong, which are also poised to create an ideal controlled zone for the world of cryptocurrencies.

However, between July 2020 and June 2021, the UAE had a trading volume of $26 billion (Chainalysis 2021). In this way, the UAE risks being placed as one of the most dynamic crypto showcases in the world and dangerous due to its unregulated nature.

Faced with this situation, in the US, US Commerce Kraken proposes to select a Middle East and North African CEO in Abu Dhabi. This choice is a strong signal for the UAE, guaranteeing its intentions to collaborate at the level for greater regulation, including in the VASP market. Such a scenario serves as a guide for Middle Eastern countries, leading them to continue following in the UAE's footsteps and fully control cryptocurrencies to attract investor confidence.

regulatory, and operational measures. The FATF is also responsible for drawing up guidelines for the implementation of standards and drafting best practice documents. The FATF has revised Recommendations in 2012 and, lastly, amended in 2022.

The FATF regularly holds a round of evaluations on Recommendations, and it assesses how effectively countries have implemented its Standards.

The topic of VAs has been taken into consideration by the FATF in recent years and to date, the organisation has issued the following standard and guidelines:

– Amendment to the FATF Standard (FATF 2019): FATF amended its Recommendation with the addition of the two new definitions to the Glossary, 'virtual asset' (VA), and 'virtual asset service provider' (VASP) and by clarifying how the Standards apply to VAs.
– Amendment to FATF standard (FATF 2020b): FATF, through an interpretative note to Recommendation 15, clarified how the FATF requirements should apply in relation to VAs and VASPs. In particular, it clarified the following aspects: the application of the risk-based approach to the VA business and VASP; supervision or monitoring of VASPs; licence or registration; preventive measures, such as customer due diligence, record keeping, and reporting of suspicious transactions; sanctions and other enforcement measures; and international cooperation.
– FATF Guidance for a Risk-Based Approach for VA and VASPs (FATF 2021a): the FATF adopted the Updated Guidance to provide details on the full range of obligations applicable to VASPs and VAs under the FATF Recommendations.

– Twelve Month Review of Revised FATF Standards on Virtual Resources and VASP (FATF 2020c): FATF report setting out the results of a review of the implementation of its revised standards 12 months after finalising these changes. The report found that although progress has been made, the vast majority of jurisdictions around the world have either not implemented these standards or they are not fully implemented. The jurisdictions examined are therefore not representative in this respect.

– By this evidence, there is a need for a 'Regulatory Perimeter' and the experience of the Financial Conduct Authority (FCA) in the United Kingdom could be seen as an example.

In 2019, the FCA published guidance on the regulatory boundary in relation to cryptocurrencies to provide clarity to market participants and stakeholders on the types of cryptocurrencies that fall under the FCA's regulatory mandate. From the study carried out by the FCA, the United Kingdom is a country with very different business models in the cryptocurrency space. Since January 2020, the FCA has become the AML/CFT supervisor for certain cryptocurrency activities and the same authority has been entrusted with the task of registering any business that falls within the scope of the regime created by the regulations on ML, financing of terrorism, and the transfer of funds (MLR). With many registration applications received, the FCA has created a 'cryptocurrency perimeter' for registration cases involving complex activities. Likewise, the FCA observed companies that acted as cryptocurrency traders, allowing consumers to access the cryptocurrency ecosystem. The FCA has carefully examined how these models work, looking for detailed information including cryptocurrency exchange contracts and how fees/commissions were paid to make a decision. The determination of a regulated company, according to its business model, more or less complex, however, is based on a case-by-case assessment for which the FCA has provided more detailed guidance.

One of the most important FATF actions is the Travel Rule (TR). Through Recommendation 15, FATF imposes the so-called Travel Rule, meaning entities subject to the TR must share certain information such as names, addresses, and account numbers of both originators and beneficiaries for cryptocurrency transfers and such sharing is a must. While TR is now well known in the cryptosystem, there is an area where significant diversity is observed between jurisdictions and the need for a more consistent approach and oversight. For example, with regard to the transfer of funds, the 'TR' has been a requirement in the United States for both banking and non-bank financial institutions since 1996 for payments of US$3,000 or more with the receiving financial institution or MSB.

With regard to VAs transfers, a number of jurisdictions remain uncertain about how to enforce the 'TR', as the infrastructure available to support compliance for banks is attentive to cryptocurrency providers, making compliance technically feasible for them but far less efficient than banks. Consequently, the regulatory implementation of the relevant requirements is complex, and it may create grey areas for non-traceable transfers. International cooperation appears to be crucial to get 'TR' implementation. Moreover, private industry efforts are underway to develop a solution or protocol that enables TR compliance.

Building Cyber Resilience

Cyber resilience refers to the ability to protect electronic data and systems from cyber-attacks, as well as to quickly resume business operations in the event of a successful attack.

Cyber-attacks are a serious threat to all of us and given the high level of interconnectedness within the financial sector, they can also pose a threat to the stability of the overall financial ecosystem.

It is therefore essential that banks, other financial institutions, and financial market infrastructures, as well as central banks such as the ECB, have an adequate level of cyber resilience to ensure their own protection and that of the entire ecosystem.

While awareness of cybersecurity has grown, cyber resilience metrics are not yet mature. A useful tool for jurisdictions and regulators to assess cybersecurity performance and the resilience of regulated institutions is comparable indicators to those available for financial risk and resilience. Most banking supervisors and regulators very often carry out cyber resilience and security assessment on reported incidents, surveys, penetration tests, and on-site inspections. There is a need to emerge forward-looking resilience indicators. Another problem in analysis methodologies is the widespread use of retrospective indicators to predict the future. In fact, jurisdictions (and often regulated institutions themselves) focus on retrospective performance indicators of the technology function (BCBS 2018).

Retrospective indicators comment on past performance as an indicator of future performance, which is reasonable when institutions' operations and the risk environment are relatively stable over time and more or less independent of external influences. However, cyber-risk nullifies this because the adversaries are dynamic, they adapt themselves to the responses and protective measures of the institutions, and sometimes they change their tactics and strategies even in the space of a single cyber-incident. While retrospective metrics continue to be important, jurisdictions increasingly recognise the need for forward-looking indicators as direct and indirect resilience metrics, which indicate whether a regulated entity is likely to be more or less resilient should risk crystallise.

Regulated institutions are also looking to improve resilience metrics more broadly (Crisanto and Prenio 2020).

Several jurisdictions (e.g., Australia, Canada, ECB-SSM, Hong Kong, Singapore, UK, and US) analyse survey responses to assess the capabilities of regulated institutions and report on prioritising follow-up work. For example, Australian poll results are subsequently published to influence industry behaviour. In the UK, thematic results are often shared with participating companies for the same purpose.

Future Scenarios on VASPs

The future of cryptocurrencies will depend on a variety of factors that we summarise here.

More Transparency and Legal Clarity through Regulation and Bans

By 2022, many countries are expected to release a statement on how they will manage crypto assets. In essence, countries will have to decide whether to tighten restrictions and introduce bans, like China, or to adopt a crypto-friendly approach, as seen in El Salvador, which adopted Bitcoin as its official currency along with the US dollar in September 2021 and Central African Republic (CAR) from April 2022. Furthermore, the entry into force of the Markets-in-Crypto Assets (MICA) regulation will provide a unified legal framework at the European Union level and create greater legal clarity for service providers and issuers of cryptocurrencies. Therefore, it can be assumed that Europe and North America are following the fundamentally 'crypto-friendly' route: CPSs protocol accepted, as long as anti-ML legislation is respected (Adrian and Weeks-Brown 2021).

AML Policy

Regulators will focus on issues such as AML, KYC (Know your Customer), taxes, and stablecoins, which will lead to the explosion of the feasibility of decentralised finance (DeFi) regulation in exchanges with regulators of other jurisdictions.

The Digital Euro Is Currently an Unprecedented Announcement on a Large Scale

The digital euro can theoretically exist as a CBDC, as a trigger solution or as a stablecoin. However, the European Central Bank (ECB) is expected to issue a CBDC no earlier than 2026. CBDCs already exist in smaller countries like the Bahamas or Nigeria. As a trigger solution, the digital euro will already exist in 2022 for the first European commercial banks and will be made available to industry and the financial sector.

Environment and Cryptocurrency

Issuers of exchange-traded products (ETPs), cryptocurrency exchanges, mining companies, and financial institutions are interested in offering green products and services to their customers. To date, many potential cryptocurrency investors have been reluctant to invest in Bitcoin due to the relatively high carbon footprint of Bitcoin mining. Overall, the energy mix used for blockchain network operations is becoming greener and greener. Mining companies are increasingly exploiting renewable energy sources, such as geothermal or solar energy, due to the cost structures offered by those energy sources.

The debate over which enabled blockchain ecosystem will prevail has slowly ended in 2021. The prevailing view is that we will live in a multi-chain world where multiple blockchains can transfer information and value to each other; but what type of blockchain?

Closed Blockchain infrastructures, which only a few years ago should have found application in an enterprise context (corporate blockchains or authorised blockchains) and to which considerable importance had been attached, are playing a minor role. In fact, public blockchains have won the race.

Adoption by Institutional Investors and Large Companies

Recently, there has been an interest from institutional investors and large companies throughout 2021. These include hedge funds, asset managers, and family offices, but also pension funds or institutions.

Decentralised autonomous Organisations (DAOs) as an Opportunity for Social and Economic Coordination

DAOs are blockchain-based decentralised organisations that are collectively owned and managed by their members, according to pre-defined rules, via voting using tokens. These create exciting use cases, such as crowdfunding, social clubs, human resources, or collective investment projects. In 2022, countless new DAOs will emerge. In theory, the DAO authoring tools allow anyone to create a DAO for any purpose. DAOs will increase although it remains to be seen how they will be affected by existing regulations and in which jurisdictions they must respond in case of doubt.

References

Adrian, T., Weeks-Brown, R. 2021. 'Crypto assets as national currency? A step too far'. *IMFBlog, International Monetary Fund*. Available online: www.meetings.imf.org/en/IMF/Home/Blogs/Articles/2021/07/26/blog-cryptoassets-as-national-currency-a-step-too-far.

Aldasoro, I., Frost, J., Gambacorta, L., Whyte, D. 2021. 'Covid-19 and cyber risk in the financial sector'. *Bank for International Settlements – BIS Bulletin*, Vol. 37. Available online: www.bis.org/publ/bisbull37.pdf.

Åslund, A. 2019. 'Western economic sanctions on Russia over Ukraine 2014–2019'. *Cesifo*, Vol. 20, p. 14.

BCBS 2018. 'Cyber resilience: Range of practices'. *Bank for International Settlements*. Available online: www.bis.org/bcbs/publ/d454.pdf.

Chainalysis 2021, 'The 2021 Geography of Cryptocurrency Report', October 2021.

Coelho, R., Fishman, J., Garcia Ocampo, D. 2021. 'Supervising crypto assets for anti-money laundering'. *FSI Insights on Policy Implementation*

N.31, Bank for International Settlements – BIS. Available online: www
.bis.org/fsi/publ/insights31.pdf.

Crisanto, J.C., Prenio, J. 2020. 'Financial crime in times of Covid-19 – AML
and cyber resilience measures'. *Bank for International Settlements – BIS,
FSI Bries* n.7. Available online: www.bis.org/fsi/fsibriefs7.pdf.

ENISA 2021. 'ENISA threat landscape 2021'. *European Union Agency
for Cybersecurity.* Available online: www.enisa.europa.eu/publications/
enisa-threat-landscape-2021.

FATF 2019. 'FATF annual report 2018–2019'. *Financial Action Task
Force.* Available online: www.fatf-gafi.org/media/fatf/documents/reports/
FATF-annual-report-2018-2019.pdf.

FATF 2020a. 'COVID-19-related money laundering and terrorist financing –
Risks and policy responses'. *Financial Action Task Force*, Paris, France.
Available online: www.fatf-gafi.org/publications/methodandtrends/
documents/covid-19-ML-TF.html.

FATF 2020b. 'FATF annual report 2019–2020'. *Financial Action Task
Force.* Available online: www.fatf-gafi.org/media/fatf/documents/
brochuresannualreports/FATF-annual-report-2019-2020.pdf.

FATF 2020c. '12-month review virtual assets and VASPs'. *Financial
Action Task Force*, Paris, France. Available online: www.fatf-gafi.org/
publications/fatfrecommendations/documents/12-month-review-virtual-
assets-vasps.html.

FATF 2021a. 'FATF annual report 2020–2021'. *Financial Action Task
Force.* Available online: www.fatf-gafi.org/media/fatf/documents/
brochuresannualreports/Annual-Report-2020-2021.pdf.

FATF 2021b. 'Virtual assets and virtual asset service providers. Updated
guidance for a risk-based approach'. *Financial Action Task Force*, Paris.
Available online: www.fatf-gafi.org/publications/fatfrecommendations/
documents/Updated-Guidance-RBA-VA-VASP.html.

Flitter, E. and Yaffe-Bellany, D. 2022. 'Russia could use cryptocurrency to
blunt the force of U.S. sanctions'. *New York Times*, available online: www
.nytimes.com/2022/02/23/business/russia-sanctions-cryptocurrency.html.

Hunter Christie, E. 2015. 'Sanctions after Crimea: Have they worked?'. *NATO
Review.* Available online: www.nato.int/docu/review/articles/2015/07/13/
sanctions-after-crimea-have-they-worked/index.html.

Lallie, H. S., Shepherd, L. A., Nurse, J. R. C., Erola, A., Epiphaniou, G.,
Maple, C., Bellekens, X. 2021. 'Cyber security in the age of COVID-
19: A timeline and analysis of cyber-crime and cyber-attacks during the
pandemic'. *Computers and Security*, 105, 102248.

Paşca, V. R., Simion, E. 2018. 'Challenges in cyber security: Ransomware
phenomenon'. *Cyber-physical systems security*, Cham: Springer, 303–330.

PART III

The Power of Distributed Ledgers in Payments

6 | DLT in Payments
New Course of History Ahead?

ALESSANDRO AGNOLETTI AND
GIANCARLO SFOLCINI

Introduction

Since at least three million years, as demonstrated by the discovery of the first tools[1] humanity invents and applies techniques to make new products, solve problems, and improve its living conditions. In short, it pursues the technological progress that is at the basis of changes in society, with impacts on values, culture, behaviours, and relationships.

---

[1] Conflict of Interest: All of the data which this document is public and the information therein is the result of analyses conducted by Nexi S.p.A. ('Nexi') and may derive from a variety of sources.

Such sources are considered to be reliable and in good faith; nevertheless, no representation or warranty, either expressed or implied, is made by Nexi as to their accuracy, completeness or correctness. The evaluations, opinions, forecasts, or estimates contained in this document exclusively refer to the date of the document with the evaluations, opinions, forecasts or estimates included herein. All the information contained in this document may, subsequent to the date of its drawing up, be subject to amendment or update by Nexi, without any obligation on its part to communicate such amendments or updates to those parties to whom this document was previously distributed. This publication is provided for information and clarification purposes only and is purely indicative and under no circumstances does Nexi, by means of this paper, intends to solicit, promote, advise, or carry out any other activity aimed at the public about the use of digital currencies, therefore, Nexi shall not be responsible for any use whatsoever of digital currencies that may occur as a result of the publication of this document. Furthermore, in the absence at present of a clearly defined legal/regulatory framework on the subject, Nexi does not guarantee the legal/regulatory aspects of the evaluations contained herein. That being said, the contents of the document exclusively reflect the opinions of the authors and they do not imply any responsibility on the part of Nexi. Neither Nexi nor its directors and employees can be held responsible for any damages, either direct or indirect or of other nature, also deriving from inaccuracies and/or errors, that may be caused to third parties when using this document.

'3.3-million-year-old stone tools from Lomekwi 3, West Turkana, Kenya' – Nature, 20 May 2015.

The *exchange of value* is one of the countless examples where the influence of technology can be appreciated. From the introduction of precious metal coins around 700 B.C. to representative value coins in the seventeenth century, digital payment solutions and infrastructures exploded in the twenty-first century, thanks to the Internet and other technologies accessible to the general public.

DLT represents the latest innovation that promises significant transformations in daily life. The exchange of value, and in particular payments, is probably the area that will be most involved. After an initial phase of immaturity, low usage, and limited application of concrete use cases, in recent years, the adoption curve of the DLT has steepened. This phenomenon has been driven by some well-known cases, including that of Bitcoin. Born in 2008 with the promise of becoming a secure and efficient digital payment system without the need for financial intermediaries, the market and real-life experience have made it a speculative investment asset, poorly suited to its original function. Throughout the chapter, key concepts related to the fate of DLT applied to payments, focusing on *crypto-assets*, will be explored, and then let History take its own course. The concepts of trust and inclusion, the role of institutions and intermediaries in governing complexity and supporting transformation, cases of adoption and sustainable and secure development of crypto-assets in payment for the benefit of people and machines will be discussed in depth.

Crypto-assets: Digital Representation of Value Enabled by DLT

For the first time in the history of information technology, through DLT, it is possible to create a digital representation of a value that is: uniquely associated with a subject (anonymous, pseudonymous, or fully identified according to the specific implementation), non-duplicable, transferable between two parties, with a high level of security. This is made possible by multiple factors, including the duplication of data across nodes in the underlying network, the implementation on the network of a distributed and shared ledger, and the presence of multiple consensus mechanisms. These factors ensure, among others, the correct updating of the ledger according to the specific rules of a certain business application (e.g., avoiding double spending), the impossibility for a single network participant to modify the ledger itself (inalterability), and the possibility for each node to independently verify the content of the ledger (transparency). Digital representations of value with these characteristics are referred to as crypto-assets,[2] since they are based on cryptographic techniques (asymmetric cryptography model, based on a pair of public and private keys).

Trust in Payments, from Cash to DLT

To understand how *crypto-assets* affect payments, it is important to remember what a payment is.

Payment is defined as the action that relieves one party (the payer) of a debt to another party (the payee). The debt arises from the fulfilment by the payee of a certain obligation (sell a good, provide a service) towards the payer. In the case of a payment settled in money, a transfer of value occurs between the payer and the payee by transferring cash or transferring a credit held at a financial institution (i.e., scriptural money or bank money).[3] In case of cash, the value is held by the payer and the mere possession of cash in sufficient quantity is the only condition the payer must meet to make the payment. In case of transfer of credit, the value is held by the financial institution in the form of a debt to the payer, and the payer is asked to prove ownership of that value (a credit from its perspective), thus ultimately its identity. The use of crypto-assets as a means of payment blends the flexibility of digital payments with the direct interaction between payer and payee that is typical of cash payments. The possession of both the private key referred to by the crypto-assets and the address of the beneficiary (derived from his public key) is all that the payer needs to carry out the transaction. Moreover, the possibility of configuring the so-called self-hosted digital wallets to manage private keys allows independence from third parties. Interestingly, the necessary assumption of trust in a payment is realised: from trust in the instrument (cash), to trust in the intermediaries (bank money), to trust in the network (DLT) as shown in Figure 6.1.

---

[2] Term used in the European regulation.
[3] All bank payments based on cards, checks, etc. always end up in debiting an account and crediting another.

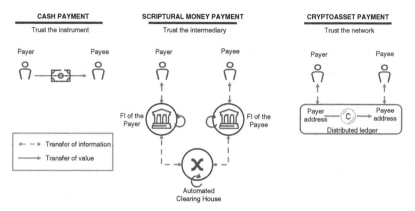

Figure 6.1 Source of trust in different payment methods
Source: elaboration by Nexi.

Categories of Crypto-assets Relevant to Payments

The evolution of technology and business models allowed different categories of crypto-assets to emerge. Crypto-assets whose use is more related to payments can be classified as shown in Table 6.1.

Crypto-assets are considered a true novelty among the payment instruments available since the invention of scriptural currency. Stablecoins, in particular, are receiving attention as potential effective means of payment, given their promise to overcome the problem of volatility.

It is important to note that crypto-assets are not considered 'funds' as defined in PSD2 and therefore do not fall under that directive, with the possible exception of e-money tokens (Paragraph 4).

As illustrated in the chart in Figure 6.2, DLT can shorten the time required and reduce the technical complexity for users to make payments using assets other than funds.

Market participants are experimenting with possible use cases to legitimise this innovation and justify the investment needed to develop and scale.

High-Potential Areas

Market evidence supports the belief that DLT-based payment systems will complement traditional ones. It comes in particular from legitimisation of DLT by the general public, to technology investments by tech companies, and to experiments carried out by public and private entities.

Table 6.1 *Categories of crypto- assets most relevant in payments*

The value of the crypto-asset depends only on demand/offer dynamic	Cryptocurrencies	First-generation crypto-assets (Bitcoin, Ether, etc.).
	Algorithmic stablecoins	Crypto-assets whose value is kept stable by adjusting demand/offer dynamic acting on the available amount of crypto-assets
The value of the crypto-asset is linked to the value of other physical or digital assets	Asset-backed stablecoins	Crypto-assets whose value is kept stable by referring to a portfolio of real assets (fiat currencies, bond, shares, and commodities) or other crypto-assets
	e-Money tokens	Crypto-assets issued and managed according to the same rules of electronic money with 1:1 ratio to the fiat currency they refer to

Note: Nexi elaboration. For this category is adopted the definition given by the ECB: '*a new type of asset recorded in digital form and enabled by the use of cryptography that is not and does not represent a financial claim on, or a liability of, any identifiable entity*'. European Central Bank, Crypto-assets – trends and implication, June 2019.

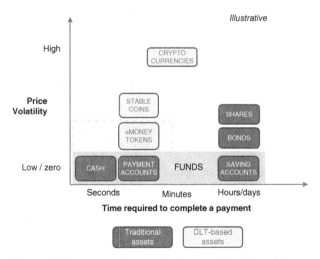

Figure 6.2 Execution time and price volatility of different payment instruments
Source: elaboration by Nexi.

This innovation is gaining legitimacy in some high-potential areas in particular:

- **Cross-border payments.** Using crypto-assets for payments across different jurisdictions and different currencies can reduce both costs and settlement times,[4] compared to current payment solutions.
- **Delivery versus payment.** It offers the opportunity of having on the same ledger the tokenised representation of a real asset and a payment instrument, allowing real-time delivery versus payment as an atomic[5] transaction without the need for a trusted counterparty. The case is easily associated with the capital market (Toast 2022), but is growing in importance in the so-called *metaverse* where crypto-assets (especially Stablecoins) are the ideal payment means for digital contents.[6]
- **Inter-company cash management.** Companies are exploring the use of DLT to optimise cash management across multiple branches.[7]
- **Machine-to-machine payments.** Unattended devices are entitled to manage digital wallets, and autonomously make event-based payments (e.g., parking time, refuelling, maintenance, or upgrades).
- **Micro-payments.** Crypto-assets can stimulate and simplify, among other business cases, low-value (<€1) pay-per-use digital content, such as online media content (e.g., music, news, and magazine) and related royalties and copyrights.
- **Programmable payments.** It corresponds to the broad concept of triggering a payment upon the occurrence of a specific event. The existence on the same network of the payment instrument (crypto-asset) and the rules that determine the payment condition (usually in the form of a smart contract) add a significant level of flexibility and innovation.

---

[4] Examples of private initiative Ripple (www.ripple.com) and pilots managed by institutions like Project Jasper-Urbin developed by Bank of Canada, Bank of England, and Monetary Authority of Singapore.
[5] In this context, the term 'atomic' is intended as a set of operations on the ledger such that either all occurs, or nothing occurs.
[6] Meta plans for a new payment token specifically designed for the metaverse was published by Financial Times in April '22.
[7] See as an example: *J.P. Morgan Creates Digital Coin for Payments* – J.P. Morgan company website, 1 February 2021, www.jpmorgan.com/solutions/cib/news/jpmorgan-creates-digital-coin-for-payments.

Aiming at Full Legitimacy

In order to achieve full legitimacy and be made available to the market in a simple, secure, and inclusive way, DLT still needs to resolve several issues. Focusing on payment applications, it is worth considering:

- **Accessibility.** For a new technology to be widely adopted, it must be easy to use for as wide a range of potential users as possible, with no barriers to entry (cost, digital skills, etc.);
- **Data management.** DLT has transparency as one of its core values, which must be balanced with privacy protection requirements.
- **Environmental sustainability.** There is a growing concern about the energy consumption of public blockchain platforms based on proof-of-work (PoW).[8] Alternative solutions are available but have not yet replaced PoW.
- **Governance.** A payment system based on crypto-assets requires a proper governance model to ensure compliance with relevant regulations, support participants, and properly manage risks and liabilities.
- **Integration.** Crucial to merchants' adoption of a new digital payment method is a low impact on their day-to-day operations, reducing the complexity and cost of integration with their existing payment and accounting systems as much as possible. Integrating legacy information systems with the DLT infrastructure poses some specific challenges.
- **Interoperability.** DLT solutions are usually 'silos' and interoperability between different DLTs is an issue that several initiatives are trying to address.[9]
- **Performance.** DLT protocols need to increase throughput (i.e., number of transactions per second) to meet the requirements of a payment system. So-called layer 2 protocols, such as the bitcoin lightning network, are addressing this issue.

---

[8] Proof-of-Work is a decentralised consensus mechanism based on mathematical problems whose solution requires high computing power and consequently a high energy consumption.
[9] Within ISO is active the working group ISO/TC 307/SG 7 – Interoperability of blockchain and distributed ledger technology systems. Among other initiatives we can cite Polkadot (polkadot.network) supported by Swiss Web3 Foundation and Cosmos (cosmos.network) supported by the Interchain Foundation.

- **Regulation.** Crypto-assets have been developed in a *grey area* of regulation or even outside of regulation itself. In order to develop a legitimate market, it is necessary to establish a solid legal framework that establishes the right safeguards for all stakeholders.
- **Security.** DLT protocols have features that promote security, but a complex DLT-based payment system has security risks that must be properly managed. A clear example is the management of private keys[10] and the possible roles of third parties tasked with key management by users (custodian).
- **Sustainable business model(s).** Existing payment systems, especially card-based systems, are based on robust business models that ensure reasonable profits for the parties involved. Entities active in crypto-assets payments adopt traditional business models, while new business models have yet to prove their profitability.

To overcome these limitations, a combined effort by regulators, financial intermediaries, and technical vendors is needed to move from pioneering to maturity.

Regulators' Commitment to Governing Complexity

The role of regulators at both the national and transnational levels is of paramount importance, to ensure the stability of the financial system and the protection of individuals, businesses, and institutions themselves.

Facebook's (now Meta) attempt to develop a stablecoin with a global footprint (project Libra, then Diem) was a wake-up call to policymakers and regulators around the world, who were faced with a new challenge with unexpected impacts (Dwoskin and De Vynck 2022).

This has led to varied reactions. Some jurisdictions, including China, have formally banned the use of cryptocurrencies, while many others, particularly in the Western world,[11] have been much

---

[10] In absence of a custodian, a lost private key cannot be recovered in any way, resulting in the loss of the related crypto-assets.

[11] In April '22, the UK Government announced plans to make Britain a global hub for crypto-asset technology and investment starting from regulation action

more supportive, showing proactivity in defining rules to govern the phenomenon with a risk-based approach. The European Market in Crypto Asset Regulation (i.e., MiCAR)[12] and the 'Guidance on virtual assets and virtual assets service providers' updated by the Financial Action Task Force[13] (FATF) are two examples. European institutions are also active in raising consumers' awareness of the risks related to crypto-assets. The bankruptcy of operators such as Genesis, FTX, Three Arrows Capital, and Voyager Digital demonstrated how this market is subject to turmoil with major impacts on investors.

In jurisdictions allowing use of crypto-assets, there is a general trend to identify and empower entities that govern cryptocurrencies or act as gateways between cryptocurrencies and the traditional financial world, that is, Crypto Asset Service Providers (CASPs) in the European regulatory definition.[14]

Regulators tend to refer as much as possible to existing regulatory frameworks and models, for example, the Principle for Financial Market Infrastructure (i.e., PFMI) to reduce complexity and create a level playing field according to the 'same service, same risk, same rule' principle (BIS-IOSCO 2012).

The phenomenon of market transformation underway is highlighting the opportunity for the regulator to coordinate and continue to enhance the contribution and role of all parties involved.

Everyone, from those who provide technology, products, infrastructure, and control solutions, must be able to recognise themselves and have clear and shared rules. The common goal is to develop a payment offering that guarantees high standards of innovation, inclusion, adoption, and security, to the benefit of people, businesses, and institutions themselves.

---

to make stablecoins an acceptable form of payment. At the same time the US Senate started discussing a new regulatory framework for stablecoin issuers in the United States.

[12] Regulation (EU) 2023/114 of the European Parliament and of the Council, 31 May 2023.

[13] FATF (www.fatf-gafi.org) is an inter-governmental body that sets international standards that aim to prevent money laundering and terrorist financing.

[14] It uses the definition adopted in MiCAR. Other definitions, such as Virtual Assets Service Providers, can be found in other sources with the same meaning.

Intermediaries Supporting the Transformation

The Future That Comes from the Past

One of the unexpected consequences of Bitcoin, conceived primarily to support the disintermediation of the payment chain, has been the emergence of new types of intermediaries (e.g., exchanges, brokers, and wallet providers) that respond to the need to offer new digital solutions to support the fruition and use of the crypto-assets themselves.

The phenomenon has expanded and strengthened with the advent of new types of crypto-assets, from *store of value* assets, to *Memes* to *Non-fungible Tokens (NFT)*, among others.

Considering the use of crypto-assets in payments, this confirmation of intermediaries as supporting transformation is appreciable from the perspective of both merchants and consumers.

Merchants' Growing Interest

Merchants show a growing interest in crypto-assets acceptance as a way to increase transaction volumes from both new customer segments (e.g., people with new purchasing power, usually young and/ or unbanked) and current customer segments increasing their spending, thanks to, for example, new availability of funds and targeted marketing campaigns.

Furthermore, some merchants see in cryptos a way to overcome some limitations of traditional payment systems for large value payments[15] combined with a potential reduction in costs and execution times, especially for cross-border transactions, as well as a reduction in fraud and/or chargeback[16] associated with card payments.

Merchants willing to accept payments in crypto-assets can adopt two different approaches, as shown in Table 6.2

Most merchants tend to take a 'hands-off' approach as long as crypto-assets payments continue to be a fraction of traditional payments relying on CASPs as shown in Figure 6.3.

---

[15] A monthly payment platform is usually set for cards, while payment services based on credit transfer sometimes have a sub-optimal user experience.

[16] Chargeback is a powerful instrument to protect consumers. Nevertheless, it is commonly acknowledged that it is sometimes abused up to the point of trespassing the fraud threshold.

Table 6.2 *Possible merchants' approach in managing crypto- payments*

Approach	Pros	Cons
Hands-on Merchant sets up a crypto wallet and directly handles the acceptance of crypto and the subsequent management	• Additional profit opportunity • Flexibility	• Crypto price volatility • Accounting and tax implication • Technical complexity • Need for specific expertise far from core business
Hands-off Merchant establishes a partnership with a specialised company to manage cryptocurrencies on his behalf	• Removing of volatility risk (bore by the partner) • Reduced technical and operational complexity	• Definition of an effective contractual agreement with the intermediary • No opportunity for additional profits

Note: Nexi elaboration.

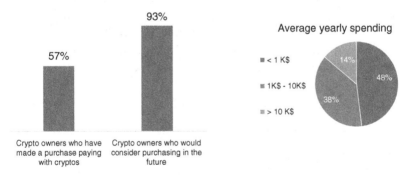

Figure 6.3 Crypto-payment in hands-off approach
Source: elaboration by Nexi.

Consumers' Attitude towards Use

From a consumer perspective, recent market analysis shows that crypto-assets holders consider and value the possibility of using them as a payment instrument as shown in Figure 6.4.

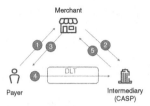

1. At checkout the payer selects the option to pay with cryptocurrencies
2. The Merchant routes the request to the CASP to get the equivalent price in Crypto. To remove volatility issues the CASP guarantees an exchange rete fiat/crypto for the time needed to complete the transaction managing the underlying risk
3. Price in crypto is presented to the payer
4. The payer transfers cryptos to the CASP
5. The CASP settle to the Merchant in fiat money

Figure 6.4 Customer attitude towards crypto-payments
Source: elaboration by Nexi on data from Cryptocurrency Payments Report, Paymts.com & BitPay. May 2021.

The reasons for this attitude are mainly to be found in the following:[17]

- Possibility to monetise earnings;
- low-cost, easy-to-use alternative for cross-border payments and remittances;
- perceived anonymity of crypto-assets; and
- unique digital payment tool available in certain jurisdictions for some specific consumer groups (e.g., tech-savvy youth in developing countries with weak banking systems).

With the growing adoption of crypto-assets, newcomers are always looking for reliable intermediaries (again, the CASPs) to assist them in accessing this new market, taking on the technological and operational complexities (like custody of private keys) that *first movers* manage on their own.

Crypto-Assets Service Providers, Who They Are and What They Do

Entities that perform the role of CASPs in a crypto-asset payment workflow can be reduced to three categories. The first category includes crypto exchanges and brokers that provide the acceptance services as a complement to their core business. Some of these entities use acceptance service as a channel for increasing crypto-asset availability to support their trading activities, in some cases offering acceptance service without commissions.

---

[17] Some of these features could be revised in the near future, such as anonymity.

The second category is made by pure crypto-assets specialists focused on acceptance service and implementing the typical business model of an acquirer with a commission-based pricing model.

The third category includes traditional PSPs, usually in partnership with CASPs, who see crypto-assets acceptance as an extension of their business, leveraging their customer base and integration with legacy payment services. CASPs perform many of the typical tasks of financial intermediaries in traditional payment systems, at the request of regulators and the market.

Managing Risks on Behalf of the Parties

The chart in Figure 6.5 shows how the costs of a transaction are split between the parties involved in a payment with crypto-assets.

Within the payment flow, the CASP assumes the risk of fixing a defined and guaranteed Crypto-Fiat exchange rate to both the customer and the merchant for the time it takes to complete the transaction; performing mitigation actions to prevent fraud, and providing protection to both the payer and the payee, in the event of a malfunction in the payment process.

Supporting Interoperability with Legacy Platforms

Intermediaries provide seamless interaction between crypto-assets and traditional financial infrastructures. For example, a growing number of banks offer their clients the ability to buy and sell crypto (so called 'ramp on/ramp off') integrated into their home-banking services.

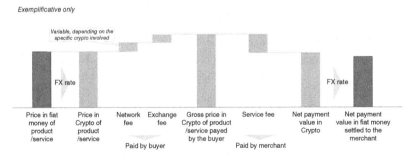

Figure 6.5 Split of transaction cost among the parties involved in crypto-payments
Source: elaboration by Nexi.

Providing Know Your Customer (KYC) and Customer Due Diligence (CDD)

As occurs with traditional payment systems, the regulatory trend is towards limiting anonymous payments. The already mentioned FATF guidance states:

Providers in this space [virtual assets] must comply with the requirements of Recommendation 16 (i.e., the 'travel rule'). This includes the obligation to obtain, hold, and submit required originator and beneficiary information associated with VA [i.e., Virtual Assets] transfers in order to identify and report suspicious transactions, take freezing actions, and prohibit transactions with designated persons and entities. The requirements apply to both VASPs [i.e., Virtual Assets Service Providers] and other obliged entities such as FIs [i.e., Financial Intermediaries] when they send or receive VA transfers on behalf of a customer (FATF 2012–2022).

The recommendation will be implemented in the future amendment to the European Funds Transfer Regulation.[18]

In the case of a transfer of crypto-assets made from a self-hosted address, the crypto-asset service provider of the beneficiary shall obtain and hold information referred to in article 14 (1) [originator data] and (2) [beneficiary data] and ensure that the transfer of crypto-assets can be individually identified[19]

According to the current formulation, the CASP of the beneficiary will need to perform KYC on the payer. Since this could lead to some limitations on the use of non-hosted wallets in person-to-business payments, it is also expected that consumers will be driven to turn to qualified CASPs.

Being the Regulatory 'Operating Arm'

Crypto-assets payments are at risk of illicit use, therefore subject to anti-money laundering and anti-terrorism regulations. Analysis tools are available to CASPs both to trace the source of crypto-assets and

---

[18] 'Proposal for a regulation of the European Parliament and of the Council on information accompanying transfers of funds and certain crypto-assets (recast)'. On 5 October 2022, the Council of the European Union sent to the European Parliament the final version of the regulation proposal.

[19] Text of the final release of the proposal for regulation sent on 5 October 2022 by the Council of the European Union sent to the European Parliament.

to identify the destination address, in order to intercept and possibly deny suspicious transactions and to provide supervisory authorities with proper reporting.

Investing in (Cyber)Security

The cryptocurrency ecosystem is a prime target for hackers, who have succeeded in several attempts to steal significant amounts of crypto in the past (Zeitchik 2022). Trusted intermediaries can dedicate the appropriate resources to prevent attacks and provide protection to customers (e.g., reimbursement of losses).

Educating and Supporting Users

CASPs are challenged to invest time and resources in educating merchants, primarily to help them fully understand the opportunities and limitations of crypto-assets and support them in developing a proper marketing strategy to attract customers.

If You Cannot Beat Them, Join Them: Opportunity of e-Money Tokens

Limiting Factors to e-Money

Electronic Money is defined in Directive 2009/110/EC as: '*Electronically, including magnetically, stored monetary value as represented by a claim on the issuer which is issued on receipt of funds for the purpose of making payment transactions [...] and which is accepted by a natural or legal person other than the electronic money issuer.*'

The definition envisions the development of a payment system based on a digital representation of value, backed by bank money on a 1:1 basis, exchangeable between participants in the system.

The Directive enabled the development of a series of payment services, mainly based on pre-paid cards, by leveraging existing networks and rules for card payments, which have had a positive effect on the diffusion of digital payments as shown in Figures 6.6a and 6.6b.

However, the technical and practical limitations of traditional technology have made the effective 'circulation' of electronic money among users complex, preventing the effective development of a true alternative payment system.

eMoney Issuer

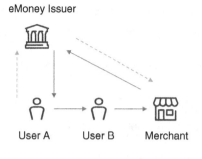

User A   User B   Merchant

⟶   e-money
----►   Other Funds

Figure 6.6a Theoretical e-money model
Source: elaboration by Nexi.

e-money Issuer

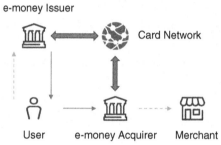

Card Network

User   e-money Acquirer   Merchant

Figure 6.6b Actual implementation of e-money model
Source: elaboration by Nexi.

Potential Evolution of Stablecoins

Stablecoins constitute a specific category of crypto-assets particularly suited for payments, overcoming the volatility of cryptocurrency prices while maintaining their flexibility.

To date, however, algorithmic stablecoins have yet to prove their effectiveness,[20] while theoretically more robust asset-based stablecoins raise concerns about the quality or even existence of collateral.

A further interesting evolution is the e-money token introduced by MiCAR:

---

[20] The case of TerraUSD crash in May 2022 was a clear example of the maturity problems of algorithmic stablecoins.

A type of crypto-asset the main purpose of which is to be used as a means of payment and that purports to maintain a stable value by maintaining a portfolio which ensures that the token maintains the value of a fiat currency that is legal tender; e-money tokens which maintain the value of a fiat currency of the Union [e.g. Euro] shall be deemed to be electronic money as defined in Article 2 (2) of Directive 2009/110/EC.

A payment based on e-money token allows DLT to be tied to traditional finance, as e-money tokens are denominated in the same unit of account as cash and bank money, fully integrated with the economic and financial system, redeemable at par by the issuer at the request of the holder (no volatility risk).

Based on these characteristics, it is possible to implement all the use cases described in the Paragraph 1.3, with the added value of having an operational and regulatory compliant 'cash leg' that provides instant settlement.

Support for Greater Inclusion

An e-money token payment system can become a powerful tool to promote inclusion by empowering each person to produce new value for its community, through a payment, and in the future through the ability to generate savings and obtain loans.

Inclusion can be further stimulated due to the increasing diffuse digitisation, which, can foster the offering of digital payment systems for basic services at competitive costs and facilitate access to more advanced financial services (savings, loans, etc.), thanks to the easy convertibility between e-money tokens and bank money.

It will also be important for each community to enable every person to benefit from digitalisation, including, among others, people with disabilities, living in rural areas, low-skilled or poorly educated.

Towards a European e-Money Scheme

The main limitation of e-money is that there is generally only one issuer, limiting the ability to scale an e-money payment system. This is why all existing solutions leverage the infrastructure and rules of card networks.

The flexibility of DLT could make it possible to create a payment system with a plurality of issuers operating on the basis of a multi-side contractual agreement implemented through smart contracts.

A payment system based on this paradigm could share the investments needed and leverage multiple customer bases both on consumers' and merchants' side, speeding up the achievement of network effect. I would also provide a reliable infrastructure upon which to develop innovative use cases and services (like programmability) as well as mimic in a regulated and secure environment the paradigms of decentralised finance.

Conceiving and implementing an appropriate governance model would be quite a challenge, even if similar experiences are under development.[21]

Nevertheless, exploiting e-money token applications could become an opportunity for the European financial ecosystem to make DLT-based payments reach full maturity, as well as a countermeasure to future initiatives from Big Techs.

Nexi Group's Involvement in the Crypto-Asset Space

Nexi Group is a European Paytech leader resulting from the merger of Nexi with Nets and Sia. The Group has an extensive presence in more than 25 European countries representing about 65 per cent of European consumption and promotes domestic and cross-border digital payment solutions and central system connectivity services.

Nexi drives progress by supporting its customers to pay and accept digital payments through a complete and personalised range of simple, intuitive, and secure solutions.

The Group is #1 merchant acquirer in Europe by number of merchants and transaction value, #1 card processor by number of cards and transaction volume and #1 by EBITDA and provides connectivity services for financial and central institutions as shown in Figure 6.7.

Nexi Group sees growing demand from its customer base for digital payment solutions, also supported by new payment methods, including crypto-asset acceptance, and new DLT-based market infrastructure.

---

[21] Worth noticing the cases of Finality International (fnality.org) whose purpose is to deliver the means of payment-on-chain for wholesale banking markets and USDF (usdfconsortium.com), a consortium of a group of US banks and fintechs to issue and use stablecoin for payment transfers and other digital assets over blockchain.

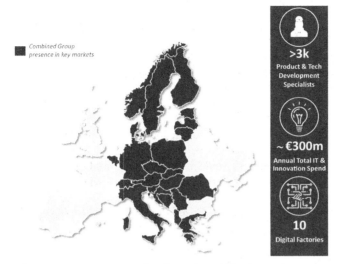

Figure 6.7 European market footprint of Nexi
Source: Nexi, October 2022.

The Group's commitment is to offer innovation to people, businesses, and institutions, at high standards of security, ease and in full compliance with the Digital Finance Package, the AML Package, and other related regulations.

Nexi is proud to be able to do this by leveraging its know-how and assets, such as talented people, technology solutions, network, and services, which are fundamental to fostering a more innovative and inclusive society.

Conclusions

DLT and the resulting crypto-assets are a constantly evolving phenomenon, and it is here to stay, offering interesting opportunities for innovation to the financial and payments industry, particularly through the development of new offerings, rules, and technologies.

The collaboration of all parties involved, from institutions to intermediaries, is essential to foster a massive adoption of this innovation and to address its related high levels of risk and uncertainty.

Nexi is at the forefront in supporting a secure and easy transition to a better society, aiming at 'distributed' inclusion and safeguarding both the interests of all private and public stakeholders and regulatory clarity.

References

Bank for International Settlement – IOSCO 2012. 'Principle for financial market infrastructure'. Available online: www.bis.org/cpmi/publ/d101a.pdf.

Dwoskin, E., De Vynck, G. 2022. 'Facebook's cryptocurrency failure came after internal conflict and regulatory pushback'. *The Washington Post.* Available online: www.washingtonpost.com/technology/2022/01/28/facebook-cryptocurrency-diem/.

FATF 2012–2022. International standards on combating money laundering and the financing of terrorism and proliferation. FATF, Paris, France. Available online: www.fatf-gafi.org/recommendations.html.

Toast, A. 2022. 'CBDC and DLT in debt capital markets: why the Banque de France's French government bonds experiment was a significant step forward'. *Clifford Chance.* Available online: www.cliffordchance.com/insights/resources/blogs/talking-tech/en/articles/2022/02/cbdc-and-dlt-in-debt-capital-markets--why-the-banque-de-france-s.html.

Zeitchik, S. 2022. 'Hackers hit popular video games, stealing more than $600 million in cryptocurrency'. *The Washington Post,* 29 March 2022. www.washingtonpost.com/technology/2022/03/29/axie-infinity-cryptocurrency-hack/

7 | Central Bank Digital Currency Rationales, Design Considerations, and Implementation Using the Algorand Blockchain Technology

ANDREA CIVELLI, CO-PIERRE GEORG,
PIETRO GRASSANO AND NAVEED IHSANULLAH

Introduction

In this chapter, we talk about three main topics. We first define the issues that a Central Bank Digital Currency (CBDC) could address and the reasons to enhance our understanding of CBDCs. Second, we discuss the optimal design principles of a CBDC as they arose from various conversations with central banks, national and supranational authorities, market participants, and academics in various jurisdictions. Finally, we propose a well-rounded and robust solution for a retail CBDC based on Algorand technology that meets these design principles. Most of the content of this chapter is borrowed from Civelli et al. (2022). In that paper, we extensively cover the CBDC design and issuance topics, informed by our recent participation in various pilots, studies, and round-table conversations on these topics.

Why a CBDC?

The digital economy brings with it great opportunities for the economic growth of both developed and emerging economies. However, this new economy also introduces new challenges that will soon impact the way central banks have traditionally operated because the digital economy does not have a well-developed financial infrastructure yet. Several countries, notably China, are vying for dominance in this new arena by providing competing, globally accessible financial infrastructure. To embrace the opportunities provided by the digital

155

economy and to maintain their monetary sovereignty, central banks should carefully consider the issuance of CBDCs.[1]

Today, central banks rely on the banking sector as the primary channel of monetary policy transmission and to enforce financial sector regulation. But in the future, new digital business models will contribute to the progressive shift of financial intermediation away from traditional commercial banking into new types of intermediaries, which follow different financial incentives, may respond in different ways to monetary policy, and upon which regulation may be difficult or impossible to enforce. Asset tokenisation and decentralised finance (DeFi) made possible by the development of next-generation scalable and secure blockchain technology, resulted in an exponentially increasing demand for digital forms of money, which can be used to settle digital assets and make payments on the blockchain. The multiplication of new types of private money with these capabilities reflects the limitations of standard central bank money in the digital economy. To embrace the opportunities provided by the digital economy and to maintain their monetary sovereignty in this new economic environment, central banks should continue to renew their financial infrastructure. CBDCs based on blockchain technology provide the correct solutions to build a new piece of financial infrastructure for the digital economy. In terms of efficiency improvements, we want to highlight here only some of the current system bottlenecks: those related to the cost of cash, the cost of cross-border transactions, and the cost of liquidity management and collateralisation in wholesale transactions via centralised systems. Aside from supporting the growth of the digital economy and ensuring monetary sovereignty, central banks also investigate retail CBDCs to reduce the long-term cost of cash. In 2012, the European Central Bank estimated that, in the EU, the total cost of retail payment instruments to society is about 1 per cent of GDP (139B Euro), almost half being cash

---

[1] We do not enter here into the debate about the institutional nature of Central Bank money, which is still far from being over among economists (for more detail, we point the reader to the contributions of Goodhart 1988 and Paniagua 2017). We simply take as a working hypothesis the idea that money is an institution, an 'imagined order', in the sense the Israeli anthropologist Yuval Harari mentions in his 2011 book 'Sapiens' (Harari 2011). A specific representation of 'money' becomes widely accepted if people believe it will present the features required.

alone (Schmiedel et al. 2012). This percentage is likely a lower bound from a global perspective, as the price of cash in emerging markets is much higher. A McKinsey's report highlights two reasons for this: the extension of cash distribution networks to underserved regions and the fact that cash distribution remains manual and is therefore labour-intensive.[2] In emerging markets, security concerns are amplified and substantially add to the cost of cash, both for central banks and commercial banks and for their customers. Despite incremental advancements to the existing central bank payment infrastructure, the cost of cash management shows no signs of change as cash continues to account for over 90 per cent of all transactions in emerging markets. However, the advancements in speed, security, and usability of blockchain technology have created the necessary platform for central banks to radically improve their cash management and distribution at scale.

Similarly, the costs of foreign exchange operations for participants are high, which is a problem, especially for emerging markets. These costs are mostly due to the lack of competition for cross-border payment services. Payment services are concentrated in a handful of very large brokers, as is the design of correspondent banking systems, where transaction validation and settlement must go through a long chain of intermediary domestic banks and the SWIFT cross-border confirmation system. For instance, a study by Hau et al. (2019) estimated forex fees as high as 0.5 per cent, with large asymmetries between larger and smaller traders. The SWIFT network is even more expensive. A report by the Financial Stability Board estimated that the typical fee for a $200 international remittance on the SWIFT network was seven per cent in 2019.[3]

Another type of cost of the current settlement system is related to banks' liquidity and collateral management in the security markets. An estimate by Hartung et al. (2019) finds that holdings of high-quality liquid assets for collateralisation can cost banks up to 50 basis points. This corresponds to approximately €13.5bn per year just

---

[2] See Brugge J., Denecker, O., Jawaid, H., Kovacs, A., Shami, I. 2018. *Attacking the Cost of Cash*. McKinsey Insights, Available online: www.mckinsey.com/industries/financial-services/our-insights/attacking-the-cost-of-cash.

[3] See Financial Stability Board. *Enhancing Cross-border Payments Stage 1 report to the G20: Technical background report*. Available online: www.fsb.org/wp-content/uploads/P090420-2.pdf.

for the holding of assets above the Basel III minimum requirements. Blockchains able to perform truly atomic transactions with immediate finality can significantly lower counterparty risk, reduce costs, and enable more collateral to be put to work versus being allocated against securing transactions. All of this reduces transaction costs and enables new business models.

A critical requirement for the viability of CBDCs is the inalterability of the core blockchain infrastructure, both now and in the future. Blockchains rely on modern cryptography to guarantee their security. New technologies on the horizon, such as quantum computers, may break the assumptions that many of today's blockchains are built on. This has the potential to expose end-users (citizens) to massive losses of value. Therefore, it is essential that a blockchain solution for CBDC be quantum resilient, a task that few blockchain organisations are well positioned to execute today and in the future.

The Algorand blockchain provides the foundation for the future of economic exchange with global-scale performance on par with centralised solutions while also delivering the safety, security, and resilience that can only come from a truly decentralised system. We'll go into more detail in the fourth section of this chapter.

Design Principles of a CBDC

It would be a significant understatement to consider CBDCs just a new method of payment. A CBDC model that embeds the correct economic and technological principles would provide a country with a new general-purpose digital infrastructure, of which payments is one component. The introduction of a blockchain-based CBDC represents an opportunity to overhaul the entire payment system and make it more efficient, accessible, and secure. However, while the building of a new payment infrastructure is not an unprecedented task.[4] Introducing a CBDC is more complicated than previous iterations of payment system innovations.

Real-time gross settlement systems (RTGS) connect a fixed set of counterparties, typically banks, and facilitate a small number of use

---

[4] The introduction of electronic fund transfers in the United States in 1918 and the move from telegraph to telex to computer networks between 1960 and 1990 have many hallmarks of the current overhaul of national payment infrastructure, for instance.

cases. In contrast, many CBDC proposals include a much broader set of entities involved in the distribution of CBDC to the general public. This extension is intended to improve the competitiveness of the financial system but simultaneously increases the CBDC's implementation complexity.

Algorand's approach to CBDC has, therefore, been inspired not by the development of products but by the creation of general-purpose infrastructure like roads, railroads, harbours, bridges, and the Internet itself. We believe that the history of the Internet provides a useful blueprint for the design of CBDC. For example, Clark (2018) outlines the 'hourglass model' of the Internet structure, with TCP/IP as the two common standards that implement the Internet as a packet transport system at the centre. On top of the common standards is the highly diverse Internet experience, including all the possible applications such as the Web, email, video, and games. Below the common application standards are supporting physical transport technologies like broadband, Wi-Fi, Ethernet, and cellular networks, which are also highly diverse. The private, permissioned Algorand blockchain achieves for CBDCs what TCP/IP has achieved for the Internet: provision of a common standard for a plethora of user-facing applications and facilitation of a wide range of different deployments depending on the central bank's requirements.

On top of the hourglass are all the different applications that can be built on Algorand's technology. In our complete CBDC White Paper, we provide details of the Algorand protocol features, facilitating the easy development of applications on top of the distributed ledger.

An extensive and rapidly growing ecosystem of applications building on the Algorand public blockchain is testimony to Algorand's ability to facilitate innovation. On the bottom of the hourglass, where in the Internet example there are different physical layers of network infrastructure, in the CBDC case there are other national real-time payment infrastructures. While most countries use RTGS systems, each country has specificities, both regulatory and technical, that are unique to them.

In that sense, a CBDC, like the Internet, is a piece of infrastructure, and it is useful to study proposals for CBDC designs in this light. Looking for high-level common denominators among all these infrastructures, we find at least three (see also Kasper 2015) as follows:

- The infrastructure needs to be efficient in the sense that it must solve a real problem in a way that is both cost-effective and fit for purpose.
- It needs to be universally accessible.
- It needs to be secure for the user.

These principles naturally apply to existing RTGS payment systems as examples of a more general economic exchange infrastructure. However, to ensure they also apply to CBDC, it is essential to correctly define the design principles a blockchain-based CBDC system should follow. We identify the following six key points:

1. How to ensure trust in the new payment instrument and the central bank;
2. How to achieve scalability for a seamless user experience;
3. How to maintain the privacy of low-value transactions while ensuring full auditability for high-value transactions;
4. How to achieve full inclusivity;
5. How to guarantee the interoperability of the system;
6. How to incentivise competition.

How to Ensure Trust in the New Payment System

The key challenge when issuing a CBDC is to create trust in the new payment instrument to ensure it maintains value at least as well as its physical counterpart. This is one of the main reasons why cash issuance is so expensive: trust in cash as a payment instrument requires the central bank to ensure that notes cannot be counterfeited and that the cash supply chain is secure.

Eliminating cybersecurity risks is essential for digital currencies. Counterfeiting CBDC issued on a distributed ledger is impossible thanks to the ledger's cryptographic primitives. By contrast, entries on centralised ledgers can be manipulated if the ledger's database is hacked or otherwise compromised. We believe that the additional cost of ensuring a centralised ledger's security offsets some of the efficiency gains of a central bank's digital currency issued on that platform.

Transacting in cash has immediate settlement finality. The digital analogue of cash must, therefore, also have immediate settlement finality. Otherwise, the instrument would carry counterparty risk, again undoing some of the benefits of introducing a CBDC. While most blockchains do not have immediate settlement finality – and some do not have settlement finality at all – Algorand's Pure Proof-of-Stake (Pure PoS) protocol implements this natively.

Another advantage of a CBDC over cash is that it is much easier to monitor the circulation of CBDC and detect fraud. The ledger's transparent nature makes it possible for central banks to use sophisticated data analytics to detect irregularities and fraud.

How to Achieve Scalability for a Seamless User Experience

Most blockchains to date, particularly those based on a proof-of-work (PoW) algorithm like Bitcoin, have been plagued by scalability issues and an insufficient number of transactions per second to meet even the light loads placed on them by early adopters. However, to reliably handle the transactions for a larger country with about 50 million CBDC users, each of whom transacts about two to three times per day, the CBDC would have to handle on average 1,500 transactions per second. This is 100 times more than the standard PoW blockchains processing capacity.

Algorand is designed to scale and easily achieves more than six thousand transactions per second in a decentralised system. Decentralisation is a function of the number of participants in the consensus protocol, hardware requirements, topography, and the number of people who own a stake in the consensus protocol itself. Algorand, unlike other platforms, has decided that to run critical infrastructure, enabling decentralisation at every level is key to avoiding single points of failure. For example, standardising on a single type of GPU/CPU/ASIC/LSIC for your network infrastructure significantly increases the likelihood that your network will be susceptible to a particular hardware attack. Having a lower threshold for hardware ensures diversity in machines upholding the network and, therefore, mitigates the impact of any individual targeted vulnerability from taking down the entire system.

Scalability is key to a seamless user experience, which, in turn, is key to the adoption and acceptance of the new payment instrument. If users must wait several seconds even for low-value transactions to clear, many essential use cases for cash will be inaccessible for a CBDC. However, most central banks' stated goalposts in evaluating the issuance of retail CBDC are to find a payment instrument that can complement cash in circulation.

The flipside of scalability is the network structure. It is not difficult to have two computers next to each other and thereby achieve a relatively high number of transactions per second. However, such a setup would not be secure, whereas decentralisation can eliminate systematic and cybersecurity risks. Algorand has proven to be highly scalable even on a globally decentralised level with its MainNet and valuable experience designing systems that are both fully decentralised and highly scalable.

How to Maintain Privacy for Low-Value Transactions While Ensuring Full Auditability for High-Value Transactions

Privacy is a human right and a necessary condition for broad adoption of CBDCs. As such, it is paramount, particularly in the context of retail CBDCs, to balance this right carefully with the regulatory need to ensure transactions are KYC/AML compliant.

This requires a layered approach to privacy with adjustable limits for fully private, partially private, and fully transparent transactions. Importantly, central banks must have full control over the thresholds between the different layers of privacy and be able to change them as necessary. Algorand does not impose a one-size-fits-all solution to this privacy/transparency continuum. Instead, Algorand provides a flexible framework that allows governments and central banks to specify their own tiers of privacy and delegate, as needed, identity to authorised Identity Providers in their system, using a combination of built-in features and high-performance/powerful Layer-1 smart contracts.

This layered approach to privacy is both practical and in stark contrast to the approach private crypto-assets like Bitcoin and Ethereum have chosen, where there is no native notion of privacy. These blockchains rely on pseudonymous addresses to protect user privacy. This approach to privacy is in direct conflict with existing KYC/AML requirements. We believe that, rather than fixing this protocol flaw, it is better to design for privacy from the beginning. Our permissioned Algorand blockchain for CBDC allows us to thread the privacy-compliance needle carefully.

How to Achieve Full Inclusivity

For a payment instrument to be universally accepted and trusted, it needs to be available to everyone in a country. A CBDC would rely on portable devices such as smartphones for accessibility, but this is a significant challenge for central banks because smartphone penetration is far from perfect. Even in the United States, it stands at about 80 per cent, and the situation is even more difficult in emerging markets like India, where smartphone penetration sits at around 37 per cent (Newzoo 2019). Consequently, any retail CBDC design must make provisions for users without smartphones. Achieving full inclusivity is crucial for retail CBDCs and wholesale CBDCs, depending on the use case (e.g., to ensure that all participants in a transaction comply with KYC/AML regulations).

Achieving full inclusivity faces two related challenges: identity and access. Especially – but not only – in emerging markets, users do not always have identity documents. In their 2016 paper, 'A Blueprint for Digital Identity', the World Economic Forum highlights the importance of building digital identity infrastructure for the future of financial infrastructure. Central banks issuing CBDC will have to seek broad stakeholder engagement to solve the digital identity challenge, amplified by the lack of access, the second challenge to full inclusivity.

With limited smartphone penetration and the resulting lack of digital identity, a substantial fraction of the population will not only struggle to transact using CBDC, but even to gain access to it. This is especially important for unbanked people in emerging markets. For no other group is this challenge as prevalent as for refugees. Algorand embraces *radical inclusivity*, for example, by also providing access to basic financial services for refugees and facilitating the inclusion of users without smartphones.

To enable access, solving identity is fundamental to scaling economic inclusivity. One of Algorand's core design principles is to create generalised and flexible tools that can be applied to many different problems. Algorand has worked with identity companies to create on-chain identity attestations. These attestations can be used in line with many emerging identity standards, such as W3C Decentralised Identifiers, so that identity can be portable across many different platforms. In working with companies such as FlexFinTx and Republic, all the individual's personal and confidential information resides off-chain. Still, the account's ability to own a particular asset is published on-chain. With the attestation issued on-chain, asset issuers can enforce logic that requires these attestations to be presented at a particular moment in time, for example, at time of purchase, or to be required as part of a routine compliance check, for example, the address is still owned by an accredited investor. A practical example: If address ABC does not have an identity attestation token in their custody issued by an identity provider, then freeze the assets in their control and block any transactions of this asset or asset class until the attestation has been restored.

In our White Paper on CBDC, we outline solutions that we have designed to allow users with intermittent connectivity and without smartphones to be included on an entirely equal footing with users with good connectivity and smartphones, highlighting Algorand's focus on radical inclusivity for CBDCs.

How to Guarantee Interoperability of the System

The hardest part of designing new financial infrastructure is developing the protocols and processes in a robust and resilient way that is compatible not just with legacy systems but also with future requirements. In the ecosystem view adopted by Algorand, this work is front-loaded and has informed the fundamental design of our open-source blockchain technology.

Algorand's 'openness-by-design' architecture creates an ecosystem where the protocol facilitates the seamless interaction of various ecosystem partners (banks, e-money companies, payment providers, etc.).

Consequently, we have front-loaded the demanding work of creating protocols and processes to allow a diverse set of ecosystem players to interact without any one party's ability to create barriers to entry. This is vastly different from other approaches, notably by consulting firms and the Diem Association (formerly Facebook's Libra Association), which effectively implement walled gardens.[5] Algorand has created an open platform that prevents capture by any private

---

[5] A 'walled garden' is defined as '[...] a limited set of technology or media information provided to users with the intention of creating a monopoly or secure information system' (see Technopedia at www.techopedia.com/definition/2541/walled-garden-technology).

actor while giving central banks and government agencies full control over which users and use cases are allowed on the platform.

How to Incentivise Competition

The rise of private digital assets has set off a flurry of innovation among small startups, large banks, and big tech companies alike. Within Algorand's first years, the rapidly growing ecosystem had over 700 organisations join the tens of thousands of companies innovating in the broader digital asset space. A lot of this innovation, however, happens outside of the purview of existing regulatory bodies. Consequently, billions of euros worth of transactions are happening outside of official sight and then settled in fiat. An official state-sponsored digital currency can allow much more of this digital innovation to happen 'in the light of day'.

To foster competition, an open system without barriers to entry is paramount. No walled garden solution can achieve this because, in such solutions, a provider can never commit not to create barriers to entry further down the line. The rules of a walled garden can be modified at any time by the solution provider. Algorand's open protocol, enforced by decentralised validation, ensures that any system built on our platform will always incentivise competition while curbing regulatory arbitrage. Only the network of the authorised parties can collectively alter the system's rules once established.

Lastly, a CBDC system would create a more level playing field between traditional financial institutions and big tech companies. The BIS (Bank for International Settlements) Annual Economic Report (2019) outlines the challenge big tech companies pose to existing financial institutions in an increasingly digital economy. Big tech companies have a massive advantage over traditional financial institutions, and this advantage can translate into cheaper services outside of existing regulatory frameworks. A CBDC will enable financial institutions to innovate more rapidly and compete on a more level playing field with the big tech companies.

Leveraging Algorand Technology to Provide a Solution Consistent with the Design Principles

As mentioned above, the advancements in speed, scalability, security, and usability of next-generation blockchain technology make available the necessary platform for central banks to radically improve their cash management and distribution at scale. On the retail side, this technology would make it possible to lower the cost of cash and provide a more resilient infrastructure for cross-border payments and remittances. An efficient way to model the coexistence of Central Bank and Commercial Bank money (for instance, in the logic of a regulated stablecoin) could be designed utilising the primitives of such an infrastructure. On the wholesale side, the availability of a blockchain able to perform truly atomic transactions with immediate finality can substantially lower counterparty risk, therefore reducing costs and enabling more collateral to be put to work instead of being allocated against securing transactions.

Moreover, we also mentioned that a critical requirement for the adoption of CBDCs is the inalterability of the core blockchain infrastructure, both now and in the future. The cryptography on which such an infrastructure would rely to guarantee its security needs to be future-proof, and threats on the horizon like quantum computers need to be addressed today to protect end-users (citizens) from massive losses of value.

The Algorand blockchain provides the foundation for the future of economic exchange with global-scale performance on par with centralised solutions while also delivering the safety, security, and resilience that can only come from a truly decentralised system.

Conceived and built by an MIT team led by Turing Prize-winning Professor Silvio Micali, Algorand is the world's first Pure PoS blockchain platform. Pure PoS refers to the system's ability to resolve transactions in a secure and expeditious manner. In blockchain parlance, this is called 'Consensus'. Algorand's novel consensus mechanism is designed to ensure that transactions are fast, instantly final, while also ensuring that the blockchain never (soft) forks. Soft forking is when there is the possibility of two 'legitimate ledgers' existing in parallel. During a soft fork, network participants can append transactions, such as payments and cash distribution, to a fork of the chain that is ultimately deemed incorrect, thus negating all transactions that were appended to the 'wrong fork'. Thus, preventing soft forking, being fast, and being secure are critically unique capabilities for a technology that provides the immutability essential for a CBDC. Additionally, thanks to Algorand's research team leading the development of state-of-the-art post-quantum cryptography,

Algorand's blockchain will be safe and secure, even if quantum computer technology continues to make significant advances.

Algorand has built the technical infrastructure for CBDCs to move from an experiment to real-world implementation and scale to global adoption.

The CBDC model that we propose is a hybrid model, built on a private instance of the public Algorand blockchain in a two-tier retail system. In this model, central banks have full control over the CBDC. Simultaneously, licensed service providers (LSPs), such as commercial banks, remittance providers, and other fintech companies, can facilitate distribution and transactions. This model also allows a central bank to delegate customer service responsibilities to institutions with that capability.

Compared to traditional bank accounts, a blockchain-based retail CBDC can reach a broader base of consumers, including those in the informal economy who might face difficulty opening a conventional bank account and who are, thus, unable to use digital services offered by banks. Compared to a traditional account-based digital currency, Algorand's proposed design will be simpler and more economical to implement and manage for central banks at scale.

Algorand's approach to retail CBDC proposes the creation of a retail digital asset similar in characteristics and purpose to cash that is issued and fully backed by the central bank as legal tender. This positioning allows for a widely accessible, easy-to-manage currency, exchangeable by consumers and businesses in a peer-to-peer fashion. By adopting 'digital first' distribution, cash treasuries can be managed programmatically, significantly reducing the cost of cash management and providing standard interfaces to streamline foreign exchange through atomically swapping CBDCs that represent different fiat currencies.

It is worth mentioning that our proposed model will not destabilise existing systems. Being an open platform that is easily integrated via standard APIs, Algorand's infrastructure and network complement current systems and would be able to work alongside physical cash. As an example, Algorand's CBDC model can be fully integrated with local RTGS payment systems, or with any regulated stablecoin. Thanks to Algorand's standard asset controls, such as asset creation and transaction approval, a CBDC issued on Algorand's platform can programmatically receive instructions from the RTGS to issue the digital currency to service providers and the public.

Our approach to designing CBDC systems follows an open system approach, with the open-source Algorand blockchain at its core. Unlike many enterprise blockchain providers who effectively build a walled-garden and lock central banks to a single solution provider, the Algorand system is designed to have open APIs that foster competition and prevent vendor lock-in. By introducing competition, central banks can better serve their constituents by embracing innovative designs that ultimately drive the cost per transaction down.

To be clear, open-source should not be interpreted as open-access. While anyone can develop applications that integrate with Algorand's standards, each network, asset, and application can implement 'Role Based Access Controls' (RBAC). These controls can determine, under what conditions an entity/individual is allowed to join the network, under what conditions can an entity/individual can create an account and receive CBDC, and under what conditions can an entity/individual participate in financial applications such as peer-to-peer lending and borrowing. These controls follow a defence-in-depth strategy and provide the Central Bank with a programmatic way of protecting their citizens while also fostering open innovation from the technology community.

To create a suitable environment for innovation, the architecture of the Algorand-based CBDC system would consist of two networks: a pre-production BetaNet and the actual MainNet. BetaNet can be used by all institutions to program their products/services against a 'beta-CBDC' for end-to-end testing. After sufficient review and approval from the Central Bank, and/or review from the broader community, applications launched in the BetaNEt can be promoted and deployed to the MainNet. To date, Algorand's implementation of the model described above has involved collaboration with both local consortium partners and global technology companies to deliver a solution tailored to each country's specific characteristics and needs. By employing an open-source design, such as Algorand's, all participants benefit from open competition while adhering to systematic protections.

One of the defining characteristics of Algorand's standards is that they would facilitate interoperability between a public and private Algorand network if the Central Bank so chooses. The Algorand Foundation has built and developed a public and permissionless blockchain network using the Algorand open-source code.

The public and permissionless platform has developed a vibrant economy with over 700 organisations, millions of users, and billions of dollars' worth of assets available to its ecosystem. The private instance on which a CBDC is issued would be fully interoperable with the Algorand Foundation's network due to the same standards being employed in both networks. This interoperability provides central banks with the best of both worlds: complete control over the private network, its validators, and the geographic location of the infrastructure, while also facilitating a connection to the public domain for access to a broader ecosystem of digital goods and services. By virtue of the two networks being interoperable, central banks can utilise a public infrastructure, and the assets created on it (e.g., stablecoins denominated in other currencies or other CBDCs) at their sole discretion.

As new innovations continue to occur, this unique capability provides central banks with a future-proof path to ensure that their CBDC will benefit and will be interoperable with all infrastructure connected to any Algorand network. In the same way that central banks can define the conditions under which an entity or organisation can acquire their CBDC, they can also define the requirements for their CBDC to be transacted against other CBDCs. This is a unique value proposition that only Algorand's technology can provide to central banks.

Conclusions

In this short chapter, we reflect on the experience Algorand had participating in various CBDC projects around the globe. We propose a hybrid, two-tier, retail CBDC model, built on a private instance of the public Algorand blockchain. In this scenario, central banks always retain full control over their CBDC, while distribution and transactions can be facilitated by LSPs, such as commercial banks, remittance providers, and other fintech companies.

A blockchain-based retail CBDC can reach a broad base of consumers, including those without a traditional bank account. We propose the creation of a retail digital asset similar in characteristics and purpose to cash, issued and fully backed by the central bank as legal tender, but which can allow for cheaper, easier, and more convenient transactions than cash itself.

The Algorand network could also be used for wholesale CBDCs. In this case, our CBDC system could offer significant cost savings for market participants by enhancing liquidity management and collateralisation requirements. The quantum-resilient Algorand blockchain is the ideal platform to realise these savings while maintaining the highest level of security.

The Algorand blockchain is a powerful financial technology that enables central banks to issue both wholesale and retail CBDC seamlessly. Our approach to designing CBDC is quite different from that enterprise blockchain providers, which aim to build a walled-garden and achieve vendor lock-in. Our open-system design prevents vendor lock-in and facilitates competition and financial innovation on a level playing field, while ensuring the central banks are still ultimately in control of this critical financial platform.

We believe that this open systems approach is the best design to empower central banks globally to issue retail and wholesale CBDC on our best-in-class blockchain platform.

References

Bank of International Settlements 2019. 'Big tech in finance: opportunities and risks. Annual Economic Report'. Available online: www.bis.org/publ/arpdf/ar2019e3.htm.

Civelli, A., Georg, CP., Grassano, P., Ihsanullah, N. 2022. 'Issuing Central Bank Digital Currencies Using Algorand'. *Working Paper*. Available online: www.algorand.com/resources/blog/report-issuing-central-bank-digital-currency.

Clark, D. 2018. *Designing an Internet*. MIT Press.

Goodhart, C. 1988. *The Evolution of Central Banks*. MIT Press Books. The MIT Press, edition 1, volume 1, number 0262570734.

Harari, Y. 2011. *Sapiens: A Brief History of Humankind*. Harper Editions.

Hartung, G., K. Rutter, and G. Stroemer. 2019. 'A solution for managing high-quality liquid assets: How distributed ledger technology can benefit the securities lending market'. *Journal of Securities Operations and Custody*, Vol. 11, No. 4, 282–291.

Hau, H., Hoffmann, P., Langfield, S., Timmer, Y. 2019. 'Discriminatory Pricing of Over-the-Counter Derivatives'. *IMF Working Paper*, 19/100.

Kasper, E. 2015. *A Definition for Infrastructure – Characteristics and Their Impact on Firms Active in Infrastructure*. PhD Thesis, LMU Munich. Available online: www.d-nb.info/1071370057/34.

Newzoo 2019. *Global Mobile Market Report – 2019*. Available online: www.newzoo.com/insights/trend-reports/newzoo-global-mobile-market-report-2019-light-version.

Paniagua, P. 2017. 'The institutional rationale of central banking reconsidered'. *Constitutional Political Economy*, vol. 28, no. 3, 231–256.

Schmiedel, H., Kostova, G., Ruttenberg, W. 2012. 'The social and private costs of retail payment instruments: A European perspective'. *ECB Occasional Paper Series*, vol. 137. Available online: www.ecb .europa.eu/pub/pdf/scpops/ecbocp137.pdf

8 | Opportunities, Challenges, and Design of CBDCs
The Italian Approach to a New Technology

SILVIA ATTANASIO AND PAOLA DEL VITTO

Introduction

Over the last few years, the use of Blockchain and DLT paradigms has continued to grow, bringing out a certain maturity in the applications that make use of them. This has contributed to scaling back some of the hype that was created in recent years. As a result, ecosystems have emerged that aim for greater value creation using the technology paradigm. This growth also stems from an increased awareness of the potential that lies in Blockchain and DLT.

A PwC's research published in October 2020 exploring the impact Blockchain technology can have on the global economy shows that, by 2025, most companies will be using it, creating value in many sectors, and leading to a potential increase in global GDP of $1.760 trillion in 2030 (or about 1.4 per cent of global GDP).

Approaching a new technology also brings with it some hurdles to overcome. Among them, the proliferation of Blockchain/ DLT initiatives has been complicated by the absence of a harmonised regulatory framework. Indeed, especially at the European level, there is a fragmentation of sometimes conflicting provisions and regulations among individual EU member states.

However, in the last couple of years, regulation related to Blockchain and DLT has taken numerous steps forward.

With a view to fostering the development of these technologies to initially support financial services and products, the Italian Banking Association is calling for an Italian national strategy on artificial intelligence to be harmonised and integrated within a wider European strategy in order to achieve homogeneity at the EU level.

In this scenario, there is growing attention on Central Bank Digital Currencies (CBDCs), a new form of digital currency issued by central banks with intrinsic value, accessible to all, and not intended as a substitute for cash. Many central banks are already active in study initiatives or experimentation on the subject (86 per cent out of a sample of 60 according to the survey on CBDCs by the Bank for International Settlements, representing about one-fifth of the world's population), to gain insight and understand the possible advantages that this currency could bring to the international economic and monetary system, such as financial inclusion, operational efficiency, and security in payments. The CBDC – DLT binomial seems to find growing support at the international level. The issue of direct interoperability in exchanges between central banks is considered critical, as it would require identifying forms of compatibility between the architectures chosen by each jurisdiction.

To date, the landscape is not complete. In particular, various aspects linked to the technological and IT standards to be implemented to meet the requirements of scalability, interoperability, security, privacy, and circularity, as well as compliance with standards and supervision, are still being examined.

The European Central Bank (ECB) is actively working on this topic, including through the document submitted for consultation on 12 October 2020, following the publication of the 'Report on a digital Euro', an in-depth study on the digital Euro prepared by the Eurosystem's High-Level Task Force on Central Bank Digital Currency (HLTF-CBDC) and approved by the Governing Council.

The ECB considers it appropriate to prepare for the possible launch of a digital Euro for three strategic reasons:

- To support the digitisation of the European economy;
- to respond to the move away from the use of cash as a means of payment; and
- to respond effectively to a scenario of increased use of digital currencies issued by private entities or by central banks in other countries. Hence the digital Euro, a central bank liability offered in digital form that complements cash and deposits at central banks.

In October, the ECB published its 'Report on a digital Euro' and launched a consultation. This is a detailed document that sets core principles and specific requirements that need to be considered in the possible future advancement of the digital Euro project. The ECB considers it appropriate to prepare for the possible launch of a digital Euro for three strategic reasons: to support the digitisation of the European economy; to respond to the move away from the use of cash as a means of payment; and to respond effectively to a scenario of increased use of digital currencies issued by private entities or by central banks in other countries. Hence the digital Euro, a central bank liability offered in digital form, which complements cash and deposits at central banks.

In this context, the Italian banking sector has been working since 2017 on the Spunta DLT project, which went into production in 2020 and will be explained in detail in the following section. In addition, at the end of 2020, the Italian Banking Association, in collaboration with Associazione Bancaria Italiana (ABI) Lab, ABI's innovation research centre, launched an experiment in the context of the digital Euro project. The initiative aims to actively contribute to the public debate and to support banks operating in Italy in the path of preparation for the future scenario, which will be described in the following paragraphs.

From both experiences, it is possible to draw useful indications and insights for the future ahead.

Italian Banks and DLT: Spunta DLT

Faced with disruptive technologies, or better still, technologies that explicitly aim to disintermediate traditional banks, there are three possible reactions: you can simply ignore them, you may hope they disappear, or you can try to understand and embrace the change. Italian banks clearly chose the third option and started the Spunta DLT project, promoted by the Italian Banking Association – ABI and coordinated by ABI Lab, the association's research and innovation centre.

The Spunta DLT project is a private, permissioned DLT-based project for interbank reconciliation promoted by ABI, and coordinated by ABI Lab. The project began in December 2017.

In essence, the project is about the matching of correspondent (or bilateral) accounts that involve two different banks. In Italy, the interbank reconciliation procedure is linked to processes traditionally carried out by back-office structures aimed at reconciling the transaction flows generated by accounting entries in the bilateral accounts and managing pending transactions. After the automatic matching, the operators deal with the suspended movements. The implementation of a new process using a private permissioned DLT for interbank reconciliations makes it possible to automatically detect non-matching transactions using a shared algorithm, standardised both the process

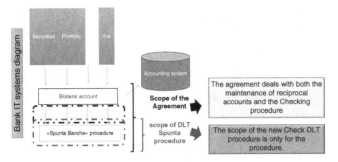

Figure 8.1 Bank IT systems diagram
Note: The project verified how the application of DLT technologies has improved some specific aspects of current operations, which can cause complex discrepancies for banks to manage.
Source: authors' elaboration.

and the single communication channel, and provides a comprehensive view of the transactions among the interested parties (Figure 8.1).

The project started with an initial working group composed of 18 pilot banks, representing 78 per cent of the Italian banking sector in terms of employees. The project saw the commitment of technical partners like NTT Data as an application designer and developer and SIA as an infrastructure operator, in addition to R3 with the Corda Enterprise platform.

Therefore, the principles of the new Spunta project envisage full visibility of transactions, including those of the counterparty; rapid management of flows with daily, rather than monthly, reconciliations; shared rules for the symmetrical reconciliation of transactions between counterparty banks; and the integrated management of communications and processes in the event of an imbalance.

The interbank reconciliation process is a niche back-office process that was seen as an excellent candidate to test with this technology for its limited impact on the IT systems of the bank, the fact that it does not impact final customers, and the need for a better standardisation. The process is ruled by an interbank agreement, issued by ABI itself, whose first formulation dates to 1978. After the redesign of the process, an important milestone of the project was reached in May 2019 when the Executive Committee of ABI approved the new interbank agreement, officially starting the path to the production phase for the entire Italian banking sector.

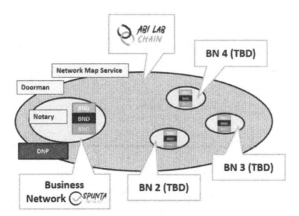

Figure 8.2 ABI Lab, conceptual diagram of the ABILabChain business zone
Note: In this model, nodes are not explicitly considered: each one identifies a bank and its management model does not affect the overall governance.
Source: authors' elaboration.

After the simulations and 1,680 tests carried out between the end of January and the beginning of February 2020 by the final operators in the back offices of the pilot banks, all the time targets were reached. From the beginning of March 2020, on time with the deadlines stated one year before, the process became operational for the first 32 banks. The tests showed that the query of the data and the execution of the simplest operations were performed in less than a second, even in the most complex cases, while the report generation phase lasted half a minute. During the tests, 103 reciprocal accounts (technically speaking, bilateral registers) were generated and fed with seven million movements in terms of real data.

Today, nearly 100 banks are in the production phase and use the Spunta DLT daily, each with its own DLT node (distributed in nine different cities across Italy). To April 2021, the DLT application processed 455,592,838 million transactions; thanks to the information matching algorithm discussed and agreed by the workgroup of banks, the average automatic match rate is 98.3 per cent (Figure 8.2).

The main factors that set the Spunta DLT project apart are:

– **An incremental, flexible approach**: the incremental approach adopted for the project made it possible to concentrate initially on functional aspects of process and governance. Attention was then shifted to the technological aspects, including high reliability, back up, performance, etc., and finally, to the legal and contractual aspects. This approach, combined with the adoption of a flexible, rapid approach ('fail fast'), which made it possible to face all challenges effectively, was also continued into the production roll-out, which took place in various waves.

- **Collaborative approach to innovative technology**: by facing the technological challenges posed by DLT's highly innovative nature collaboratively, it was possible to steer and solve all the issues thanks to a collaborative approach with all players involved. Concrete evidence of this teamwork is the sharing of intellectual property of the developed software between the banks participating in the first phases and ABI Lab.
- **Constant project alignment**: the constant alignment and active involvement of the banks involved kept individuals' focus on the project high throughout the process.
- **Ongoing improvement**: the creation of a monitoring process enabled ongoing improvement of the Spunta DLT application and underlying infrastructure.
- **Governance model**: a governance model distributed over multiple levels was created, making it possible, for example, to manage project activities and decisions with a clear view of roles and establish the responsibilities for each level; to ensure observance of distributed governance; to segregate roles to maximise their openness to competition in future initiatives; and to rationalise the contractual model through the pivotal role played by ABI Lab.
- **Shared environment**: awareness that test management, deploy management, and application maintenance function in a distributed environment that is very different from centralised, isolated, and autonomous environments. In a decentralised environment, there is high interdependence among use cases.
- **Processes and procedures**: given the number of participants that need to be involved and the various technological levels, processes and procedures were created to enable the automation of most of the test management, deploy management, and application maintenance activities and their monitoring.
- **Identification of indicators**: the KPIs and KPOs were identified, and all SLAs were negotiated in a collaborative manner.

- **Security and compliance**: the security of the distributed system, rep-licated over multiple nodes, was ensured. Many important decisions were also made, such as the choice of the network, the securing of the machines and data, the connection with banking systems, and the access of banking operators to the infrastructure.
- **Operating model**: the formulation and creation of a distributed operating model that ensures reliability through disaster recovery and back-up of ledgers for all nodes included in the infrastructure, in full accordance with banks' security levels.
- **The nodes**: participating banks were allowed to choose whether to install the node in managed mode at third-party data centres or service centres or on their own premises, or whether to manage it fully autonomously.
- **Multi-platform infrastructure**: the infrastructure was designed to host multiple DLT platforms at the same time.
- **Infrastructure console**: creation of an infrastructure monitoring system capable of understanding the state of functioning of distributed infrastructure to identify possible problems.
- **Function dashboard**: creation of an application monitoring system capable of understanding the state of functioning of the application to identify possible problems.
- **Collaboration**: throughout the various phases, the individuals from each bank and the technology partners that participated suc-ceeded in cooperating as effectively as possible towards the project's success.
- **Creation of a community**: a group of individuals with technology skills, who acquired a working method that made it possible to achieve the result.
- **Understanding of the technology**: compared to centralised solutions, the time devoted to training operators proved crucial. In addition to creating a technological solution, operators were specifically trained and given all information needed to understand the technology.

In conclusion, it is possible to summarise that distributed technology implies distributed governance: decisions were made together, by vot-ing, and ABI Lab acted as a facilitator of a highly complex community that needs and wants to cooperate. Working in synergy is essential. Sometimes, it can be particularly hard, especially because each bank must abandon its own procedures to adopt a common process with a view to pursuing standardisation. Moreover, the two main streams of the project, the technical one and that related to processes, must always be kept aligned. It should also be kept in mind that DLT introduces a new paradigm through software, so it is important to leverage it to transform processes.

Finally, it is important to note that DLT is not just about efficiency or making things cheaper or quicker than ever. This innovation is introducing a new paradigm through software that will reshape the way we work and make transactions.

ABI's Position Paper on CBDC

In parallel to the Spunta DLT project, in June 2020, even before the publication of the ECB's Report, the Executive Committee of the Italian Banking Association approved general guidelines on its position concerning digital currencies and CBDCs. At the same time, Italian banks declared their willingness to participate in projects and experiments on a CBDC, contributing to facilitate the implementation of a European-level initiative in a pilot national banking sector, thanks to their expertise developed in a concrete implementation of distributed infrastructure and governance. This position is the result of the analysis conducted by a dedicated expert group established by ABI to explore digital currency and crypto-assets. In detail, the 10 CBDC observations that summarise the Italian banks' position in 2020 are provided below:

– Monetary stability and a full respect for the European regulatory framework are a priority.
– Italian banks are already working on a distributed ledger infrastructure thanks to the Spunta DLT project. They want to be part of the change stemming from such an important innovation as digital currency.
– In the financial environment, a programmable digital currency represents an innovation capable of profoundly modifying the way we conceive currency and exchanges. This transformation can potentially deliver a great added value in terms of efficiency for both operational and support processes. This is why it is extremely important to put our heart and soul, quickly and in collaboration with the entire ecosystem, into new instruments to primarily support the development of the Euro area.

- It is necessary that people put their trust in digital currencies. To this end, it is essential that the utmost regulatory, security, and supervisory standards are fully respected.
- Thanks to the key role played by the ECB, a CBDC represents the instruments that, more than others, can satisfy the innovation needs in keeping with the current framework of rules, existing instruments, and interoperability with the analogue world. At the same time, this instrument may reduce the attractiveness of similar instruments issued by private or (in the fully decentralised implementation) non-identifiable players, as a result of their higher inherent risk.
- To take maximum advantage of the transformation potential of such instruments, the possibility, currently under consideration, of issuing a retail European CBDC, that can represent an evolution of cash, is particularly interesting. Thanks to the role of banks, it is possible to identify technical solution and an operational framework capable of preserving the current characteristics of cash, while adding several typical benefits of the digital world (already satisfied by digital payment instruments), such as the ability not to lose money and, in this period where sanitary risk takes centre stage, to operate contactless.
- By analysing every detail, it would be possible to define how to distribute, store, and exchange digital currency so as to combine customer needs with the need to ensure that the monetary policy is transmitted to the real economy, as well as compliance with the regulatory framework. Clearly, the banks' role is crucial in each of these objectives.
- A key success factor for the adoption of CBDCs is a seamless user experience, capable of ensuring at the same time full interoperability between digital and analogue processes and a complete circularity among all ecosystem players.
- Depending on the technological choices that will be made, particular attention should be devoted to the protection of personal data.
- Looking ahead, the availability of a CBDC will pave the way for several very interesting use cases: to foster peer-to-peer value transmission, supporting money exchange between person and machine and in a machine-to-machine scenario; to facilitate cross-border transactions settlement, reducing interest rate, exchange, and counterparty risks; to promote, thanks to the programmability of this instrument, the automatic execution of payments when predefined situations arise, streamlining administrative processes.

ABI's Experimentation Path

The 10 observations that make up ABI's position were the food for thought from which, in the following months, ABI began to conduct the reflections that, today, are leading the reasoning on the possible issuance of a CBDC. Indeed, thanks to the progress on the Spunta DLT project, and inspired by the ECB Report and by the continuously evolving international context, in December 2020, the Italian banks and the Italian Banking Association, in cooperation with ABI Lab, started an experimentation on a programmable CBDC.

The aim of the initiative is to proactively contribute to public debate and support banks operating in Italy as they prepare for the future. The project focuses on enhancing the role of banks in the ECB's digital Euro environment. The digital Euro differs from the existing electronic payment means mainly due to its programmability. The project also aims to demonstrate the technical feasibility of a digital Euro based on blockchain DLT, a system of distributed ledgers, in addition to exploring new value-added services that will become possible thanks to the currency's programmability.

The experimentation initiative takes inspiration from the principles shared with the banks and which form the basis of ABI's response to the ECB's consultation 'Report on a digital Euro', and specifically:

1. the need for the D€ to be functionally different from an electronic payment instrument, to complement and not compete with commercial bank money, bank initiatives, and investments (especially in the field of payment services);
2. the importance of safeguarding the intermediation role of banks for the economic system.

   The preference for the use of DLT – DLT to exploit the great potential of this new technology and provide functionalities based on distributed technologies: a D€ built on DLT, thanks to its programmability, could balance, on one hand, the full control and governance of issuance by the ECB/Eurosystem and, on the other, allow banks to provide and offer new services, or provide services already offered in a much more efficient way.

The experimentation path linked to the digital Euro is structured in two parallel strands:

- **Infrastructure and distribution model**: the experience gained with the Spunta DLT project has prompted the creation of a set of distinctive values that underlie the important maturity reached by banks in Italy and that can be put at the service of the experimentation of a Euro Digital solution. The expected output of the enhancement of the elements characterising the ABILabChain distributed infrastructure, which has 100 DLT nodes in production, has been the drafting of an analysis document showing the value-added elements of the operational infrastructure.
- **Programmability**: with the dual objective of enhancing the role of the banks in the event a programmable digital currency becomes available and promoting a digital currency that is different from the electronic payment means already available, the second strand dedicated to programmability is broken down into four use cases chosen by the banks adhering to the initiative.

Regarding the first strand, a document analysing the main components of the ABILabChain infrastructure has been drawn up. This document illustrates the experience of the Spunta DLT project and the relative design approach, which can provide useful ideas in the experimentation of a digital Euro.

Among the benefits highlighted in the document, it appears that the governance model adopted for the coordination of the entire project can be of reference to draw useful ideas even in the definition of the future governance structure of the digital Euro. In addition, the value of the community involved in the Spunta DLT project emerges as a strength, as it put together several banks, different skills, and a shared decision-making method, which contributed to the creation of a DLT system.

The second work stream has been divided into four working groups that will focus on as many use cases and will work in collaboration with the banks and digital partners Fabrick, NTT Data, PWC, and Reply, which have made their resources available to the project. This stream has been dedicated to programmability through the identification of four areas of application that enhance the role of banks and the differentiating value of technological aspects.

The selection criteria adopted for the choice of the use cases were as follows:

- enhance the role of banks in the distribution of a possible digital currency;

- enhance the programmability of the currency, as a differentiating factor compared with existing means of payment;
- Identify clear and concrete use cases, with a visible impact in favour of citizens and the European digital economy; and
- make sense for programmable money and, specifically, for the digital Euro (very different from cryptocurrencies).

To demonstrate how the Italian banking sector would use the digital Euro to offer value-added services, the development of the four use cases led to the four proofs of concept illustrated below:

- **SimplyHome**: performance of multiple payments expected at the time of purchasing a property through the granting of a mortgage. The execution of payments (to the seller, to the property agency, to the notary, to the seller's bank to pay off a previous mortgage, etc.) through the enabled functionality of split transaction (making a single transaction divided into multiple payments) will simplify and automate the management of transactions towards the various players involved in the process of buying and selling a property, giving enhanced certainty to the entire process.
- **Safe return**: within the process of returning a purchase made through an e-commerce website, thanks to the implementation in a distributed ledger of instructions that are binding and executable only on the occurrence of predetermined conditions (so-called Smart contract), it is possible to make the return process more reliable and consumer-friendly. At the time of delivery of the returned goods by the client, the sum of money can be blocked and kept in an escrow account managed by a bank, which will only release it after confirmation or rejection of the return, respectively to the consumer or to the seller.
- **Culture pass**: culture pass is an initiative linked to the bonuses granted by the government to support specific types of expenses (i.e., books, electric scooters, kindergarten, etc.). The development of this case will lead to the creation of specific smart contracts linked to the digital Euro, which will make it possible to incorporate the logic and purpose of expendability of these tokens and therefore to use the bonus only in compliance with the terms and conditions defined by the issuing entity. In addition, a simplified prototype linked to the provision of money to minors (pocket money) will be developed, to limit the expendability only to the categories of purchases allowed by law.

– **Pay&Split**: execution of payments for products on consignment. The case provides for the transparent management of the execution of payments for products on consignment in the so-called short supply chains, using the split transaction functionality (atomic and instantaneous transactions). At the time of purchase, a single transaction is divided so that payment is directed to the seller of the product and to the various producers making up the supply chain.

The use cases implemented are not intended to encompass all possible applications of the digital Euro, but merely to offer a robust demonstration as a basis for further work moving forward.

All use cases show the transformational potential of the implementation of a distributed register of binding instructions that may only be executed upon the satisfaction of predetermined conditions ('smart contracts') connected to the currency and thus capable of rendering the currency programmable. These application logic and conditions may also be structured into a multi-level system (e.g., at the level of the central bank, the retail bank offering the service, and the user). It is thus possible to achieve extreme simplification of complex processes involving multiple players, who will then be able to interoperate with one another without being forced to rely on the same service provider.

The main benefits associated with the use of programmable money on DLT compared to traditional technologies that emerged from the four use cases were:

– **Interoperability**: the digital Euro could be a platform that brings interoperable services to the currency level, regardless of the supporting Payment Service Providers (PSPs).
– **Composability**: native compatibility with other use cases without intervention on applications and with potential changes made by the ECB to the digital Euro which are immediately transmitted to all use cases.
– **Native auditability**: native and atomic check of rule execution and transactions through real-time smart contracts, in addition to the ability to install audit nodes to verify real-time smart contracts, for example.
– **Simplicity**: streamlining of the processes, which are automatically described and codified in the logic of a smart contract, even in real time (the configuration of the rules is enabled by the service

provider and can be tailored by the client according to his/her needs, within predefined patterns).
- Privacy: with DLT it is possible to natively provide for the visibility of information based on the need-to-know principle (only those involved in the transaction have access to the information).

The Launch of the Digital Euro Project

In the meantime, on 14 July 2021, the Governing Council of the ECB approved the launch of the Digital Euro Project.[1] The aim is to deepen and address central aspects regarding the design and distribution model associated with the digital Euro. The final decision on the actual issuance of the digital Euro will be made at a later stage. According to Fabio Panetta, the new digital currency would complement cash without replacing it.

The duration of the investigation phase is set at 24 months, to be followed by the actual implementation phase, estimated to last 36 months.

The launch of the project follows the exploratory activities conducted so far by the Eurosystem between September 2020 and March 2021. These have been divided into four streams[2]:

- 'Scale the existing': use of existing infrastructures, with reference to the centralised TIPS infrastructure; accounts open to citizens have been simulated on this infrastructure, even in a pseudonym scenario to preserve confidentiality, to then carry out the issuance, distribution, and withdrawal of the digital Euro. *Published by Banca d'Italia in cooperation with NCBs (Austria, France, Germany, Greece, Lithuania, Netherlands, and Portugal) and ECB.*
- 'Combined feasibility': testing the feasibility of a combination of centralised and decentralised architectures (i.e., DLT and non-DLT). The objective is to understand the possibility of reusing existing infrastructures while enabling the implementation of innovative

---

[1] See European Central Bank 2021. *Eurosystem launches digital euro project.* Press Release. Available online: www.ecb.europa.eu/press/pr/date/2021/html/ecb.pr210714~d99198ea23.en.html.

[2] See European Central Bank 2021. *Digital euro experimentation scope and key learnings.* Available online: www.ecb.europa.eu/pub/pdf/other/ecb.digitaleurosc opekeylearnings202107~564d89045e.en.pdf.

functionalities. This approach was verified according to two models, one that places the two architectures on par and the other that articulates them on two hierarchical levels. First model 'Flat Approach' *Published by Bank of Italy in cooperation with NCBs (Austria, France, Spain, and Luxembourg) and ECB* and second model 'Tiered Approach' *Published by Banque de France in cooperation with NCBs (Austria, Belgium, Italy, Lithuania, Luxembourg, and Spain) and ECB.*

- 'A new solution': analysis of a new solution based on a decentralised platform (i.e., DLT) for all phases of issuance, distribution, and withdrawal of the digital Euro. This strand also delved into the interaction with existing digital identity solutions. Compliance with existing AML/CFT regulations has also been assessed. *Published by the Central Bank of Estonia in cooperation with NCBs (Germany, Greece, Ireland, Italy, Latvia, Netherlands, and Spain) and ECB.*
- 'Bearer instrument': deepening of a bearer instrument, based on a model in which transactions take place without internet connection (offline). *Published by the Bundesbank in cooperation with NCBs (Spain, Netherlands, Italy, France, and Finland) and the ECB.*

The Investigation Phase of the Project

In this context, to facilitate the design and implementation of the digital Euro from the private sector perspective, the ECB has set up a Market Advisory Group (MAG), which will be called to contribute the views of users and distributors of the digital Euro during the investigation phase of the project.

The objective of the MAG will be to contribute to the Eurosystem's reflections by providing input on (i) the concrete design and distribution of the potential digital Euro from an industry perspective and (ii) how the digital Euro can add value for the different types of players involved.

MAG's meetings will be held at least quarterly, starting in November 2021, throughout the planned two-year duration of the pre-trial phase. Written consultations will be organised between meetings by the ECB. Identified issues will also be brought to the attention of the steering body for euro retail payments established by the Eurosystem and chaired by the ECB, the Euro Retail Payments

Board (ERPB). The ERPB is composed of high-level representatives of European trade associations on the supply and demand side of payment services and represents a wide range of stakeholders (banks, IMELs, payment institutions, information and device service providers, PA, industrial, retail, and e-commerce companies, ECAs). In addition, the Eurosystem will involve the public and merchants through dedicated surveys, such as focus groups, and will continue to hold technical workshops with the industry.

In early 2022, work continued on what use cases could be enabled by a digital Euro to achieve the Eurosystem's policy objectives, also considering the evolving needs of citizens, merchants, and all stakeholders at the European level; on the possible remuneration model; on the integration with payment services and systems; and on the integration with the acceptance network., Finally, assuming that different degrees of protection of users' personal data can be technically guaranteed, the privacy implications of possible intermediation, and settlement models were also examined.

From ABI's reflections in the working group, it emerged that the functionalities capable of promoting innovation and competitiveness of the digital Euro essentially depend on two interconnected factors: the architecture envisaged for the distribution of the digital Euro and programmability. To be able to compete effectively with comparable instruments offered by private entities or other foreign central banks, it is desirable that the digital Euro enables exchanges beyond the mere transfer of money. Moreover, for the digital Euro to be successful, it must enable the provision of value-added services, thereby supporting competition without displacing private initiative, primarily in digital payments, and avoiding the risk of disintermediation. To this end, the digital Euro could be an innovative platform, provided by the Eurosystem, where banks and other PSPs could have the opportunity, leveraging on the technical features of this platform, to offer new services.

Conclusion

With the ECB's Governing Council starting the investigation phase of the digital Euro project, we are looking forward to months in which fundamental issues related to the definition of the technical characteristics and distribution of a digital Euro will be discussed.

Trusting that the digital Euro may represent a platform on which private operators can develop and offer innovative solutions, it will be crucial to adopt an open approach for the next steps, involving from the very beginning different players of the payment industry. To this extent, the Italian Banking Association and Italian banks are willing to actively contribute to the upcoming phases of experimentation that the Eurosystem may conduct.

ABI's aim is to ensure that whatever technological choice the Eurosystem adopts, it does not undermine the role of banks as intermediaries or their ability to offer innovative services such as those tested in 2021.

This transformation will take shape within a future international scenario which stands on three pillars: the development of technology as infrastructure, the inclusion of cryptocurrencies and stablecoins in a robust regulatory framework, and the advent of CBDCs in advanced countries.

9 A Proposal for an Asia Digital Common Currency (ADCC) Applying Distributed Ledger Technology (DLT) and Blockchain Technology (BCT)

TAIJI INUI AND WATARU TAKAHASHI[1]

Introduction

A proposal for Asia Digital Common Currency (ADCC) is explained hereinafter. ADCC is a regional common currency (examples of ancient asean currencies are provided in Figure 9.1) to be issued as a regional common currency without establishing a monetary (currency) union or regional central bank utilising blockchain technology (BCT) and distributed ledger technology (DLT).

Now, a digital form of common currency ADCC is proposed in ASEAN+3 now. ASEAN+3 consists of 14 economies which are 10 ASEAN states as well as China, Japan, Korea, and Hong Kong China.

In the early 2000s, the Asian Currency Unit (ACU) and/or Asian Monetary Unit (AMU) was proposed based on the lessons learned from the Asian Currency Crisis that happened in 1997 but failed. Following is the brief explanation of ACU and AMU (author's understanding).

The Asia Currency Crisis may have happened because of the so-called double mismatches, that is, currency mismatches and maturity mismatches. This double mismatch was damaging as the significant depreciation of their currencies inflated borrowers' debt burden. This led foreign lenders to refuse rolling short-term debt, which then triggered massive defaults of banks and firms.

In order to mitigate the negative impact of currency mismatches depending too much on USD, a common currency based on Asian

[1] This research is supported by JSPS KAKENHI Grant Number 20H05633.

Figure 9.1a Yongle coin
Note: Asia had a common currency named 'Yongle coin (永樂通宝)' centuries ago in Ming Dynasty circulated wide area in Asia including Japan.
Source: commons.wikimedia.org/wiki/File:Eiraku-Tsuho.jpg. This image is licensed under the Creative Commons Attribution-Share Alike 3.0 Unported license (CC BY-SA 3.0).

Figure 9.1b Chinese 100 yuan
Note: Same 'Kanji character (圓)' originated from ancient China' is still used as the denomination of currency in China, Hong Kong China, Japan, Korea, and Chinese Taipei.
Source: flickr.com/photos/jsjgeology/49792393672. This image is licensed under the Creative Commons Attribution 2.0 generic license (CC BY 2.0).

currencies was proposed since the majority of trading counterparties in ASEAN+3 are located inside the region. However, differences of a variety of issues such as economic growth (financial and capital) market structures, population, access to education, poverty rate, government debt, and governance structure were too big compared to those in Europe. Therefore, the weight of currencies consisting of the common basket currency was hard to agree. Also, if the Asian common basket currency was supposed to be used as a local currency, paper-based banknotes were necessary since digital currency was not

Figure 9.1c Japan 1 yen
Note: Same 'Kanji character (圓)' originated from ancient China' is still used as the denomination of currency in China, Hong Kong China, Japan, Korea, and Chinese Taipei.
Source: commons.wikimedia.org/wiki/File:Bank_of_Japan_silver_convertible_one_yen_banknote_1885.jpg. This image is licensed under the Creative Commons Attribution-Share Alike 3.0 Unported license (CC BY-SA 3.0).

Figure 9.1d 500 Taiwan dollar
Note: Same 'Kanji character (圓)' originated from ancient China' is still used as the denomination of currency in China, Hong Kong China, Japan, Korea, and Chinese Taipei.
Source: commons.wikimedia.org/wiki/File: 500_New_Taiwan_Dollar.jpg. This image is licensed under the Creative Commons Attribution-Share Alike 4.0 International license (CC BY-SA 4.0).

mature yet from neither technological nor business perspective. Then, the Asia common basket currency was not realised.

Currently, many central banks in the region are planning to issue CBDC. Then, we can utilise the technology for digital currency, in particular that for CBDC to issue ADCC. From this perspective, the proposal to issue ADCC will be possible.

Differently from Europe, it is definitely a proposal to issue common currency in Asia without establishing the regional central bank in Europe by utilising BCT including DLT as well as remaining local currencies in particular CBDCs in the region co-existing with the ADCC, which is different from the introduction of euro as the single currency in Europe.

Categorisation of ADCC from Technological and Business Perspective

Taking a look at the current trend, many central banks are tackling CBDC initiatives not only in Asia but also globally. Cooperation of central banks for enhancing interoperability of CBDCs is also coordinated by the BIS.

Digital currencies, particularly CBDCs, have been studied for years. As a result, many related papers have been published including the 'Central Bank Cryptocurrencies' from BIS. BIS 'Central bank digital currency' explains design features of CBDC from availability, anonymity, transfer mechanism, interest-bearing, and limit (or cap). These design features are applied for ADCC as shown in Table 9.1.

There are different types of digital currencies. Electronic money is a kind of digital currency already used and prevails in many countries. Also, technologies developed for electronic money are applied to

Table 9.1 *Key design features of ADCC*

	Existing central bank money		CBDC		
	Cash	Reserves and settle balances	General purpose token account	Wholesale only token	ADCC token
24/7 availability	✓	X	✓	(✓)	(✓)	✓
Anonymity vis-à-vis central bank	✓	X	(✓)	X	(✓)	✓
Peer-to-peer transfer	✓	X	(✓)	X	(✓)	✓
Interest-bearing	X	(✓)	(✓)	(✓)	(✓)	X
Limits or caps	X	X	(✓)	(✓)	(✓)	✓

✓ = existing or likely feature, (✓) = possible feature, X = not typical or possible feature.

digital currencies. General features of electronic money are explained in Appendix for reference purpose.

ADCC is token-based type, distributed type, and local type. At the same time, ADCC is also recorded based on the ID of a digital wallet, the same as an account-based type and managed centrally at a central bank and government agency. ADCC is also stored remotely at the centre of the central bank.

Background of the Proposal for ADCC

There were significant positive opinions to introduce a common currency in Asia. As a matter of fact, significant supply chain networks were developed in line with the increase of direct investment to the region after the 1990s, which promoted integration of industries and trades in the region just like the situation in Europe. In the case of Asia, dependency on USD for trade increased even for intra-regional trades, which didn't fit the Asian sentiment very much in some sense. Also, there was some expectation of a common currency which could prevent the attack on 'weak currencies' considering the lessons learned from the Asia Financial Crisis that happened in 1997. Actually, based on the lessons learned, the currency swap network (so called Chiang Mai Initiative) was established. Introduction of common currency could further enhance such safety net in the region. On the other hand, there were some negative opinions, to introduce common currency in the region as follows: (i) political integration (cooperation) was not deep enough compared to that in Europe and (ii) stages of economic developments were different country by country, in particular that in the financial sector. The financial crisis in Europe caused by the Global Financial Crisis was also a negative factor. As such, there were negative reasons to introduce common currency in Asia. Then, discussions on common currency in Asia have been inactive for years. Even under such a situation, the authors would like to propose introducing common currency in Asia for the following reasons: First, digital currency can be issued without paper banknotes. Second, integration and interrelation in the field of industry and trade in Asia have progressed drastically, backed (boosted) by the rise of China in the 2000s. Third, development and penetration (prevailing) of mobile devices not only in developed countries but also developing countries decreased the differences of financial services in the region which could contribute to financial inclusion. Fourth, political relationships in ASEAN countries as well as regional cooperation such as the progress of the Chiang Mai Initiative in ASEAN+3 have been further strengthened. Last and most important, new technologies including DLT and BCT enabled the implementation of common currency by solving challenges.

Considering the above, conditions to introduce ADCC have been fostered and prepared very much compared to the situation of the past.

Contrary to the impression that Asia's common currency is trying to follow the experience in Europe, the common currency existed historically in Asia. In the Middle Ages in Asia, Chinese currency was used (circulated) widely prevailing in Asia (outside China including Japan). For almost 500 years, there was no domestic currency in Japan using (prevailing) the Chinese coin (yuan). Japan was a 'yuanised country'. One of the reasons why Chinese yuan prevailed outside the country was based on the demands from merchants actively trading goods widely in the region instead of the political policy of China.

Business Flow of ADCC

Issuing and distributing procedures and mechanisms of ADCC are to be explained as follows: First, each country in the region provides its government bonds to the international organisation. Then, the international organisation issues ADCC (denominated) bonds backed by the government bonds as assets and returns the ADCC bonds to the central banks. The ADCC bond is recorded on the asset side of the balance sheet of the central banks. The central banks issue ADCC and distribute the ADCC to the general public. Concept to issue ADCC is shown in Figure 9.2.

ADCC is recorded on the liability side of the balance sheets of central banks. When the ADCC returns back to the central bank which issued the ADCC possibly through other central banks, the ADCC is no longer the currency, and the data are stored at the central banks and the international organisation as well. By using such stored data, counterfeit ADCC should be identified (found). Specific flow of providing government bonds from ASEAN+3 central banks, issuing ADCC bonds, and issuing ADCC is illustrated in Figure 9.3.

1. Central banks in the region provide government bonds to an international organization.

2. The international organization issues ADCC bonds backed by the Gov. bonds

Note: "**ADCC bond**" is "ADCC (denominated) bond"

3. Central banks issue ADCC backed by the ADCC bonds

Figure 9.2 Concept to issue ADCC
Source: authors' elaboration.

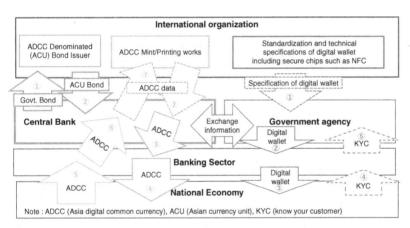

Figure 9.3 Asia Digital Common Currency (ADCC): issuing processes
Source: authors' elaboration.

Technological Features of ADCC Particularly Digital Wallet

Technological features of a digital wallet using contactless IC (NFC chip) are to be discussed here. Contactless smart cards with Near Field Communication (NFC) chips are widely used for a variety of purposes as a matured technology in Japan and globally. A point of sale (POS) terminal (contactless IC card reader/writer) emits electromagnetic waves to the card with an antenna inside. When the

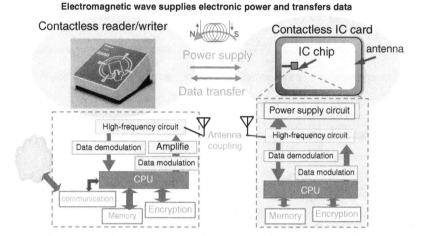

Figure 9.4 Outline of electronic money transfer (payment) at merchant shops
Source: authors' elaboration on NTT Data.

electromagnetic wave crosses through the antenna (or the antenna moves in a magnetic field), electric current is induced (electricity is generated),[2] which supplies electric power to the NFC chip inside. Under this scheme, electric power is provided from POS terminals to digital wallets as well as information necessary for payments being transferred. In other words, no battery is necessary inside the contactless IC card, which means almost maintenance free for the wallet. Outline of technological features is shown in Figure 9.4.

Security of ADCC

One of the most important issues for digital currencies may be to ensure both security (preventing illegal activities) and privacy. The former may be preventing counterfeit money (duplication of ADCC) from happening. AML/CFT may also be an important issue for security. The latter may be securing anonymity.

With respect to the security of ADCC, a tamper-resistance device such as NFC chip is used to make off-line payment securely as explained above, which means DLT can't be applied for off-line payments. Also, payment records (history of payment) are kept by

---

[2] Fleming's right-hand rule (theory).

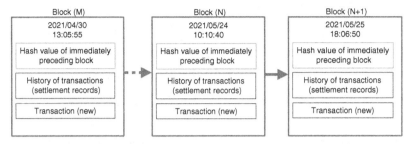

Figure 9.5 Outline of transaction records by applying blockchain technology
Source: authors' elaboration.

utilising BCT to further strengthen the security.[3] More specifically, payment-related information such as amount, time when the payment completed, digital device IDs of digital wallets for both payer and payee, etc. are processed by hash function and recorded as shown in Figure 9.5.

In order to prevent transaction records (history of payments) from being longer which could cause system performance problem when transferring the ADCC from one digital device to other, banks are encouraged to return ADCC to the central bank soon after receiving them from merchants to clear the transaction records replacing the ADCC to new one, which will make the transaction process faster and rapid again. Also, this kind of market practice will make illegal activities be captured sooner. KYC information such as the name and related personal information of payer and payee may be very useful to capture illegal activities such as money laundering as well as counterfeit ADCC. However, if such personal information is held by (disclosed to) central banks, anonymity may not be guaranteed. Therefore, the KYC information such as the owner of digital devices (digital wallet, mobile wallet, digital vault, etc.) is managed and controlled not by the central bank but by a relevant government agency, which may need to be newly established for this purpose. Outline image is shown in Figure 9.6.

---

[3] With respect to the security measure to identify and prevent counterfeit ADCC, a method (original method) using PKI is proposed by the author: refer to JP2009020848A – Electronic money issued by central bank or institute having equivalent function as legal tender – Google Patents. Available online: www.patents.google.com/patent/JP2009020848A/en.

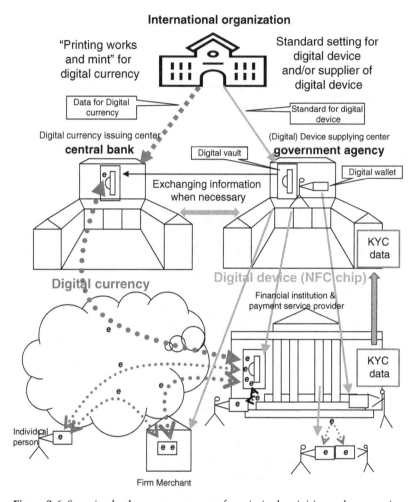

Figure 9.6 Securing both countermeasures for criminal activities and anonymity
Source: authors' elaboration.

If a central bank finds a counterfeit digital currency, it should
be reported to the police agency immediately as well as to the government agency storing KYC information on digital devices to
identify the owner of the device which could be the source of the
illegal activity. Countermeasures for AML/CFT are also conducted
by the cooperation of relevant authorities such as the central banks
and government agencies together with banks and merchants by

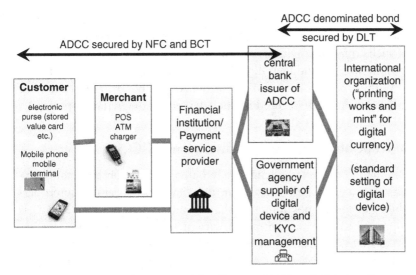

Figure 9.7 An image of issuing and distributing ADCC and digital wallet
Source: authors' elaboration.

distributing blacklists of digital devices which are used for such illegal activities. As explained above, the ADCC proposal can secure both anonymity and anti-criminal activities appropriately by establishing an institutional framework.

The ADCC returned to the central bank will be sent to the international organisation to check the integrity of the ADCC. An image of distribution and return of ADCC and digital wallet is shown in Figure 9.7.

When the ADCC returned to the central bank and/or international agency, the authenticity of the currency is checked as follows: first, trade history records of ADCC are checked by the central banks.[4] Then, the returned ADCC is sent to the international organisation where all records of issued ADCCs are stored in a database.

The international organisation checks the ADCC with the records in the database. If a fraudulent ADCC such as duplication of ADCC is found, investigation on the issue will be conducted by informing the police agency and government agency recording and managing KYC

---

[4] Each ADCC keeps record of trades (history) including ID numbers of digital wallets in which the ADCC was stored. Central banks have information on digital wallets such as black list of it.

of digital wallets. Survey and investigation for such illegal activities should be conducted thoroughly. Also, in order to prevent recurrence of such criminal activities, relevant measures such as distributing information (list of fraudulent digital wallet ID numbers) are to be taken.

With respect to the handling of the ADCC bonds, the integrity of information can be secured by the DLT preventing data tampering.

Interoperability and Standardisation of ADCC

One of the biggest challenges may be harmonisation and standardisation of digital currencies from the viewpoint of global interoperability including possibility of sharing infrastructures. The ADCC is supposed to co-exists with local currencies. Considering the current trend that digitalisation of local currencies will also progress, it may be an important issue that ADCC can be exchanged with local currencies conveniently and user friendly. Therefore, interoperability among digital currencies and sharing system infrastructures of common currency will be an important issue for the benefits of users to enjoy the advantages of digital currencies. Following are possible issues for standardisation of digital currencies.

1. Digital currency should be protected by a device with physical tamper-resistance such as NFC chip by adopting 'stored-value' type.
2. Payment records (history of payments) are kept by using a hush function and BCT[5] to prevent tampering.
3. In order to secure both anonymity and security measures for illegal activities such as counterfeit digital currency and Money Laundering and Financing of Terrorism (ML/FT), institutional framework is to be introduced that is separating the role of digital currency issuer (central bank) and KYC managing authority[6] (government agency).
4. With respect to network protocols and telecommunication technologies and specifications, the conventional measures which are already used for electronic money systems are to be adopted as much as possible.

---

[5] BCT here is not a DLT. Payment records are kept by using PKI or hash function as a history of payments. But such records are not shared with other nodes (digital devices).

[6] The authority is responsible for information of the owner of digital devices to prevent and identify illegal activities when happening.

It may be a possible (necessary) way to utilise International organisations for Standardisation such as ISO/TC68 AG5 (digital currencies) and SC2WG17 (security of digital currencies).

Considering these kinds of challenges, in particular the importance of interoperability with the highest level of security, close communication and cooperation among central banks and government agencies together with the international organisation are necessary and most important to provide secure and safe ADCC.

Providing Assets from ASEAN+3 Countries

In order for the international organisation to issue ADCC-denominated bonds, member countries provide government bonds of individual countries to the international organisation (ADB or AMRO for example in ASEAN+3). Following may be an example of such process. In case of Thailand, the international organisation opens securities account at the Thailand Securities Depository (TSD) which is the Central Securities Depository (CSD) in Thailand. The international organisation obtains the government bonds from Bank of Thailand or Thai government. Also, in case of Japan, the international organisation opens securities account at Bank of Japan (BOJ) and obtains Japanese government bonds being transferred from BOJ or Japanese government through BOJ-NET. As such, the international organisation needs to open securities accounts at the government book-entry systems in ASEAN+3 countries. Also, the international organisation may need to be a participant of Real-Time Gross Settlement (RTGS) system opening current account at central banks of individual countries in ASEAN+3 as a direct participant or entrusting a direct participant as an indirect participant without opening current account depending on the rules and regulations of each country.

More specifically, first, the international organisation such as AMRO opens a security account at the CSD (book-entry system) for government bond in each country in ASEAN+3 to obtain government bonds from central banks in ASEAN+3 as shown in Figure 9.8.

In case, the country can issue government bonds by utilizing DLT, the tokenised government bonds can directly be provided to the international organisation without through CSD.

Figure 9.8 Image of providing government bonds from each economy to AMRO
Source: authors' elaboration.

Issuing ADCC Bonds Utilising DLT and BCT

There may be some possible ways for the international organisation to issue ADCC (denominated) bonds by utilising the latest technologies such as DLT and BCT. The most possible option may be issuing the ADCC bonds as security tokens utilising DLT and BCT.

Outstanding amount of ADCC bonds is directly related with the value of ADCC and stability of it as well. Also, issuing ADCC bonds may correspond to the 'European Currency Union' established based on the Maastricht Trade agreed by member countries to issue euros. Certainly, though issuing ADCC may be very much different from the currency union in Europe in terms of historical background, scale, influence, etc., the issuance of ADCC will have significant meaning and role to have stable common currency in Asia. ADCC bonds are to be issued in a form of digital securities without depending on its transfer of ownership (entitlement) on a CSD located in a country.

Legal and regulatory framework to issue digital securities has already been stipulated in some countries. In the case of Japan, the amendment of 'Financial Instruments and Exchange Act' in May 2020 clearly defined digital securities including 'Electronic record transfer right' and 'security token offering', etc. In other words, 'security token' is defined as 'digital securities'. Also, 'electronic record transfer right' explained as something like 'deemed securities (security token)'.

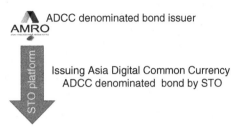

Issuing ADCC

Figure 9.9 Image of issuing ADCC-denominated bonds using CSDs.
Source: authors' elaboration.

Issuing digital securities (security token) may be generally the same with that of conventional securities. The international organisation is an issuer and central banks in the region are investors obtaining the securities (ADCC bonds). Considering the nature of the issuance, it is not a public offering since the investors are just the central banks. The important point is that creditors are managed by the bond registry based on the blockchain platform establishing the ownership (entitlement) of the bonds without depending on a CSD located in a certain country. Definitely new technologies including DLT and BCT enable this kind of advantages.

Important issues such as operator of the blockchain platform, paying agency, rating of the ADCC bonds, etc. may be decided based on the discussions at the international organisation by member central banks and government agencies. An image of issuing ADCC bonds is illustrated in Figure 9.9.

Member central banks are connected with the international organisation and with each other by a peer-to-peer network to transfer (obtain) the ADCC bonds from the international organisation through the blockchain platform.

Issuing ADCC Backed by ADCC Bonds

Issuing ADCC is to be done by central banks (or relevant government authorities) in ASEAN+3. The international organisation (AMRO or

ADB for example) may work as a kind of mint and/or printing bureau[7] to issue ADCC for ASEAN+3 countries in this case.

When the central banks issue ADCC, the ADCC is recorded on the liability side of the balance sheet of the central banks. When the ADCC is withdrawn by a commercial bank, the same amount is debited from the current account of the commercial bank opened at the central bank. In this case, outstanding balance of ADCC may need to be backed by ADCC bonds[8] because the central bank may not be the last resort of ADCC as a currency.

During the initial phase of the ADCC issuance, the exchange rate of ADCC may be decided by adopting the AMU calculated by Research Institute of Economy, Trade and Industry (RIETI), which may be one of the most important challenges for ADCC to be studied. Having said that, the rate (value) of the ADCC will be decided by the markets soon or later because ADCC will be traded freely in the markets. For more detail, please refer to the 'Asia Digital Common Currency (ADCC) challenges and opportunities – particularly (i) common currency-denominated bond issuance and (ii) calculation of currency denomination' published (in Japanese).

With respect to the wholesale payments, ADCC may be distributed through blockchain platforms just like the ADCC bonds. Having said that for the general purpose (retail) payments, ADCC may be distributed through digital devices such as smartphones as digital wallets. Interoperability and standardisation for transferring ADCC between the central banks are very important issues. The central banks and government agencies need to cooperate and discuss the issue at the international organisation. Issuing and transferring ADCC may be hybrid (on-line and off-line) having ADCC ledger mainly in central banks in the region. Possible patterns for issuing and distributing ADCC may be shown in Figure 9.10.

---

[7] In case AMRO plays a role of a mint or printing works in ASEAN+3, ADCC is delivered as data from AMRO to central banks (electronic vaults) in ASEAN+3 through a network which connects AMRO with the central banks. The data for ADCC don't have value as currency until issued by the central banks. AMRO does not have such a function and/or role currently, nor does ADB.

[8] Outstanding amount of ADCC does not necessarily be covered by ADCC bonds by 100 per cent but may be covered up to a certain percent by the assets depending on the agreed rule to keep the value and stability of ADCC.

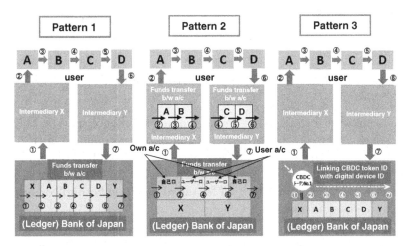

Figure 9.10 Possible patterns of CBDC ledger
Source: authors' elaboration on Bank of Japan data.

In case of off-line mode, essential information to be saved in contactless IC chips which are to be installed in digital devices (mobile wallet and electronic purse, etc.) is to be provided under the standardisation by the international organisation to ASEAN+3 government agencies. Specifications of the IC (NFC) chips are to be standardised.

Advantages of ADCC: Monetary Policy and Financial Stability

Advantages of digital currency from a macroeconomic perspective may be (i) enabling settlement digitally and (ii) ensuring effectiveness of monetary policy operation. Other than these, when ADCC is introduced as a regional currency, not only the advantages of digital currency within the country but also the benefits as common currency to be used for cross-border payment. Also, the advantage as officially controlled currency is different from private crypto currencies.

Enabling Settlement Digitally

One of the advantages of ADCC is to enable settlement immediately with less cost. In Asia, the digitalisation of the economy has been developed and expanding all over the countries globally. Digitalisation of business processes of trade has also been promoted. Introduction of digital currency may meet such trends and requirements.

Reduction of Fee (Commission) for International (Workers) Remittance

As mentioned before, cross-border worker remittance may be able to be securely completed freely with little or no commission (fee). Particularly, when international remittance with mobile phones is implemented, cross-border transferability of ADCC will be secure and convenient. Also, it may be used for micro-financing both to conduct finance and get refunded.

Furthermore, with ADCCs, remittance between companies will be cheaper than before. In the ASEAN+ 3 region, since the supply chain is well developed, the production and sales of companies are already integrated across the border as a region. Institutional development such as the FTA (Free Trade Agreement) has promoted intra-regional trade. Meanwhile, financial services were segmented. The development of intra-regional payment systems using a digital common currency will provide financial services that respond to the progress of economic integration in production and trade.

Stable Monetary Policy Implementation for Developing (Dollarised) Countries

If ADCC is adopted as a legal tender in a country whose monetary policy is not stable, ADCC may offer a reasonable way to conduct stable monetary operation. As already mentioned, stable seigniorage will be secured for the countries.

Reduction of Social Cost

By introducing ADCC, social costs may be reduced. Generally, digital currency like ADCC has high user-friendliness and convenience reducing service time at a merchant such as operation time for POS machines, etc., which could reduce workload and time for payment. Also, if ADCC is widely accepted, it could be an alternative payment instrument for physical coin, which will also reduce handling cost and workload of physical coin.

Securing Safety and Security

ADCC is much more secure than the private virtual coin stored and managed by virtual currency exchanges, because ADCC is protected by not only cryptographic measures (encryption) but also physical hardware with tamper resistance (IC chips such as NFC). ADCC will also have measures to address the requirements from Financial Action Task Force (FATF) and Bank Secrecy Act (BSA) without having negative effects for anonymity.

Prevention of Direct and Physical Transmission of Infectious Diseases

When cash is used as a payment method, it is generally handed over, and there is a risk that viruses and pathogens could be physically and directly transmitted via cash or credit card.[9] On the other hand, when using digital currencies such as ADCCs, (i) getting closer a card or mobile device with a built-in NFC (contactless IC chip) to a POS terminal (less than 10 cm), (ii) mobile device or terminal by reading QR code with the attached scanner, and (iii) electronically transferring between mobile devices, etc., the currency (data) is transmitted without physical intermediaries, and payment is completed. Therefore, by using ADCCs, direct transmission of viruses and pathogens can be considerably avoided.

Providing Fair (Equal) Services (Financial Inclusion)

Some countries in ASEAN+3 issue a unique card linked with a unique number such as national ID and social security number for all people (nationals) of the countries. If such a national ID and/or social security number can be stored safely in a chip (NFC for example), ADCC can also be saved in the chip securely. As such, all people (nationals) in the country will be able to have an electronic wallet for ADCC. Government payment and expenditure such as social welfare and pension can be transferred to the electronic wallet. The wallet can be

---

[9] Auer et al. (2020) point out 'Scientific evidence suggests that the probability of transmission via banknotes is low when compared with other frequently touched objects, such as credit card terminals or PIN pads'.

used for receiving workers remittance from outside the country, too. Financial inclusion is one of the most important issues for a government to provide as fair services.

Vitalizing Regional Activities and Enhancing Globalisation

Through the discussions by the government agencies and central banks particularly by the international organisation in ASEAN+3, regional activities will be enhanced. ADCC may be a feasible topic of discussion if environmental conditions become mature in the near future. In such a case, it may be an important issue that large and small countries have equal voices. ADCC will be a global economic infrastructure that can avoid the inadequate situation in which large powers dominate discussions.

This concept may be applicable for a more global range if ASEAN+3, ADB/AMRO, and ADCC are replaced by G20, BIS/IMF, and Special Drawing Right (SDR), respectively. Then, global digital common currency (GDCC) can be sent and received globally (refer to Figure 9.11).

'Common Currency' and Not 'Single Currency'

In this proposal, it is assumed that ADCC and national currencies are simultaneously circulating in each country.

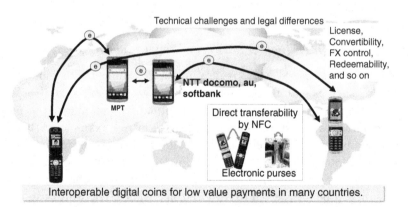

Figure 9.11 International remittance and cross-border payments using ADCC
Note: This slide shows only a possible future image and does not explain any current solutions.
Source: authors' elaboration.

In the case of Europe, in 1998, the national currencies were integrated into a single currency, the euro. At the same time, it aimed to make the European financial market a single market. This reflected the strong political will towards economic integration in Europe at that time. The single currency had the great effect of making Europe's financial markets efficient, but it was regarded as a drawback to deprive the member countries of monetary policy freedom. On the other hand, the situation in which a common currency coexists with national currencies is complicated and inferior to a single currency in terms of financial market integration. However, such a situation would be more appropriate because it is a more flexible system that maintains the degree of freedom in monetary policy to some extent, and that political will is relatively weak in Asia compared to Europe.

Remaining Challenges and Possible Opportunities

In order to actually implement the ADCC, there are still many remaining challenges. The following are some of them.

Risk of Capital Flight

As an issue inherent to digital currency, policy-related challenges including capital flight need to be discussed. It may be pointed out that capital flight could happen more easily because of digital currency if circumstances exceed some limit and if no effective measures are taken just as happened in some countries in Asia. Bitcoin increased publicity in East Europe because it caused capital flight there. This kind of capital flight is a serious threat against financial stability. However, being different from Bitcoin which does not have central control mechanisms, the ADCC which has central control mechanisms can be regulated by central banks and monetary authorities of member countries proactively.

Asset-Backed ADCC

Since issuing ADCC for a central bank is not the issuance of its own currency (legal tender), ADCC may be issued backed by the ADCC-denominated bonds as security deposit for issuance. How much the deposit needs to be secured would be another challenge. By the way, in Japan one half of the outstanding balance of electronic money needs to be entrusted to a reliable third party as a security deposit for issuance by a private company (stipulated by Payment Services Act). Also, when the international organisation issues the ADCC bonds, to what extent government bonds from member countries need to be held as assets would also be discussed.

Other Challenges

When ADCC is actually being used, there remain many challenges. One of the challenges is penetration of mobile wallets with secure IC chips such as NFC in ASEAN+3. With respect to the general acceptability, it is expected to provide (distribute) contactless smart cards with secure chips such as NFC having national ID inside to entire people (nationals) free by the government in ASEAN+3. Also, distribution of terminals and/or tablets to read such information from the smart card for payment and other business purposes. The physical location (country) of ADCC operation centre (Digital coin issuing centre and Digital device supplying centre) and its backup site could be a serious political challenge. Interface specifications and application interface (API) for the POS terminals and with other devices will also be a challenge. In order to make the ADCC concept upgrade to actual implementation initiative, some technical challenges remain. Following are possible remaining challenges from business practice perspective: (i) the framework for each government and central bank invest to the international organisation (legal background, budget, and process), (ii) laws and regulations for the international organisation to conduct such an operation as a printing bureau/mint of ADCC, (iii) cooperation and competition with other CBDCs, (iv) competition with current banking system in particular with big banks, and (v) possible impact to monetary operations. When issuing ADCC as currency in ASEAN+3, a basket currency unit such as ACU may be considered. Having said that, considering the enormous workload and time needed for starting the euro in Europe, it may be extremely difficult to issue ADCC. Therefore, so many challenges need to be solved.

Conclusions

Issuing digital currency itself has already reached a practical stage of implementation technologically. However, it may need further discussions to issue it as the legal tender of a country. Having said that, considering the characteristics of the digital currency, it may be a possible way if it is used (i) as a measure for small value cross-border remittance and (ii) prepaid 'value-based' payment instruments, circulating in ASEAN+3 region. Considering the trend in ASEAN+3 where financial and economic activities across the border have been increasing drastically, the introduction of regional digital common currency such as ADCC would be beneficial for the region supporting cross-border transactions providing a convenient way of payment and remittance to the people working in different countries. Furthermore, if ADCC is well accepted by the society and has increased creditworthiness, AMRO may be able to issue ADCC exceeding the asset obtained from the ASEAN+3 governments and central banks in the future.

Many people kindly provided the authors' valuable information, advice, and comments. The authors would like to express their sincere gratitude to the people who kindly provided such information as well as made insightful comments and advice. Also, this chapter is written based on such information and advice, but the opinions expressed here belong to the authors and don't reflect any official views of JICA, CBM, ADB, Osaka University of Economics, Kobe University, and/or any other organisations.

Appendix to Chapter 9. Electronic Money and Digital Currency

Taiji Inui and Wataru Takahashi

Electronic money has similar functions and provides similar services with digital currency though electronic money is categorised as a prepaid instrument legally and widely used as a daily payment instrument in Japan and globally. Electronic money systems have been operated without serious incident for many years. Outline of the electronic money (Suica) network is illustrated in Figure 9.12.

The electronic money system can provide payment and settlement services at merchant shops off-line (locally) without being connected with the centre server of the system. The 'stored value (electronic money)' can be transferred from a 'digital wallet' to a POS terminal based on NFC technology. From this perspective, electronic money may be categorised as 'token-based type' digital money at the merchant

---

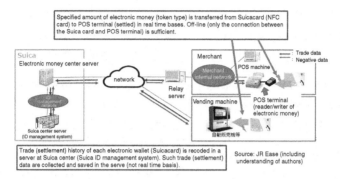

Figure 9.12 Outline of electronic money (Suica) network
Source: authors' elaboration.

shop. More specifically, the NFC chip with tamper-resistance security is used as the digital wallet to store the value (electronic money). The electronic money (balance) is safely recorded to the NFC chip. The value (electronic money) is transferred from a wallet (with NFC chip) to a POS machine (with NFC chip) just like handing over banknotes. A unique ID is allocated to each NFC chip which represents a digital wallet (also to a chip stored in a POS machine).

Whereas, the electronic money system is managed by the centre server system, centrally and remotely. Information including balance of stored value (electronic money amount) stored in the NFC chip is tried to be recorded and managed by the centre server based on the ID allocated to the wallet (and POS server). This means electronic money is managed just like an account-based type of digital currency, though replication of the information from POS machines of merchants to the centre server is not real time (possibly one a day or more frequently). The ID of the NFC chip (digital wallet) is not always linked with the owner of the wallet (personal information) unless registered as a commuter pass, credit card, bank card, and/or mobile phone. As such, electronic money systems may be categorised as token-based, distributed, and local type of digital money at merchant shop side as well as account, centralised, and remote type of digital money at centre server system side, which could be regarded as hybrid type of digital money.

Electronic money is stipulated as a prepaid instrument by Payment Services Act in Japan, which means that electronic money is not a legal tender or having unrestricted use power. As such, electronic money could be refused when used for payment or asking to exchange to legal tender. Also, electronic money (in Japan) doesn't have complete transferability between end users depending on the electronic money system (even though technologically possible). Therefore, electronic money can be used the same as cash (banknotes) but has some differences.

Bibliography

Adrian, T., Mancini-Griffoli, T., 2019. 'The Rise of Digital Money'. FinTech Notes, No. 19/001, *International Monetary Fund.*

Asian Development Bank 2020. 'Next steps for ASEAN+3 CSD-RTGS linkages, A Progress Report of the CSIF'. Cross-border Settlement Infrastructure Forum (CSIF).

Auer, R., Cornell, G. Frost, J. 2020a. 'Covid-19, cash, and the future of payments'. BIS Bulletin No3. *Bank for International Settlement.*

Auer, R., Cornell, G. Frost, J. 2020b. 'Rise of the central bank digital currencies: drivers, approaches and technologies'. BIS Working Papers No 880. *Bank for International Settlement.*

Bank of Thailand 2018. 'Project DLT Scripless Bond'.

Bank of Thailand 2019. 'Inthanon Phase2'.

Brunnermeier, M.K., Harold, J., Landau, J.P. 2019. 'The Digitalization of Money'. Working Paper 26300. *National Bureau of Economic Research.*

Carney, M. 2019. 'The Growing Challenges for Monetary Policy in the current International Monetary and Financial System' Bank of England. Central Bank Speech.

Cheng, J., Lawson, A.N., Wong, P. 2021. 'Preconditions for a general-purpose central bank digital currency'. FEDS Notes, Federal Reserve.

Committee on Payment and Settlement Systems and the Group of Computer Experts of the central banks of the Group of Ten countries 2019. 'Security of Electronic Money'. *Bank for International Settlements.*

European Central Bank 2020. 'Report on a digital euro'.

Hyperledger 2018. 'Hyperledger Fabric'.

Inoue, T. 2020. 'Digital Yen- the time when the Bank of Japan issues Digital Currency (in Japanese)'. Nihon-Keizai-shimbunsya.

Inui, T. 2007. 'Electronic money issued by central bank or institute having equivalent function as legal tender'. Google Patent. Available online: patents.google.com/patent/JP2009020848A/en.

Inui, T. 2010. 'A proposal to start a survey on electronic coins as a common currency issued by an international organisation choosing SDR as the currency unit'. (Proposed to BIS).

Inui, T. 2014. 'Common Electronic Coin'. (Proposed to IMF).

Inui, T., Takahashi, W., Ishida, M. 2020. 'A Proposal for Asia Digital Common Currency'. Discussion Paper Series DP2020-19. *Research Institute for Economics and Business Administration*. Kobe University.

Ishida, M. 2006. 'Exchange Rate Instability: Japan's Micro-Macro Experiences and Implications for China'. *China and World Economy*, Vol. 14, No. 2. Institute of World Economics and Politics, Chinese Academy of Social Sciences.

Ishida, M. 2014. 'Revisiting East-Asian Community – From Functional Approach to Institutional Approach'. *International Economic Review*. Institute of World Economics and Politics, Chinese Academy of Social Sciences.

Lagarde, C. 'Winds of Change: The Case for New Digital Currency'. *International Monetary Fund*.

Masashi, N. 2020. 'Virtual Currency vs Central Bank – Digital currency: who will prevail (in Japanese)'. Shincho-sya.

Masayoshi, A. 2019. 'Should the Bank of Japan Issue a Digital Currency?'. *Bank of Japan*.

Masayoshi, A. 2020. 'Central Bank Digital Currency and the Future of Payment and Settlement Systems'. *Bank of Japan*.

Nakamoto, S. 2008. 'Bitcoin: A Peer-to-Peer Electronic Cash System'.

Nakayama, Y. 1998. 'Electronic Money Technology and Patent'. Institute of Monetary and Economic Studies, Bank of Japan.

Nakayama, Y., Hitemitsu, M., Abe, M., Fujisaki, E. 1997. 'On Measures to Implement Electronic Money (in Japanese)'. Bank of Japan, Institute of Monetary and Economic Study.

Release master "Hyperledger Fabric Docs", Hyperledger Fabric, 2019.

Study Group on Legal Issues regarding Central Bank Digital Currency 2019. 'Report of the Study Group on Legal Issues regarding Central Bank Digital Currency (in Japanese)'. Bank of Japan, Institute for Monetary Economic Studies.

Study Group on the Virtual Currency Exchange Services 2019. 'Report from Study Group on Virtual Currency Exchange Services'. Financial Services Agency.

Takahashi, W. 2014. *Financial Cooperation in East Asia: Potential Future Directions*, in 'Trade, Investment and Economic Integration', Vol. 2, Ch. 2, for Globalization, Development and Security in Asia. World Scientific.

Takahashi, W. 2020a. 'Reviving Yongle coin (Eirakusen): The Future of Money and Asian Digital Common Currency (in Japanese)'. Financial Forum, Kyoto Bank Economic Research Institute.

Takahashi, W. 2020b. 'Reviving Eirakusen: The Future of Money and the Asian Digital Common Currency (in Japanese)'. Financial Forum, Kyoto Sogo Keizai-kenkyu-jo.

Takamura, Y., Syunji, I., Ryotaro, S. 2018. 'Regional Financial Coopera-
tion Related Meetings in Asia'. Ministry of Finance.
Yanagawa, N., Hiromi, Y. 2019. 'Digital Innovation, Data Revolution and
Central Bank Digital Currency'. The Bank of Japan Working Paper Series
No. 19-E2.
Yoshiyuki, A. 2018. *World First Bond Issuance Scheme Utilizing Block-
chain by World Bank (in Japanese)*, in 'Kinyuu-Zaisei-jijou'. Kinyuu-
Zaisei-jijou Kenyukai.

PART IV

Enabling Financial Inclusion and ESG with Distributed Ledger Technology

10 | Distributed Ledger Technology and Financial Inclusion

HARISH NATARAJAN AND BIAGIO BOSSONE

Introduction

This chapter is about financial inclusion – where the world stands on it, the progress achieved so far, the existing gaps, and what still needs to be solved to address the gaps – and whether DLT can offer a solution for progressing further on the way to facilitate access to finance by people that are still excluded from it.

DLT is a type of secure database, or ledger, that is replicated across multiple sites, countries, or institutions with no centralised controller. Essentially, it is a way of keeping track of who owns a financial, physical, or electronic asset, with the information being maintained and updated securely for an entire network of users by users themselves rather than by a central agency (Figure 10.1). Its name is commonly used as the generic descriptor for any distributed, encrypted database and application that is shared by an industry or private consortium, or which is open to the public.

How can similar applications help in the process of including the financially excluded? Indeed, financial inclusion is often cited as one of the many benefits of DLT by many start-ups, researchers, and companies active in the DLT space.[1] Yet, there are reasons for being more cautious, recognising that, while the potential for DLT to deliver significant benefits is there, many fundamental building blocks need to be put in place before that potential can be fully realised.

The purpose of this chapter is to identify these building blocks and discuss how DLT can contribute to financial inclusion once they are

---

[1] Just as examples, see *Inclusion through Distribution: How Blockchain Supports Financial Inclusion*, Deloitte China, Available at www2.deloitte.com/cn/en/pages/financial-services/articles/how-blockchain-supports-financial-inclusion.html; *Distributed Ledger Technologies and Financial Inclusion*, International Telecommunication Union, ITU-T Focus Group Digital Financial Services, 03/2017; Ramanathan, S. 2021. *How DLT Can Improve Financial Services*. Forbes Technology Council, 20 August 2021.

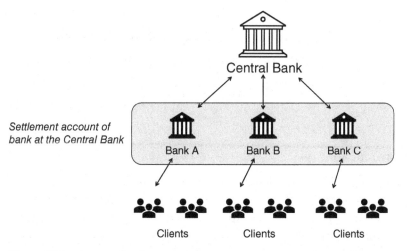

Figure 10.1a A centralised payment system
Note: DLT uses cryptography to allow participants on the network to record new transactions on the ledger in a secure way, without the need for a central certifying authority.
Source: authors' elaboration.

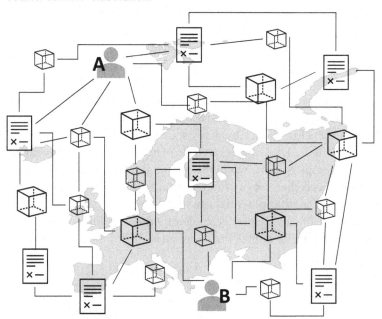

Figure 10.1b An illustrative example of a distributed ledger system similar to Bitcoin (blockchain)
Source: authors' elaboration.

established. The second section defines financial inclusion, gives an update on financial inclusion progress at the global level, and briefly recalls the basic policies that have been adopted so far to include financially excluded people. The third section discusses the role DLT can play in the context of financial inclusion and the factors that can influence such role, and the fourth section identifies use cases of DLT as a solution to support financial inclusion. The last section summarises the main issues.

Financial Inclusion: Definition, Status, and Reasons for Exclusion

Let's start by offering a working definition of financial inclusion. It is 'access to, and usage of, relevant financial services that are appropriate for, and meet the needs of, the users'. The key words here are *access, usage, relevant,* and *appropriate.*

In general, the financial services generally discussed in the context of financial inclusion include payments, savings, credit, and insurance.

Starting with payments, it must be noted that their execution requires access to a 'transaction account' that allows users to make and receive payments for the day-to-day needs and to store funds in a safe way. Even the most basic bank accounts, much as any accounts with other licensed deposit taking institutions (like credit unions and, in some countries, postal agencies) and e-money services (like prepaid card and mobile money) meet this definition.

Globally, around 69 per cent of adults have access to a transaction account (Figure 10.2). That leaves around 1.7 billion adults unbanked, nearly half-of-whom are in seven developing countries. This data is based on a triennial survey done by the World Bank (the Findex). This survey also enquires into the reasons why respondents may not have access to a transaction account. The reasons can be broadly grouped into: 'I have no need', 'it is too expensive', and 'I cannot get one'.

When we consider DLT as a solution for financial inclusion, we need to ask ourselves which one of these reasons would DLT really address. Drilling a bit further on the composition of the unbanked world population, a divide is apparent based on geography, income levels, gender, and education. Notice that the income level of a country by itself does not fully explain the financial inclusion gap

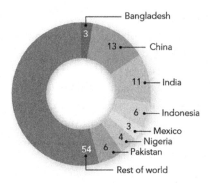

Figure 10.2a Adults without an account by economy (%), 2017
Note: Globally, of the 1.7 billion unbanked adults: 56% women, 50% live in the poorest 40% of households, 62% have a primary education or less, and 47% are out of the labour force.
Source: Global Findex Database.

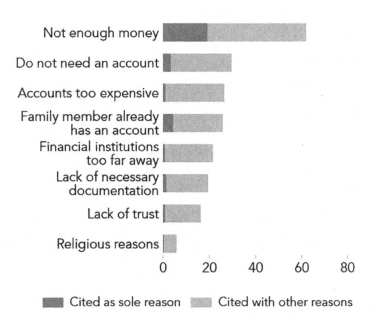

Figure 10.2b Adults without a financial institution account reporting barrier as a reason for not having one (%), 2017
Note: Respondents could choose more than one reason.
Source: Global Findex Database.

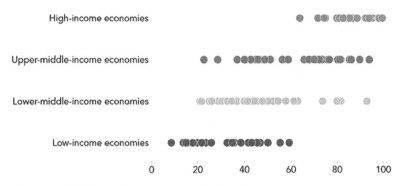

Figure 10.3 Adults with an account (%), 2017
Source: Global Findex Database.

(Figure 10.3), as even countries within a given income level show wide disparities among each other and substantial numbers of individuals and small businesses are not financially included in higher income countries. In fact, one sees a similar gap between high-income and lower-income countries and within countries between the top 60 per cent and bottom 40 per cent by income.

At a general level, looking across the range of financial services for individuals as well as for micro-small and medium enterprises, the reasons for exclusion can be explained by a combination of demand side and supply side factors (Figure 10.4). On the demand side, volatile and small incomes, geographical barriers, informality and lack of documentation and trust in financial institutions and financial literacy seem to be the most relevant factors. On the supply side, the factors include high operating costs, legacy business models, and limited innovation and competition.

In many countries, both the demand and supply side factors are being addressed in a holistic manner through a combination of policy interventions, including:

1. Legal and regulatory reforms that allow the operation of non-bank entities to directly offer basic transaction account features (like mobile money) and allow use of third-party agents, tiered know-your-customer requirements, and usage of alternative data like transaction account activity, utility bills and the like in credit worthiness assessments;

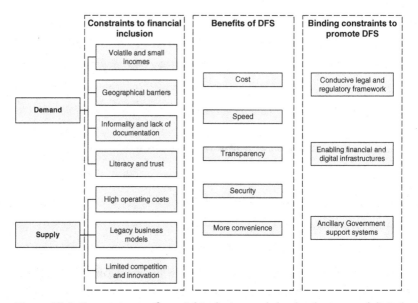

Figure 10.4 Constraints to financial inclusion and the development of digital financial services
Source: Digital Financial Services, World Bank Group.

2. the deployment of basic digital and financial infrastructure (like mobile telephony, digital IDs, payment systems, and credit reporting infrastructures); and

3. ancillary government systems and policies that encourage greater usage and access of financial services, simplify the compliance processes (e.g., filing tax returns and reporting of annual financial statements) that come with formalisation for smaller businesses, and make available data held with the government for use by financial service providers.

As a result, several developing countries have boot-strapped themselves from low levels of financial inclusion to levels where 70–80 per cent of adults have achieved access to transaction accounts over 5–10 years.

The Role of DLT

How can DLT improve on this process?

DLT offers several capabilities that, under some conditions, have the potential to address the factors impacting financial inclusion:

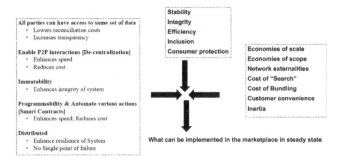

Figure 10.5 DLT features vs. economic forces vs. policy objectives
Source: authors' elaboration.

> The unified view of data enabled by DLT can lower the cost of provision of financial services.
> The potential to enable decentralisation can further lower costs by removing intermediaries and thereby lowering cost of provision of services.
> Data immutability would enable lowering reconcilition and verification costs and, in some contexts, it can increase confidence by assuring the integrity of data.
> Programmability enabled through the likes of 'smart contracts' can help automating processes and embedding financial services within real-world economic interactions, thereby lowering costs and creating more traction for users.[2]
> Lastly, the distributed nature of DLT can make the systems more resilient, thereby improving operational reliability, customer convenience, and confidence.

However, all these features must be seen against the economic forces that influence the provision of financial services and the policy decisions of the financial sector authorities. The result of the interaction of all these factors will determine what role DLT can play (Figure 10.5).

---

[2] A smart contract is a self-executing contract, whereby the terms of the agreement between the buyer and the seller are written into lines of code. The code controls the execution, and transactions are trackable and irreversible. The code and the agreements exist across a decentralised (DLT) network. Smart contracts allow for transactions and agreements to be carried out among anonymous parties without the need for a central authority, legal system, or external enforcement mechanism.

Economic forces such as economies of scale and scope, network externalities, the cost of searching for an ideal product or service, the cost
of building one's own package of financial services, and the inertia
of existing business processes and customer convenience will affect
(positively or negatively) the demand for DLT services and determine
incentives that will facilitate and possibly accelerate or, on the contrary, hamper DLT adoption.

Similarly, for all the talk of unbundling, de-centralisation and disintermediation, intermediaries like banks, custodians and payment
service providers (e.g., wallet providers) are still necessary for the
financial system to work: customers and business enterprises prefer
by far using services that are already packaged for them and sup-
plied by specialised providers (whose comparative advantage rests
precisely on their capacity to centralise, bundle, and intermediate
certain production and delivery functions), rather than having to
assemble various components of services made available separately
in various market segments (which would require investing considerable knowledge, time, and resources). Not to mention the inherent
advantages deriving for customers and businesses from the maturity
transformation, liquidity and credit creation, and risk management
services that banks and other financial intermediaries uniquely offer
to support their activities.

Thus, the demand for DLT will also be influenced by the importance that the public attaches to the role of intermediaries. And
yet, this influence will be dynamic: while service providers will not
be displaced, they may see their role in transactions change. New
providers will become relevant, and for the incumbents to remain
relevant, they will need to adapt to new activities and be ready to
service larger audiences at cheaper terms and more efficiently.[3] Also,
the idea is evolving whereby banks and nonbanks join (even multiple)

---

[3] With intermediaries facing the risk of becoming redundant, the DLT evolution
can be compared to the emergence of the Internet. Much like the economic
impact of the Internet has mostly affected consumer goods and services, DLT
could have similar implications for financial services and other products. In
the same vein, much as the Internet has caused a shift from a central platform-
based economy, where data were only infrequently used, to a decentralised
Author Hub account platform-based economy where data are a precious
commodity, the rise of DLT may cause a shift towards an economy where data
play the key role and new service providers can become relevant.

consortia – groups of companies – collaborating to develop common objectives and standards for DLT and playing different roles and offering different use cases in them.[4]

Further, the financial sector authorities will continue to shape the financial sector landscape to ensure that the public policy objectives of stability, efficiency, safety, inclusion, and consumer protection are safeguarded. For example, a permissionless model of DLT will raise policy issues, and the use of global stablecoins or foreign CBDCs will cause financial stability concerns; also, the likes of ICOs and cryptocurrency-based portfolios will bring up investor and consumer protection matters and will require the official recognition of ID mechanisms (as the recent FATF guidelines on digital ID notice[5]).

Another policy dimension that will soon become critical – and will influence, inter alia, DLT choices – is *ecological sustainability*. Under the mounting global pressure on governments worldwide to address climate change and environmental degradation issues, central banks and financial authorities will increasingly be called on to ensure that financial market infrastructures (FMIs) and services evolve consistently with ecological sustainability (Bossone and Natarajan).[6] This not only means strengthening the resilience of FMIs and financial service provision to ecological challenges; it will require making choices and inducing behaviours that reduce their ecological impact.

Also, while today authorities pursue a technology-neutral approach to oversight and regulation of FMIs and financial service provision – whereby it is for the market to choose technologies for applications to finance – they will be responsible for ensuring that the technologies adopted are ecologically sustainable. The choice for DLT or alternative solutions will thus be driven also by ecological considerations.

---

[4] Consortia offer various benefits. Through their network effects, an ecosystem has a greater opportunity to grow and become more dominant in the long run, thus gearing the incentives towards 'co-opetition' (a mix of cooperation and competition). The growth in consortia and the DLT ecosystem will create opportunities for new and incumbent providers. See The role of blockchain in banking: Future prospects for cross-border payments, OMFIF and CCB University, 2020, available at www.omfif.org/wp-content/uploads/2020/05/The-role-of-blockchain-in-banking.pdf.

[5] See Draft Updated Guidance for a risk-based approach to virtual assets and VASPs, report by the Financial Action Task Force, Sixth draft, Public consultation, March 2021.

[6] Bossone, B., H. Natarajan. *Central Banks, National Payment Systems, and Ecological Sustainability*. Unpublished data.

The net result of all these interactions will still leave several areas where DLT can help the cause of financial inclusion, subject to setting up the building blocks referred to earlier. A few illustrative opportunities are discussed next.

How Can DLT Support Financial Inclusion?

The first opportunity is cross-border payments, particularly small-value international migrant worker remittances. There is a clear linkage between these payment flows and economic well-being and financial inclusion. DLT-based approaches can enable shifts from the traditional correspondent banking model to one where transactions across a correspondent banking chain are processed in an atomic manner in real-time rather than in sequential message exchanges between each part of the chain, with an indeterminate amount of delay possible at each leg (Figure 10.6).

This could have significant cost-saving effects for businesses and individuals by improving the speed and reliability of cross-border payments. The introduction of global stablecoins and/or cross-border CBDCs on top of this could take this outcome one level further; yet, as mentioned earlier, there are financial sector policy concerns that will need to be addressed, as outlined in the recent report by the Financial Stability Board (FSB), before that becomes a feasible option.[7]

Several other innovations are underway, which should be noted. Feeling the pressure to innovate, incumbent banks and payment providers are embracing FinTech to improve their services so that consumers can conduct payments more conveniently, faster, and 24/7. For example, many incumbent banks are joining hands, in some cases also with non-banks, to develop fast payment networks and offer access to their deposit-based products via mobile apps.[8]

---

[7] See FSB, *Enhancing Cross-border Payments* – Stage 1 report to the G20, April 2020; CPMI, *Enhancing cross-border payments: building blocks of a global roadmap* – Stage 2 report to the G20, July 2020; and FSB, *Enhancing Cross-border Payments* – Stage 3 report to the G20, October 2020. FSB stands for Financial Stability Board. CPMI stands for Committee on Payments and Market Infrastructures.

[8] See, for instance, Petralia, K., T. Philippon, T. Rice, and N. Véron 2019. *Banking Disrupted? Financial Intermediation in an Era of Transformational Technology.* Geneva Reports on the World Economy 22, ICMB and CEPR.

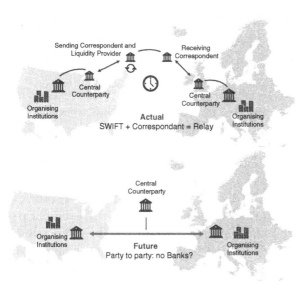

Figure 10.6a Cross-border payments
Source: authors' elaboration.

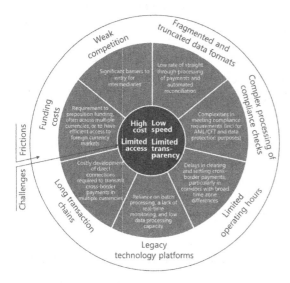

Figure 10.6b Cross-border payments
Source: Committee on Payments and Market Infrastructures, July 2020. 'Enhancing cross-border payments: building blocks of a global roadmap – Stage 2 report to the G20'. *Bank for International Settlements*, CPMI Papers No 193. The publication is available on the BIS website: www.bis.org/cpmi/publ/d193.pdf.

Furthermore, existing money transfer operators are increasingly supporting a wide variety of payment instruments and integrating them into payment systems in sending and receiving countries – including in some cases with fast payment systems.

Central banks are also increasingly considering extending access to the payment systems operated by them to FinTech players and operating their systems on a 24/7 basis, and FinTechs have extended the money transfer operator model for cross-border transfers by connecting to local payment infrastructures and banks or e-money providers on both sides of a transaction.

Closely related to this trend, a range of specialised providers have entered the market to establish white-label cross-border payment services, such as Earthport, MFS Africa, and Currencycloud.[9] Incumbent institutions and FinTechs can integrate with these white-label solutions to rapidly offer cross-border payment services to their clients.

Moreover, the global financial messaging network SWIFT has launched the Global Payments Initiative (SWIFT gpi) to bring transparency, speed, and reliability to correspondent banking transactions.[10] These initiatives could bring down fees in cross-border payments. While fees remain high for some regions, they have come down recently, and the progress is apparent, considering the range of low-cost services being introduced (as can be seen in the SmaRT indicator, which tracks the lowest cost providers meeting certain quality attributes, Figure 10.7).

In this context, it remains to be seen what additionality DLT can enable. Beyond cross-border payments, two more areas should be noted where there is very little automation, systems and processes are unorganised, and new needs have arisen as a consequence of the 'tokenisation of real-world assets' – a recent upshot of the incessant process of digital-economy innovations.

---

[9] Earthport is a company that provides cross-border payment services to banks, money transfer service providers and businesses via the world's largest independent ACH network. MFS Africa is the largest mobile money hub in Africa; it connects over 320 million mobile money wallets to enable cross-border payments for remittance companies, financial service providers, and global merchants. Currencycloud sells software for banks and FinTech firms to process cross-border payments.

[10] See *SWIFT gpi: The new norm in cross-border payments*, available at www.swift.com/our-solutions/swift-gpi.

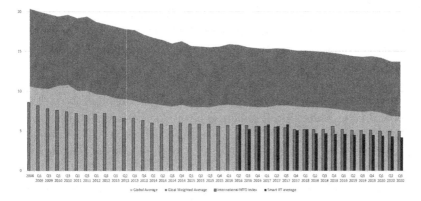

Figure 10.7 Low-cost providers are active in many markets
Note: The Global Average recorded a moderate increase from 6.67% (Q2 2020) to 6.75 (Q3 2020). The International MTO Index experienced a decrease over the quarter 6.81 (Q3 2020) from 6.95% (Q2 2020). This is the second consecutive quarter in which this figure has been recorded below 7%. The global weighted average decreased to 5% (Q3 2020) from 5.03% (Q3 2020). The Global SmaRT Average for Q3 2020 was recorded at 4.17%. Source: World Bank Remittances Prices Worldwide Database.

The first area involves **agricultural and commodity value chains**. In many developing countries, these chains are disorganised and very fragmented; they consist of a very long sequence of intermediate steps from production to final-destination markets and suffer from poor transparency (or lack thereof) from third-party stakeholders. Against this background, attention is increasing from the consumer side to proving provenance and the practices adopted in cultivation or production. The farmers or producers at the end of the value chain are unable to realise the right price for their products and are unable to prove their business potential and to secure access to the finance necessary to grow and expand their business.

DLT, along with other enablers (like access to basic payment services and identity) can help track the journey of the product and the practices adopted, thereby making it possible for the producers to extract a better price and to secure access to finance. Still, there would be a need for various trusted intermediaries to provide validation of such critical aspects as production practices and recording the journey of the product, implying that the value chain would not be fully disintermediated.

The second area involves **data management**. Worldwide, there is a strong move towards recognising that data and information concerning individuals, held by businesses and governments, do belong to the individuals to whom they relate, and, as owners, individuals need agency over these data and information. Laws are being introduced in several countries to grant this right – a case in point being the General Data Protection Regulation in the EU.[11] However, how this right should be exercised is not fully addressed. Here, DLT can play a critical role by allowing individuals to organise their own data and prove any specific attribute about themselves when needed on their own. This has implications for the usage of alternative data in credit decisioning and other processes in the financial sector.

Once again, however, one must notice that DLT is only part of the puzzle, and various other technologies and innovations are underway that can perform similar functions. As the Committee on Payments and Market Infrastructures (CPMI) and the World Bank have recently noted, selected advances in technology are proving relevant to payments, and their application to new payment products and services as well as new access channels can improve financial inclusion.[12] These include application programming interfaces (APIs), big data analytics, biometric technologies, cloud computing, contactless technologies (including quick response (QR) codes), digital identification, and the Internet of Things, which can all facilitate the delivery of new products and access modes.[13] New technologies not only offer new modes of accessing new products by means of electronic wallets, open

---

[11] See *Regulation (Eu) 2016/679 of the European Parliament and of the Council* of 27 April 2016 on the protection of natural persons with regard to the processing of personal data and on the free movement of such data.

[12] See *Payment aspects of financial inclusion in the fintech era*, report by the Committee on Payments and Market Infrastructures and the World Bank Group, Bank for International Settlements, Base, April 2020.

[13] Prominent examples of new products are instant payments, central bank digital currencies (CBDCs), and stablecoins. *Fast payments* are defined as payments in which the transmission of the payment messages and the availability of 'final' funds to the payee occur in real time or near-real time on as near to a 24-hour and seven-day (24/7) basis as possible. *CBDC* is a central bank liability, denominated in an existing unit of account, which serves both as a medium of exchange and a store of value. *Stablecoins* are crypto-assets that aim to maintain a stable value relative to a specified asset, or a pool or basket of assets (crypto-assets being broadly defined as private digital assets that use cryptography and are designed to work as a medium of exchange).

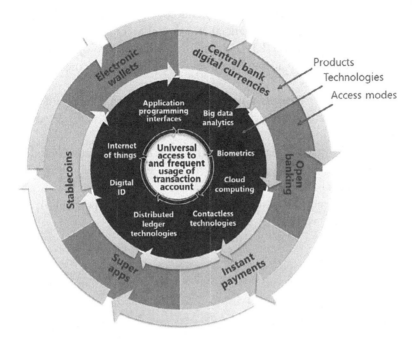

Figure 10.8 FinTech developments potentially relevant to the payment aspects of financial inclusion: the 'PAFI Fintech Wheel'
Source: Committee on Payments and Market Infrastructures – World Bank Group, April 2020. 'Payment aspects of financial inclusion in the fintech era'. *Bank for International Settlements and World Bank Group*, CPMI Papers No. 191. The publication is available on the BIS website: www.bis.org/cpmi/publ/d191.pdf.

banking, and super apps; they allow payments to be initiated via traditional transaction accounts and/or payment instruments (Figure 10.8).

Concluding Remarks

To summarise, the linkage between DLT and financial inclusion – and therefore the effectiveness of the former in supporting the achievement of the latter as a national policy objective – requires considering the following aspects:

– DLT should be seen in the context of ongoing innovations.
– DLT's link with financial inclusion is conditional on a number of building blocks and relies at a fundamental level on basic access to

payment services, ID, some key technology infrastructure (notably, mobile telephony), and financial and digital literacy.

- Further research on DLT is essential to solve for the optimal solution that takes into account economic forces and the financial sector policy objectives.
- Cross-border payments and corners of finance that have not seen much automation are prime candidates where DLT can contribute to financial inclusion.
- Consideration will have to be given to ecological sustainability issues, in particular by pursuing choices bearing minimum impact on climate change and the environment.
- There is a need to step-up international cooperation, particularly on cross-border aspects.

11 | *Banking, Blockchain, and ESG*

JOHN HO

Introduction

The popularity of cryptocurrencies and blockchain-based solutions is accelerating. Blockchain technology can help organisations drive more favourable enterprise environmental, social, and governance (ESG) outcomes. However, the technology has drawn scrutiny over energy consumption. Surging demand for cryptocurrencies and accelerating adoption of blockchain-based solutions have highlighted an important issue: the technology's growing energy consumption and its impact on our climate. Given the focus on sustainability, stakeholders such as *institutional investors* and environmental organisations have made public statements about how blockchain technology can exacerbate climate risk due to high energy consumption. But such claims are an oversimplification of highly complex and quickly evolving technological developments.

Blockchain's energy consumption, specifically Bitcoin mining, gained media attention following Tesla's *decision to suspend accepting Bitcoin* in 2021 as a form of payment due to climate concerns. The electric vehicle company further stated that it will resume allowing Bitcoin transactions once there is *confirmation of significant clean energy usage* in mining. Public, non-permissioned blockchains have created vast decentralised networks spanning across nations on which a range of goods and services are now being delivered. The value created over these networks, estimated at over US$2 trillion as at early 2022, has also created a fiercely competitive business environment to secure the digital assets awarded to actors hosting, verifying, and supporting activities on the blockchain.

The increasing interest from retail and institutional investors in digital assets such as Bitcoin, Ethereum, and other cryptocurrencies has raised growing concerns among industry participants and public bodies about sustainability and business conduct risks across some blockchain value chains.

Members of the public, policymakers, and regulators have in recent times focused largely on potential environmental impacts, notably the energy consumption of prominent networks like Bitcoin and Ethereum, but there are wider social and governance considerations. Against this backdrop, this begs a few questions:

1) Is Bitcoin and underlying blockchain or distributed ledger technology (DLT) in general bad for the environment?
2) And for companies that are proactively developing their climate transition plans, could investment in, or use of, blockchain or DLT hinder their progress?

Why Is Environmental, Social, and Governance (ESG) Import*ant?*

There are two broad schools of thought when it comes to why ESG matters; one starts from the role of investors in society and the other focuses on risk management. Many investor groups including pension funds, charities, and endowment funds see their role as more than just return-seekers. They are conscious that funding our retirements, financing societal initiatives, and contributing to the cost of education can give them a function within wider society. With this responsibility comes influence. These investor groups manage significant pools of capital; directing this capital gives them a substantial amount of authority. They decide how and where they want their funds allocated and can choose to favour investments that aim not to have a negative effect on society, or those targeting a positive effect. The other major philosophy behind ESG is rooted in risk management.

Investors who take this approach incorporate ESG factors into their investment process to help mitigate risk. For example, a potential investment in a company with low ESG standards could expose the portfolio to a variety of risks faced by the company in the future, such as worker strikes, litigation, and negative publicity, resulting in lower future returns. For investors, monitoring the ESG credentials of an investment can lead to better risk-based judgements.

Environmental, Social, and Governance (ESG) Criteria

ESG criteria are standards for a company's operations that investors have begun using to either detect potential investments that have deleterious effects (according to the criteria) or to modify the criteria for

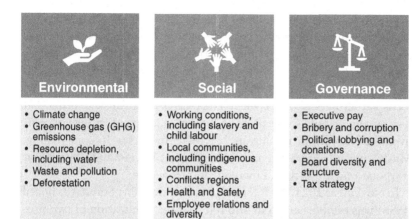

Figure 11.1 What is ESG investing
Source: Fidelity International, PRI, 2018.

making new investments that align harmoniously with the ESG criteria. Environmental considerations include, for example, a company's energy consumption, carbon footprint, and pollution. Social criteria often examine how a business carries out its relationships, including with clients and suppliers or among its employees. Governance concerns generally relate to how transparent a company is, the composition of its board and holding boards accountable for the promises that they make to their shareholders. ESG's popularity continues to grow alongside crypto-assets. ESG investing is the consideration of ESG factors, alongside financial factors, in the investment decision-making process. Different labels like sustainable investing, socially responsible investing, ethical investing, and impact investing all form part of ESG investing, with ESG factors covering a broad of issues (Figure 11.1).

In the discussion of blockchain technology's ability to support sustainability efforts, a distinction must also be drawn between 'environmental' (the 'E' in ESG) initiatives and 'sustainability' initiatives. Environmental initiatives revolve around reducing pollution and harm to the environment, while sustainability initiatives are more all-encompassing, referring to those that cover the spectrum of ESG. More and more investors are thinking about ESG issues when allocating their portfolios. Additionally, cryptocurrency is starting to capture an allocation from a growing number of portfolios.

However, some investors may hesitate due to reports that Bitcoin is not environmentally friendly, so is there any way investors can include cryptocurrency in their portfolios if they are taking ESG into consideration? Are some cryptocurrencies more ESG-friendly than others? It all depends on how you look at the space. The issue received renewed focus earlier in May 2021 when Tesla CEO Elon Musk tweeted that his company would stop accepting Bitcoin as payment, citing concerns over the 'rapidly increasing use of fossil fuels' for Bitcoin mining. Musk's tweet led to a free fall in the price of Bitcoin and other major cryptocurrencies, such as Ethereum and Dogecoin.

In November 2021, the International Sustainability Standards Board (ISSB) was established. ISSB also released the publication of two prototype documents relating to climate-related (Climate Prototype) and sustainability-related disclosures (General Requirements Prototype). The Climate Prototype sets out the requirements for the identification, measurement, and disclosure of climate-related financial information, and the General Requirements Prototype sets out the overall requirements for disclosing sustainability-related information relevant to the sustainability-related risks and opportunities faced by the entity. As these develop, we may see an impact on institutional investment in digital assets as they consider how the investment or exposure into digital assets align with their sustainable policy and objectives.

Digital Assets Energy Consumption

There is increased focus on the impact of digital assets, in particular cryptocurrencies, from an ESG perspective. However, not all digital assets such as cryptocurrencies – or their underlying blockchain or DLT platforms – are created equal in their energy demands. The goal of most major cryptocurrency platforms is to create a decentralised, distributed ledger, meaning that there is no one authority to verify the authenticity of transactions and ensure that assets are not spent twice, for example. There needs to be a trustworthy mechanism – a consensus system – to verify new transactions, add those transactions to the blockchain, and to confirm the creation of new tokens.

The primary concern stems from the environmental cost of crypto mining activities, in particular those that rely on proof-of-stake (PoS) protocol, which tend to have high energy consumption. When a group of transactions (a block) needs to be verified, all of the 'mining' computers race to solve a complex maths puzzle, and whoever wins gets to add the block to the chain and is rewarded in coins. The competitive nature of proof-of-work (PoW) consensus systems has led to substantial increases in computing power provided by institutional cryptocurrency mining operations and, with that, higher energy demands.

Cryptocurrencies' environmental impact, in particular PoS consensus such as Bitcoin (BTC), is under increasing scrutiny given the heavy energy consumption involved in mining it. As with any industry and new technology in the past, digital assets must overcome concerns regarding sustainability to achieve this potential. One aspect is the amount of energy consumed by digital assets such as the Bitcoin network. The Cambridge Bitcoin Energy Consumption Index (CBECI) estimated that the annualised electricity consumption of the Bitcoin network in 2021 was 87 terawatt-hours (TWh). This is equivalent to Finland's annualised electricity consumption for 2021 (83.7 TWh).[1]

In contrast, PoS consensus requires considerably less energy to operate. With this method, validators 'stake' their cryptocurrency for a chance at verifying new transactions and updating the blockchain Validators are randomly selected to add the following block based on their stake; the more cryptocurrency a validator has staked, the more likely they will be chosen to validate transactions and create new blocks. This method rewards long-term investment in a particular blockchain, rather than raw computing power. A validator is picked based on how much currency they have staked and how long it has been staked for. Once the block is verified, other validators must review and accept the data before it's added to the blockchain.

Regulatory Approaches

The high energy usage needed to mine cryptocurrencies that operate on PoW consensus on decentralised blockchain networks has led a number of countries to ban the mining of cryptocurrencies in their countries. China led the way in 2021 restricting onshore crypto activities in different phases. Although the country banned Bitcoin mining in 2021 for a number of reasons, one main reason was the massive energy consumption Bitcoin required and the impediment that posed

---

[1] See Cambridge Bitcoin Electricity Consumption Index, www.ccaf.io/cbeci/index/comparisons

to China's goal of carbon neutrality by 2060 (Quiroz-Gutierrez 2022). This significant event prompted many miners to move out of China to a number of countries such as the United States, Kazakhstan, Russia, and other emerging countries where the electricity costs are relatively cheaper and where crypto mining activities are permitted. In a bid to ease soaring energy prices and blackouts, other countries such as Algeria, Bangladesh, Egypt, Iran, Morocco, Qatar, Tunisia, Kazakhstan, and Kosovo have joined suit to ban crypto mining (Lee-Hood 2022). In Europe, Markets in Crypto-Assets Regulation (MiCAR) is Europe's regulatory framework for unbacked crypto-assets and stablecoins that do not fall within the existing EU regulatory regime. MiCAR is expected to take effect some time in 2024. In the context of finalising the first draft of the MiCAR, the European Parliament Committee on Economic and Monetary affairs (ECON Committee) was initially considering a ban on the crypto-assets using 'PoW' as a consensus mechanism to validate their underlying transactions. Notwithstanding some of the most popular cryptocurrencies' use of this technology (including Bitcoin), EU institutional concern is mainly based on the mechanism's high energy consumption, which consumption conflicts with EU environmental goals. However, in accordance with certain market players' advocacy, the final text of MiCAR took a 'softer' approach by generally permitting the use of PoW, subject to additional environmental disclosure requirements to be included in relevant crypto-assets white papers.

On 7 October 2021, more than 70 climate, economic, racial justice, business, and local organisations in the United States recently wrote to Congress, asking them to mitigate the considerable contribution portions of the cryptocurrency markets are making to climate change.[2] The letter cites the extreme levels of carbon emissions, energy consumption, and electronic waste generated by cryptocurrency usage, production, and mining, especially the deeply energy-intensive PoW process used by the two largest cryptocurrencies, Bitcoin and Ethereum 1.0. Since 15 September 2022, Ethereum consensus mechanism has migrated to a PoS protocol under the 'Ethereum Merge' initiative,

---

[2] Multiple Authors, 2021. *Crypto Climate – Letter to US Congress.* Available online: www.static1.squarespace.com/static/5e449c8c3ef68d752f3e70dc/t/61 5e2a00d556c53336b0e365/1633561088889/Crypto+Climate+Letter+to+Con gress.pdf.

which significantly reduces the carbon footprint as POS consensus is more energy efficient compared to PoW consensus.

Increased demand for the sophisticated mining machines, with massive computing capacity, is exacerbating a global shortage of semiconductors. Such concerns have led New York Governor Kathy Hochul to sign legislation on 22 November 2022 banning new crypto mining operations in the state that are powered by fossil-fuel generators, making New York the first state in the United States to do so.[3] The law bars for two years, in the state of New York, the issuance of new, renewed, or expanded permits for fossil fuel power plants that deliver power for PoW cryptocurrency mining, the energy-consumptive process by which digital money transactions are validated. It would not apply to plants that have already submitted paperwork for permits, and it creates no obstacles for crypto mining powered by renewables or any of the state's three nuclear plants.[4]

Role of Banks

Digital assets have increasingly gained interest from financial markets participants and citizens given the rapid development of crypto-asset markets, which reached US$3 trillion as of the end of 2021.

In parallel, ESG factors have risen to become a priority for policy makers, and regulators in the banking sector, and great societal awareness of the urgent need for action on climate and sustainability issues. The overwhelming ESG concern amongst investors is climate risk, especially post-Paris Agreement[5] and here is where crypto has faced the most backlash. The infrastructure supporting crypto-assets such as Bitcoin uses an enormous amount of energy, the quantity of which rivals the energy consumption of certain small nations. The use of renewable energy is not sufficient to curb the negative externalities given the opportunity cost for the use of renewables elsewhere in society, especially given current geopolitical conditions. Bitcoin and other digital assets are increasingly becoming part of mainstream financial markets, given the growing interconnectedness of decentralised

---

[3] New York State Senate, Senate Bill S6486D, 22 November 2022, www.nysenate
.gov/legislation/bills/2021/S6486
[4] Ibid.
[5] Paris Agreement is the global accord on climate in 2015 whereby nations
pledged to take measures to reduce GHG emissions globally.

finance (DeFi) and traditional finance (TradFi). More scrutiny is therefore expected by policy makers and regulators across all aspects of this digital asset market, including in relation to its environmental impact. PoW consensus mechanisms for the validation of transactions and associated crypto-mining are the key drivers of the carbon footprint of blockchain-based finance.

In respect of the environment, climate change is an emerging threat to financial stability of the banking sector. The physical and transition risks associated with climate change could contribute to financial instability through numerous channels, including financial intermediaries experiencing significant losses, the impairment of financial market functioning, or the sudden and disruptive repricing of assets. Climate-related financial risks can affect households, communities, businesses, and governments by damaging property, impeding business activity, impacting income, and altering the value of assets and liabilities. These risks may lead financial institutions to pull back from credit provisions, potentially amplifying the initial climate-related shock and harming financial stability. Regulators in many jurisdictions such as in European Union, United Kingdom, United States, Japan, Hong Kong, Singapore, Switzerland, and Canada have continued efforts to address climate-related data gaps; promote consistent, comparable, and decision-useful disclosures; improve assessments of climate-related financial risks and vulnerabilities; and incorporate climate-related financial risks into their risk management practices and supervisory expectations for regulated financial entities where appropriate.

Against this backdrop, at the same time, banks are making investments across a range of sectors, from marketplaces and platforms for blockchain or DLT development to services for market data and decentralised apps. The majority of these investments aim to increase consumer reach, user adoption, technological innovation, and customer experience. The challenge faced by banks is to ensure that their participation in digital assets-related activities and the adoption of the underlying blockchain or DLT does not derogate from their mandate to implement sustainability agenda and mitigation of sustainable finance and ESG risks. Most of these mandates and tasks are closely linked to the regulators' broader objective of contributing to the stability, resilience, and orderly functioning of the financial system. These mandates and tasks cover the three pillars of the banking framework, that is, market discipline, supervision and prudential requirements, as well as other areas related to sustainable finance and the assessment and monitoring of ESG risks. Given the carbon footprint and associated climate transition risks of certain digital assets, combined with negative externalities extending to the wider society, this would require multi-pronged approach by banks including management oversight of their strategy relating to adoption of digital asset-related activities (and adoption of underlying blockchain technology or DLT) and aligning them with the sustainable agenda, goals, and objectives, including transparency and disclosure to their supervisory authorities and shareholders regarding the mitigation of any environmental or other aspect of ESG impact relating to the digital asset-related activities. This could include placing caps on holdings of PoW-based digital assets and adhering to additional prudential requirements on those holdings.

The approaches that financial institutions that are active in digital asset ecosystem have taken include the following:

1. Move away from the use of energy-intensive consensus mechanisms for digital assets: while it may be challenging to determine the exact environmental impact of digital assets, it is quite clear that the energy consumption for certain consensus networks such as PoS to operate their networks is significant. Recent publicly announced tokenised bonds and other types of tokenised financial assets have shown a trend towards banks adopting more sustainable network consensus such as PoS requirements for blockchain or distributed ledger (Bitbond Report 2022). The move to PoS from PoW platforms or other enhancements will reduce computing power requirements. Hence, they could eventually reduce the environmental impact and support the mainstream usability of some of these applications – and in turn increase the potential disruption to TradFi.
2. Improve transparency into digital asset energy usage: to better inform and calibrate policy interventions, policy makers and supervisory authorities of regulated financial institutions have instituted measures to encourage digital asset participants to disclose regular, timely, and accurate data on computing power being expended on the blockchain network and provide location-specific distribution. First, crypto companies must understand their climate impacts, which requires gathering, maintaining, and transparently disclosing

high-quality data about their electricity consumption and energy mix. crypto companies will then need to calculate their Scope 1, Scope 2, and Scope 3 greenhouse gas (GHG) emissions.[6] This will enable them to design mitigation portfolios and consider targets, such as net zero.

The final version of MiCAR in Europe introduces ESG disclosure obligations. These have been included to encourage a move away from energy-intensive PoW consensus mechanisms. ESG disclosures are required in white papers and on crypto-asset service providers' (CASPs) websites, with European Supervisory Authorities tasked with developing further standards. CASPs would have to publish information related to the environmental and climate-related impact of each crypto-asset for which they offer services. This should be placed prominently on their website. In the United States, on 9 December 2022, a bill was tabled at the Congress which is designed to obligate CASPs to publish information related to the environmental and climate-related impact of each crypto-asset for which they offer services. Collectively these proposals do not amount to a ban of PoW mechanisms. However, the greater transparency on ESG factors would aim to drive investment decisions away from 'brown' digital assets and towards 'green' digital assets.

3. Carbon offset: since downstream users' emissions from the use of cryptocurrency are indirect emissions, reaching net zero emissions as a user of cryptocurrency will require the purchase of mitigation credits (or also known as carbon offsets). A carbon offset is a reduction or removal of emissions of carbon dioxide or other GHGs made in order to compensate for emissions made elsewhere. Offsets are measured in tonnes of carbon dioxide

---

[6] Scope 1 refers to direct emissions that result from an organisation's activities, such as fuel combustion from facilities (e.g., burning natural gas for space heating) and vehicles that your company owns or controls (e.g., burning gasoline or diesel for company automobiles or trucks).

Scope 2 refers to indirect emissions associated with an organisation's activities, often from the generation of purchased electricity consumed by your company (e.g., emissions from natural gas power plants that supply electricity to your local power grid).

Scope 3 refers to other indirect emissions from an organisation's supply chain, rather that its primary operations (e.g., embodied emissions in purchased raw goods, distribution and transportation, employee commuting, use of sold products, and end-of-life treatment).

equivalent. A carbon offset is generated by an activity that either prevents the release of, reduces, or removes GHG emissions from the atmosphere. Emission reduction projects around the world generate carbon offsets from activities such as renewable energy, biogas, and reforestation.

Carbon offsetting is employed by financial institutions and companies to balance emissions, including GHG, by purchasing credits to compensate and counter equivalent emissions. Carbon offsets are bucketed into two categories: voluntary or compliance, with the global carbon offset market on track to be worth somewhere between $40 billion and $120 billion, spurred much by carbon-neutral demands (Bruce 2021). For companies looking to improve carbon offsetting efforts *en route* to net zero, they must first be able to ascertain an accurate baseline of total emissions. It is key to access supply chain data to digest carbon intensity as a predicate to implementing change (Bruce 2021).

Blockchain as an auditable system of record can create standardisation and accountability in yielding a cost-effective and sustainable method to streamline operations and track, measure, and manage environmental impact data across the Scope 1, 2, and 3 emission categories – critical for companies to manage their value chain accordingly.

Further 'E' Considerations

However, adopting a more environmentally friendly 'PoS' blockchain model can be complicated by regulatory frameworks designed to ensure consumer protection. For example, the US Securities and Exchange Commission (SEC) and other global regulators believe that many crypto-assets used on blockchains have characteristics indicative of a 'security' that falls under their regulatory authority, a designation which can have an existential impact (Clifford Chance 2021). One factor the SEC weighs heavily in favour of a crypto-asset being a 'security' is the existence of a defined group of persons responsible for managing a blockchain or blockchain-related project that asset purchasers reasonably expect to rely on to realise future profits. This is due, in part, to concern that a small group of managers with power over a blockchain or access to its software can lead to informational asymmetries that managers can exploit to take advantage of unsophisticated investors. 'PoS' blockchains with centralised governance including blockchains with too small a validator pool, run the risk of creating the kinds of control and informational asymmetry issues that may cause global regulators to step in (Clifford Chance 2021).

Another avenue explored by some companies seeking to position Bitcoin mining as 'sustainable' is to procure energy from renewable energy sources or to enter into corporate power purchase agreements. However, companies must consider the reputational risks associated with 'green washing' and the focus by stakeholders on verification and reporting (which may necessitate steps such as embedding audit rights in the underlying power purchase agreements).

More than Just an 'E'

ESG concern in digital assets goes beyond climate or environmental challenges, and there is a need to address social impact and governance concerns. Less attention has been placed on the social inclusion and equality aspects of the digital industry. This will come as awareness grows and here is where the banking industry can play its part. On social consideration, the focus is on addressing inequality and financial exclusion, exacerbated by the lack of access to financial services by the unbanked or underbanked global population. Globally, approximately 1.7 billion adults remain unbanked (Demirgüç-Kunt et al. 2022).

An often-cited example is the current state of the cross-border payment or remittance ecosystem, which is expensive, slow, opaque, and inaccessible to many people due to lack of credit history or verifiable credentials. The World Bank estimates that globally, sending remittances costs an average of 6.3 per cent of the amount sent in Q3, 2022 (World Bank 2022). The use of blockchain can enable financial inclusion in underdeveloped countries facing poverty, underdeveloped economies, and inequality.

Stablecoins such as USDC and USDT have been used particularly in less developed countries or emerging markets for cross-border payments and/or to transfer funds to those who do not have access to banking services. Stablecoins are tokens whose value is tied to another asset, usually fiat currencies such as the US dollar. They seek to combine the credibility that comes from their supposed stability, with the benefits of tokenisation, that allow them to be used as payment instruments on distributed ledgers. Stablecoins are beginning to find acceptance outside of the crypto ecosystem. Some firms like Mastercard have integrated popular stablecoins into their payment services. This can be a positive development if stablecoins can make payments cheaper, faster, and safer.

Central banks around the world are also investigating or trialling the use case of a retail central bank digital currency (CBDC) to enable citizens who have no bank account to use or hold CBDCs via their digital wallets. CBDCs are the direct liability, and payment instrument, of a central bank. This means that holders of CBDCs will have a direct claim on the central bank that has issued them, similar to how physical currency works today. Countries such as The Bahamas, Nigeria, The Eastern Caribbean States, and China have launched their retail CBDCs to facilitate greater levels of financial inclusion and enable underserved people around the globe to access financial services. On the other hand, wholesale CBDCs are restricted to use by financial institutions. They are akin to the balances which commercial banks place with a central bank today. Wholesale CBDCs on a distributed ledger have the potential to achieve atomic settlement, or the exchange of two linked assets in real time. They have the potential to radically transform cross-border payments, which today are slow, expensive, and opaque.

The growing popularity and adoption of DeFi services and products have lowered the barrier of entry and enabled the mass public to access certain types of financial services in the digital asset ecosystem. DeFi platforms or protocols can facilitate borrowing, lending, and trading activities to be performed autonomously through smart contracts, potentially enhancing the efficiency and accessibility of financial services. The democratisation of access to DeFi given its decentralised nature without a centralised intermediary has attracted many investors, especially those underbanked or unbanked. DeFi has provided such individuals with better rates on their savings, eliminated banking fees, and offered the opportunity to invest in digital assets such as fractionalised art or real estate, areas that were traditionally the preserve of the wealthy.

The governance issues associated with digital assets will also need to be addressed. These range from risks such as cyber hacking and rug pulls, anti-money laundering to a lack of diversity within the community. That said, these risks are hardly exclusive to crypto. The development of DeFi and decentralised autonomous organisations (DAOs) has posed new questions for us on governance, with degrees of centralisation and the control of keys being debated across the community. The ability to choose the direction of a project through governance tokens opens new possibilities for governance and a new meaning to the term 'democratised finance'. Boards or management of cryptocurrency-exposed companies may need to adapt existing risk management policies and practices to the specific risks arising from digital assets. Many of these topics will be relatively familiar (for example, finance, cybersecurity, and anti-money-laundering policies), but new and significant risks may arise from how the coins themselves are governed. As institutional players like banks, hedge funds, and other financial institutions enter the digital asset ecosystem, the governance issues will begin to take centre stage as such institutional players will require issuers and crypto-asset service providers to take steps to address or mitigate such risks before greater institutional adoption takes shape.

In addition, digital assets also have a diversity problem. The non-profit 'Diversity in Blockchain' released an initial report at the end of 2019 highlighting the lack of diversity in the blockchain and crypto-currency space (Joseph 2019). The statistics suggest only 4–10 per cent of the workers in the crypto sector are women and that it is dominated by white and Asian men. There are industry efforts made to redress this imbalance with women's fintech or digital asset-focused groups being formed to encourage more women participation and fairer and diverse representation in the workforce. Government institutions, supervisory authorities, regulators, and financial institutions have taken concerted efforts to improve the gender imbalance and diverse representation in the banking sector. These efforts are laudable and over time, we are likely to see an increase in women and more balanced ethnic participation in the workforce.

Blockchain Technology or DLT as an ESG Enabler

One should not lose sight of the fact that the applications of blockchain technology or DLT go far beyond its use as the technology underpinning digital assets. In this chapter, we use blockchain or DLT interchangeably as blockchain is a type of distributed ledger. Bitcoin, blockchain's first application, is widely known as an environmental polluter, consuming massive amounts of energy and emitting vast amounts of CO_2 in order to validate transactions and sustain the network. However, concerns of this nature hold true only for specific applications of the underlying technology such as PoW consensus which has high energy consumption. Depending on network architecture and choice of consensus or protocols, blockchain or DLT can be deployed in more energy-efficient ways. For example, public blockchain using PoS or private blockchains using algorithms like proof-of-authority (PoA), when set up properly, do not consume more energy than traditional database solutions (OECD 2019). The core competencies of blockchain technology – transparency, data auditability, privacy, value transfer, and process efficiency and automation – can be leveraged to drive the systemic changes needed to deliver a greener, more sustainable future in finance (OECD 2019).

Blockchain in finance can contribute towards achieving the United Nations' ('UN') sustainable development goals ('SDGs'). The UN's SDGs (Figure 11.2) are commonly referred to as the framework for achieving 'ESG' goals and outcomes. Blockchain's potential ESG applications are numerous. With a focus on financial application, we discuss in particular how blockchain lends itself to the following SDGs (depicted in icon form) (McCormack et al. 2021).

Environmental: the use of blockchain or DLT can change traditional financial transaction flows and create economic return while supporting climate action. For example, through improved carbon

Figure 11.2 United Nations Sustainable Development Goals
Source: www.sdgs.un.org/goals. The content of this publication has not been approved by the United Nations and does not reflect the views of the United Nations or its officials or Member States.

emissions trading, facilitated clean energy trading, green bonds issuance, and better tracking and reporting of GHG emissions reduction.

Social: the use of blockchain or DLT can enable financial inclusion in underdeveloped countries facing poverty, underdeveloped economies, and inequality. DLT could lead to greater transparency, including for supply chains trade finance. By allowing greater transparency and accountability, DLT could help demonstrate the sustainability of supply chains from a social (or environmental) point of view. For example, initiatives are being tested around the technology's ability to support more comprehensive carbon tracing.

Governance: the use of blockchain or DLT, if properly designed, can maximise transparency, mitigate greenwashing, and build trust between financial institutions and their clients or trading counterparties to assist these firms to transition to a sustainable and greener ecosystem. The push for climate change considerations puts pressure on financial institutions to develop and use advanced technologies such as blockchain that promises improved governance.

'Greenwashing' – the making of unsubstantiated claims about the sustainability of an investment product – is high on regulators' agendas for 2023 and it is crucial that ESG capital markets are transparent for the benefit of both issuers and investors. Technology, including blockchain or DLT, and innovation have an important role to play in addressing these risks and ensuring the continued growth of the sustainable finance market, which has surged in recent years and is worth in excess of US$3 trillion. The banking sector has set bold and ambitious targets to reach net zero. Even the largest banks are recognizing that reducing carbon must sit at the very top of their agendas.

Application by Banks to Improve ESG Efforts

Here are some of the ways financial institutions can use blockchain to improve ESG efforts and facilitate the mobilisation of finance towards a more sustainable future.

Asset Tokenisation

Financial institutions are turning to blockchain technology and tokenisation to improve the shortcomings of conventional securities. Tokenisation combines both the benefit of improved security and digital native-token. Additionally, it applies it to traditional assets creating a new digitised asset that can be stored, traded, and settled on the blockchain.

A digital asset is anything of value whose ownership is represented in a digital or computerised form. This is done through a process called tokenisation – which involves using a software program to convert ownership rights over an asset into a digital token. Digital assets are typically deployed on distributed ledgers that record the ownership and transfer of ownership of these assets. A blockchain is a type of distributed ledger that organises transaction records into blocks of data which are cryptographically linked together. According to Van Gysegem and De Patoul (2001), the share of tokenised assets will take up about 40 per cent of the digital assets market by 2025. There is increased demand for green investments such as green bonds, green exchange-traded funds, green deposits, and green structured products. The World Bank issued the first ever green bonds in 2008, and today the green bond market is an estimated $1.3 trillion market, according to the Climate Bond Initiative. Green bonds are issued to finance environmental and climate projects including areas such as clean transportation, green buildings, renewable energy, and sustainable water.

It will make a significant environmental impact whether these tokenisation projects use PoW blockchains or the more modern and significantly more energy-efficient PoS blockchains. Environmentally sound and innovative regulation of the token economy would establish competitive advantages for financial innovation in Europe and ensure a sustainable environmental impact. Tokenizing green bonds can also significantly drive down the cost of green finance. According to a recent King and Wood Mallesons report (McCormack et al. 2021), the estimated cost of issuing a green bond under a standard process is just under US$6.5 million but this could be reduced by almost 90 per cent for a full blockchain automated issuance. This makes green bond issuance a far more attractive option, welcoming younger generations to take charge of their own future. Blockchain can also replace paper heavy bills of lading in trade finance through the use of smart contracts on the blockchain, allowing for faster and more efficient transactions, through:

– Real-time review of a purchase agreement and draft terms of credit by the import bank;

- digital signatures following goods inspections;
- review and approval of payment obligations through a smart contract by the export bank; and
- digital acknowledgement of receipt of goods to trigger payment by the importer. It can also assist with secure sharing of KYC information by storing customer information on decentralised blocks (McCormack et al. 2021).

By tokenizing projects through blockchain, we will also be able to add traceability and provenance to green investments. With access to more information, investors can better diversify their portfolios and tokenisation allows smaller investors to take part in further expanding the pool of green capital available. In Box 11.1, the Genesis project is outlined as an application of this technology to green finance.

Box 11.1 – Case study: project genesis

In Project Genesis, the Bank for International Settlements (BIS) Innovation Hub's first green finance project executed in conjunction with the Hong Kong Monetary Authority (HKMA), that explores green finance through combining blockchain, smart contracts, internet-of-things, and digital assets.

Together with six partners, the project achieved two prototypes that bring to life the vision that an investor can download an app and invest any amount into safe government bonds, which will develop a green project; over the bond's lifetime, the investor can not only see accrued interest, but also track in real time how much clean energy is being generated, and the consequent reduction in CO_2 emissions linked to the investment; further, the investor can sell the bonds in a transparent market.

Project Genesis's vision for a technologically driven green finance was motivated by the following objectives:

- Explore how finance can drive the transition to a green and sustainable future.
- Sustainability can be better achieved by integrating blockchain and other technology into the processes that bring financial products to market.
- Opportunities for greenwashing products will be greatly reduced and, at the same time, the technology can be utilised to control risk for both issuers and investors, thereby helping to make truly green investment the norm rather than merely novel.

The key benefits offered by the Prototype(s) for Project Genesis include:

- Automated and streamlined primary issuance system
- Efficient asset servicing during the life cycle of the bond
- Easier secondary trading for investors and asset holders
- Real-time insight into end-investor behaviour and activities
- App-based mobile access for investors
- Low denomination bond issuance
- Decreased transaction costs
- Instant and atomic settlement
- Potentially improved asset liquidity
- Positive Impact on Hong Kong's environmentally friendly and sustainable growth

In consonance with the take-away from the BIS Green Swan research report that climate change involves complex collective action problems that require increased coordination among governments, the private sector, civil society, and the international community, project Genesis was guided by a multi-disciplinary panel of experts in ESG, green finance, bond markets, law and regulation, each of whom contributed an article giving their views on key aspects of their areas of expertise.

Accurate ESG Data

Having reliable and accurate ESG data is an evermore vital concern for banks. Regulations are reaching a point where publishing data on ESG targets will be legally mandated. In Europe, the European Central Bank and the Bank of England have already launched supervisory climate risk stress tests to assess how prepared banks are for dealing with climate shocks. Similarly, supervisory authorities in the United States, Switzerland, Japan, Hong Kong, Canada, Singapore, South Korea, and Australia have provided similar regulatory expectations for the banking sectors to mitigate any climate risks faced by the banks. At the same time, initiatives like the UN-convened Net-Zero Banking Alliance (representing over 40 per cent of global banking assets), the Glasgow Financial Alliance for Net Zero, and the Principles for Responsible Banking add to the clamour for banks to provide evidence of their progress.

As such, having good data is foundational to driving the green and transition finance agenda. Financial institutions need accurate, granular data to assess and manage the environmental risks in their portfolios. Financial institutions need good data on their customers' and suppliers' carbon footprints and compliance with their respective transition targets. They also need good data on the climate-related risks their physical assets are vulnerable to. Quality data is key in the fight against greenwashing and in enabling stakeholders to make well-informed ESG-investment decisions. But the ESG data acquisition process is often manual, tedious, and costly. Access to good data sources is often fragmented, and data verification is at a nascent stage.

The demand for trusted data will only grow as regulators strengthen reporting and disclosure requirements. Yet, the availability of good data remains a big challenge. The process of ESG data acquisition is manual, cumbersome, and costly. There is also a lack of transparency in the verification and reporting process.

Blockchain is an emerging technology that is designed as a decentralised ledger and is capable of data collection, monitoring, steering, and reporting operations that fit the purposes of the reporting obligations motivated by the climate change considerations. With the growing urgency for climate solutions, blockchain technology could be a powerful tool to revolutionise green finance, especially as transparency and traceable information are critical in measuring and monitoring climate impact. Data and technology will be key to bringing the quality of green audits to the next level. If data can be standardised and made more easily accessible, technologies such as blockchain, the internet of things (IoT), and artificial intelligence may be applied to capture, process, analyse, and validate data in real time and more efficiently. The Project Genesis prototype is designed to do just that: capturing data (i.e., electricity generated by a solar farm) using smart metres at the ultimate source and using blockchain technology to preserve the integrity of the data. In Box 11.2, the Greenprint project is presented as a concrete example of constructing a Green Fintec Ecosystem.

Supply Chain Transparency

Blockchain can offer investors several benefits such as insights into value chains. Blockchain can help measure adoption-related activities such as carbon reductions initiatives in factories and agriculture.

Box 11.2 – Case study: Project Greenprint

To build a Green FinTech data ecosystem, the Monetary Authority of Singapore (MAS) has launched a collaborative effort with the financial industry called Project Greenprint. Project Greenprint seeks to build digital utilities that streamline the collection, access, and use of climate and sustainability data. It aims to help mobilise capital to sustainable projects, monitor the climate commitments made, and measure the impact associated with investments. Project Greenprint has focused on four digital utilities:

- An ESG disclosure portal: titled ESGenome, MAS is piloting the ESG Disclosure Portal with Singapore Stock Exchange (SGX), to enable listed companies to carry out baseline sustainability reporting against a set of 27 core metrics. The SGX portal allows companies' one-time inputs to be automatically mapped across a range of major sustainability standards and frameworks.
- An ESG registry of green certifications: titled ESGpedia, it uses DLT to record and maintain the provenance of green certifications issued by various sectoral bodies. This allows banks to access various green certifications through a single interface.
- A data orchestrator: this entails aggregating ESG data from multiple data sources to meet specific green and transition financing needs. This requires interoperability and consent-based access to major ESG data providers, utilities providers, sectoral platforms, and of course the ESG Registry itself. MAS has already started small-scale pilots to identify financing gaps and technology solutions for decarbonisation in priority sectors such as energy, real estate, agriculture, and transportation.
- A digital marketplace: the digital marketplace, which is scheduled for launch in 2023, aims to synergise connectivity across the Greenprint utilities and facilitate access to ESG data. It will facilitate linkages between ESG FinTech solution providers and investors, financial institutions, and corporates. It will also house an ESG Data Directory to facilitate discovery and access to the ESG datasets contributed by the Greenprint digital utilities and collaborators.

Through Project Greenprint, MAS wants to make Singapore a launchpad for ESG FinTech solutions that will help drive Asia's and the world's transition to net zero.

> **Box 11.3 – Case study: IBM's Food Trust**
>
> IBM's Food Trust uses blockchain to connect participants across the
> food ecosystem to enhance visibility and accountability across the
> food supply chain, such as growers, processors, and retailers, with
> data collected along the supply chain. This allows them to ensure that
> food safety protocols and sustainable food practices are adopted at
> each stage of the food chain. Built on IBM Blockchain, this solution
> connects participants through a permissioned, immutable, and shared
> record of food provenance, transaction data, and processing details.
> It also allows them to trace any food fraud incidents or food safety
> breaches back to their source. This use case demonstrates the benefit
> of the blockchain technology being deployed as a way to maintain
> provenance and traceability in the data.

For ESG monitoring purposes, one of blockchain's primary uses is
bringing a *bird's-eye view to supply chain management*. A more sustainable, energy-efficient supply chain could deliver profound savings
in transportation costs and the concurrent curtailing of carbon emissions that a better managed, more efficient system would bring.

With blockchain technology, transactions at every step of the supply
chain can be recorded and distributed. This brings an unheard-of level
of transparency and traceability to the movement of goods around the
globe. With automated IoT interfaces, data collection is seamless and
less contingent on overworked individuals.

This transparency also makes monitoring ethical sourcing in industries that have long presented a challenge to regulators, such as *sea-
food harvesting*, more attainable. Products, whether raw or processed,
can be tracked early in the production cycle, and the information is
available to end users long before items are even delivered – with the
journey tracked in real time via blockchain.An interesting application
to the food supply chain is provided in Box 11.3.

Humanitarian Aid

The blockchain technology has aided organisations or governments to
provide for an innovative way to disburse funds to the needy that do
not have direct access to bank accounts or TradFi to source funding.

Stablecoins have been used to transfer funds to those who do not have access to banking services. In this regard, the program developed by UNHCR (see Box 11.4) is a factual application of this technology to provide humanitarian relief to targeted beneficiaries.

Box 11.4 – Case study: UNHCR humanitarian payment using blockchain payment solutions

UNHCR, the United Nations Refugee Agency, and the Stellar Development Foundation (SDF), a non-profit blockchain organisation, announced on 16 December 2022 a new first-of-its-kind pilot program that will use blockchain technology powered by the Stellar network to reach people in need with speed, agility, and accountability. UNHCR and UNICC have partnered to pilot a new aid disbursement solution based on Stellar, which allows for the quick, efficient, and secure distribution of cash assistance to internally displaced persons in Ukraine. Persons who qualify for assistance will receive funds in USDC stablecoins directly into their Vibrant digital wallet, which they can use to access funds anywhere in Ukraine or move across borders without needing cash. They can also choose to convert their funds into cash, whether euro, dollars, or local currency at any of the global MoneyGram locations including over 4,500 in Ukraine.

The program is being piloted in Kyiv, Lviv, and Vinnytsia and will expand to other towns and cities in Ukraine. The money will provide humanitarian assistance to some of the people most impacted and vulnerable due to the war, to help them cover basic needs like rent of accommodation, food, medical care, and heating during the winter. The solution has been extensively tested over the last six months and is expected to be expanded to reach more war-affected people inside Ukraine as well as refugees from Ukraine in early 2023.

This blockchain initiative complements UNHCR's goals to further expand the systematic and rapid use of cash-based interventions. Since 2016, when UNHCR issued its first policy on cash-based interventions, UNHCR has delivered almost US$5 billion in cash assistance to some 35 million people in 100 countries. UNHCR is committed to further expanding the provision of cash, which is normally the preferred assistance modality by people forcibly displaced, as it gives them the freedom and dignity to themselves decide how to prioritise the assistance given, based on their personal need.

Box 11.5 – Case study: Carbonplace
(carbon transaction network)

A consortium of financial institutions has established Carbonplace, which is a platform that is being developed to provide settlements, infrastructure, and systems for marketplaces and exchanges in the voluntary carbon market. Carbonplace is a global carbon transaction network that will enable the simple, secure, and transparent transfer of certified carbon credits. It is built on a secure, energy-efficient DLT and due to be commercial by early 2023. Carbonplace will simplify the purchase of carbon credits for businesses committed to transition to a net zero future. Banks leading the initiative claim the platform will help to boost transparency by providing a book of record for the ownership of carbon credits, allowing owners of such credits to clearly demonstrate possession to the market, thereby reducing the risks of double counting and simplifying reporting. It also aims to provide full traceability and linkage back to the source of a carbon credit.

Carbon Credit Trading

Blockchain can also be used to enable carbon offset (see Box 11.5). Blockchain-enabled platforms allow companies to offset their carbon footprint through investment in environmental projects. Demand for carbon offset opportunities continues to surge, coinciding with the desire to decarbonise cryptocurrency. Some blockchain exchanges, venues, or platforms have taken proactive measures to collaborate to become carbon neutral, starting by offsetting the carbon caused by withdrawals of cryptocurrencies from the platforms.

MicroFinance

The UN expects that blockchain technology will play an important role in sustainable development through enhancing climate data transparency, supporting climate finance, and enabling clean energy markets (UN 2021). Leveraging blockchain networks with lower power consumption can be the key to further unlocking these opportunities to propel climate transition. Blockchain technology also can drive superior overall ESG outcomes (e.g. Box 11.6).

Box 11.6 – Case study: principles for responsible investment

Principles for Responsible Investment is an investor initiative in partnership with the UN Environmental Program (UNEP) Finance Initiative and the UN Global Compact. It was created to set out how blockchain can contribute to responsible investment and become a force for social good. In the context of enhancing social outcomes, one use case is financial inclusion through microfinance, where blockchain technology can significantly reduce the transaction cost for people in developing countries to access capital.

Carbon Meta-Registries Using Distributed Ledger Technology

At the heart of green finance and net zero goals is the Paris Agreement. The Paris Agreement is a legally binding international treaty on climate change adopted by 196 countries in Paris in 2015 and went into force on 4 November 2016.

Under the landmark Paris Agreement, countries committed to holding global temperature rises to 'well below' 2C above pre-industrial levels, while 'pursuing efforts' to limit heating to 1.5C.

However, to meet those goals, countries also agreed on non-binding national targets known as nationally determined contributions (NDCs) to cut – or in the case of developing countries to curb – the growth of – GHG emissions in the near term, by 2030 in most cases. Many countries also updated their NDCs at Cop26 held in Glasgow in 2021 relating to their national commitments to contribute to net zero emission targets, and countries responsible for about three-quarters of global GHG emissions set out long-term targets to reach net zero carbon by about mid-century. These include climate-related targets for GHG emission reductions, policies in response to climate change and as a contribution to achieve the global targets set out in the Paris Agreement. With both voluntary and compliance markets claiming emission reductions and without a global registry, it has been difficult to account for what positive environmental impact has actually taken place and who should get the credit. Blockchain can prevent double counting of carbon credits with the use of smart contracts. With smart contracts in place, carbon credits that are already issued and logged onto the blockchain, cannot be (re)allocated to another entity. However, as with all blockchain solutions,

> **Box 11.7– Case study: IHS Markit Meta-Registry for carbon credits**
>
> On 28 October 2021, IHS Markit announced the launch of the Carbon Meta-Registry, a secure online platform that seamlessly connects disparate environmental markets and registry systems around the world, enabling the exchange of carbon market data and mitigating the risk of double-counting of credits. This particular meta-registry plans to leverage DLT, which would help solve issues like double counting and ultimately, more accurately reflect a country's NDC. Programs engaged with the Meta-Registry span national programs, sub-national programs, international CORSIA-approved standards, and domestic voluntary programs, including: Acre Carbon Standard, Global Carbon Council, Gold Standard, Plan Vivo Foundation, Papua New Guinea, UK Peatland Code, UK Woodland Carbon Code, and Verra. In early 2022, the Meta-Registry will expand to offer exchange connectivity to connected programs and standards. The global carbon meta-registry reduces the risks related to double-counting, while providing critical infrastructure and seamless connectivity among markets and their participants to further enable the growth of these vital markets.

implementation of smart contracts must be carefully considered to be successful. All blockchain solutions, including in relation to technical infrastructure, must be developed having close regard to a problem statement, and must be appropriate to address that problem and its targeted deployment reach. In the coming year, we are likely to hear more about meta-registries – regional and possibly global online ledgers to help track, manage, and account for in-country and cross-border transfers of new and existing carbon credits (see the example of IHS Markit, Box 11.7), renewable energy certificates, and other 'environmental attributes' across independent carbon markets and registry systems around the world.

New Green Financial Products

The transition to green finance has spawned the creation of new green financial products notably green bonds, green loans, and sustainability-linked loans. Sustainability-linked loans aim to facilitate and support environmentally and socially sustainable economic activity and growth. Green Bonds are any type of bond instrument where the proceeds or an equivalent amount will be exclusively applied to finance or refinance, in part or in full, new and/or existing eligible green projects (ICMA 2021). Green loans are any type of loan instrument made available exclusively to finance or refinance, in whole or in part, new and/or existing eligible green projects which include green building, climate change adaptation, renewable energy projects, and environmentally sustainable management of living natural resources and land use (ICMA – Loan Market Association 2018). The fundamental determinant of a green loan is the utilisation of the loan proceeds for Green Projects (including other related and supporting expenditures, including research and development), which should be appropriately described in the finance document. Sustainability-linked loans are any type of loan instruments and/or contingent facilities (such as bonding lines, guarantee lines, or letters of credit) which incentivise the borrower's achievement of ambitious, predetermined sustainability performance objectives. The borrower's sustainability performance is measured using sustainability performance targets (SPTs), which include key performance indicators, external ratings, and/or equivalent metrics and which measure improvements in the borrower's sustainability profile (ICMA – Loan Market Association 2019). Instead of determining specific uses of proceeds, sustainability-linked loans look to improve the borrower's sustainability profile by aligning loan terms to the borrower's performance against the relevant predetermined SPTs. For example, sustainability-linked loans will often align the borrower's performance to margin redetermination over the life of the sustainability-linked loan. As regulatory focus on climate change continues to grow, there will be increased demand for the transparency and granularity of these products – which can only demonstrate positive environmental impact if the underlying data is measurable, verifiable, and able to be relied upon by third parties. Today, the monitoring of use of proceeds, underlying asset performance, and environmental impact is generally done through periodic manual processes. This leaves the potential for human error and reduces the timeliness of data. These non-digitised data sets are not easily referenced over time and do not fit neatly into future carbon accounting, or ratings and reporting regimes. Blockchain technology could provide the platform for reliable, accessible, and updated data on green bonds (see Box 11.8 for a concrete example), green loans, and sustainability-linked deals. While

---

Box 11.8 – Use case: BBVA blockchain green bond

In February 2019, BBVA issued the world's first Green Bond using blockchain, for EUR 35 million, on behalf of MAPFRE8 using a fully automated blockchain platform that allows the client to structure the instrument directly. This deal is particularly ground-breaking given its dual nature: it is both sustainable and high-tech. On one hand, the funds are earmarked to finance green projects within the BBVA's framework of the SDGs. As such, the bond has been categorised as green, according to the Second Party Opinion issued by DNVGL – a global leader in certification. On the other hand, the terms of the bond were negotiated on BBVA's internally developed blockchain platform. To be granted green bond status, an issue needs to undergo a series of audits and comply with the so-called 'Green Bond Principles'. Current technological and digital tools are allowing to significantly simplify and expedite the otherwise complex arrangements, thus contributing to drive their popularity. Indeed, the use of 'blockchain' and DLTs allows storing information in a completely secure and fully traceable, immutable manner, simplifying the transaction and increasing the transparency thereof. The use of the blockchain platform offers the following advantages throughout the process:

- It allows all participants to have access to the transaction. DLT reduces issuing time and ensures that negotiations and agreements reached are traceable and immutable. These features of traceability and immutability make it easier to demonstrate compliance with relevant regulations.
- The platform allows the client to choose between numerous product configuration options. This feature provides the client considerable flexibility in terms of designing the bond that best suits their needs.
- It works for the simplest, to the most complex products. This enables a self-service approach in which investors who know what product they want to invest in can save time and effort by limiting the definition of the different variables. Investors looking for new investment solutions can quickly and easily explore new products.
- It is an entirely digital process in which the negotiation of the structure and prices, and the creation of documentation for the bond are part of the same tool.

BBVA used the technology primarily to 'simplify the processes and streamline the negotiation time frames' with investors. BBVA used a version of Hyperledger Fabric permissioned blockchain, accessible only

> to authorised counterparties such as investors, for issuance of the first Green Bond over blockchain, with the record of the transaction written to the public Ethereum Testnet for full visibility to any observer, as with previous debt products. As well as offering customers access to their platform, BBVA also gave customers the option of hosting a node of the blockchain, which about half of them accepted. In issuing this Green Bond, MAPFRE and BBVA still underwent the traditional third-party validation process for Green Bonds, by DNV GL9.

not yet mainstream, we are likely to see increasing use of technology solutions for the monitoring of green bond and loan compliance in the coming year. One of these solutions are blockchain-based systems supported by IoT devices. With IoT devices connected to a blockchain network, real-time data can be captured, and such information would then be automatically uploaded to the green bonds used to fund it. It is a means of verifying that the data is genuine, and this would improve investors' ability to trust the greenness of their asset or portfolio.

The Path Forward

While blockchain technology's reputation as a resource intensive technology may grab the headlines, the reality is that the use of the technology goes beyond mining for cryptocurrencies. It likely will prove to be short-sighted to neglect the positive ESG impact of blockchain technology in light of the narrow energy consumption debate about Bitcoin. Blockchain will play a strong supporting role in propelling a sustainable future for finance. With powerful applications of blockchain constantly surfacing, and serious thought and invest-ment going towards reducing energy consumption and tackling social inequalities through blockchain, blockchain must not be written off as a strong means to achieving the world's sustainable goals. The prov-erb 'let us not throw the baby out of the bathwater' holds true in this context. As evidenced by real-life applications, blockchain can drive sustainability across environmental, social, and corporate governance issues through its inherent trust and transparency, its ability to create new opportunities for value creation, and next-level traceability. We must harness technology and data to drive effective climate action. The transition to a net zero economy can only be achieved with a committed and concerted effort across the public and private sectors. Blockchain technology looks set to play an integral role in supporting organisations' ESG priorities as more creative applications emerge in furtherance of a more sustainable and equitable future.

References

Bitbond Report 2022. 'Digital Assets in Action: Current Use Cases for Financial Institutions'. December 2022, 34. Available online: www.bitbond .com/wp-content/uploads/2022/12/Digital-assets-in-action-Current-use-cases-for-Financial-Institutions-Bitbond-2022-Report.pdf.
Bruce, A. 2021. 'The Near-Term Future of Blockchain: Tracking Carbon Offsets'. Forbes. Available online: www.forbes.com/sites/ forbestechcouncil/2021/08/16/the-near-term-future-of-blockchain-tracking-carbon-offsets/?sh=5aaf4a205790.
Clifford Chance 2021. 'The Impact of ESG on Emerging DLT Technolo-giesm'. Available online: www.cliffordchance.com/insights/resources/ blogs/talking-tech/en/articles/2021/11/the-impact-of-esg-on-emerging-dlt-technologies.html.
Demirgüç-Kunt, A., Leora K., Dorothe S., Saniya A. 2022. 'The Global Findex Database 2021: Financial Inclusion, Digital Payments, and Resilience in the Age of COVID-19'. World Bank, Washington, DC. Available online: www.openknowledge.worldbank.org/bitstream/handle /10986/37578/9781464818974.pdf
ICMA – Loan Market Association 2018. 'Green Loan Principles – Supporting Environmentally Sustainable Economic Activity'. Available online: www.icmagroup.org/assets/documents/Regulatory/Green-Bonds/ LMA_Green_Loan_Principles_Booklet-220318.pdf.
ICMA – Loan Market Association 2019. 'Sustainability Linked Loan Principles'. Available online: www.icmagroup.org/assets/documents/ Regulatory/Green-Bonds/LMASustainabilityLinkedLoanPrinciples-270919.pdf.
ICMA 2021. 'The Green Bond Principles, Voluntary Process Guidelines for Issuing Green Bonds'. Available online: www.icmagroup.org/assets/ documents/Sustainable-finance/2022-updates/Green-Bond-Principles_ June-2022-280622.pdf.
Joseph, S. 2019. 'State of Diversity and Inclusion in Blockchain. Diversity in Blockchain Inc'. Available online: www.static1.squarespace.com/static/ 5a7f13828a02c7e2df8e6c68/t/5e00f58ccf118b46b6fbd32c/ 1577121230490/The+State+of+Diversity+and+Inclusion+in+Blockchain .pdf

Lee-Hood, L. 2022. 'Another Entire Country Just Banned Cryptomining. Futurism'. Available online: www.futurism.com/kosovo-crypto-ban.

McCormack, U., Tear. L., Ajwani, N. 2021. 'Blockchain and ESG – Using Blockchain for Sustainability and Green Finance'. *King and Wood Mallesons*. Available online: www.kwm.com/hk/en/insights/latest-thinking/blockchain-and-esg-using-blockchain-for-sustainability-and-green-finance.html

OECD 2019. 'Financing Climate Futures: Blockchain Technologies as a Digital Enabler for Sustainable Infrastructure'. Available online: www.oecd.org/finance/Blockchain-technologies-as-a-digital-enabler-for-sustainable-infrastructure-key-findings.pdf.

Quiroz-Gutierrez, M. 2022. 'Crypto Is Fully Banned in China and Eight Countries. Fortune'. Available online: www.fortune.com/2022/01/04/crypto-banned-china-other-countries/.

UN 2021. 'Sustainability Solution or Climate Calamity? The Dangers and Promise of Cryptocurrency Technology'. UN News. Available online: www.news.un.org/en/story/2021/06/1094362.

Van Gysegem, F., De Patoul, K. 2021. 'The Tokenization of the Economy and its Impact on Capital Markets and Banks. Roland Berger Insights'. Available online: www.rolandberger.com/en/Insights/Publications/Tokenization-The-future-of-financial-markets.html

World Bank 2022. 'Remittances Prices Worldwide Quarterly, Issue 43'. Available online: www.remittanceprices.worldbank.org/sites/default/files/rpw_main_report_and_annex_q322_final.pdf

A Further Look at DLT in Banking: Lessons Learned, Current Applications, and Future Scenarios

12 | A Look into the Intermediaries of the Metaverse
Halfway between the Present and the Future

IDA CLAUDIA PANETTA AND SABRINA LEO

Introduction

Although the term metaverse is unclear and ambiguous in its defini-tion, it has been attracting growing interest in business communities (McKinsey Digital 2022). It can be framed as the inclusive dimen-sion of an assortment of innovative elements, not the exhaustive of technologies necessary for its material development. The metaverse is flanked by innovations in economic size, that is, the relationships between operators in *marketplaces* and those in the social sphere. Given its changing shape and potential, the metaverse is capturing the attention of the financial industry, among other sectors. The reason financial intermediaries are pushing in this direction, albeit cautiously, can be traced back to the promise of the metaverse being a potentially limitless dimension, allowing for different interactions from those experienced so far in virtual channels.

Banks are familiar with the use of technology in offering their ser-vices; think of home banking, through which customers can access financial services throughout the day and the week. The increase in the digital dimension has allowed customers to experience greater flex-ibility in banking services, which has prompted banks to design and develop new platform services and ways of interacting with custom-ers. The exploration of the context of the metaverse is thus a natural evolution, and a step ahead in the development of the banking indus-try, which wants to have closer relationships with its customers.

It is worth mentioning that banking in a virtual environment is nothing new in the strict sense: ABN Amro and ING, two European banks, had virtual financial centres in Second Life (OECD 2022a), a mini three-dimensional (3D) virtual state that uses avatars for social interactions. The activity of these intermediaries in Second Life lasted a few years, opening the discussion, above all and (or) still today, to reflections on the added value generated. Although the immersive experience in the metaverse pretends to be different from Second Life, in this case, too, the added value for banks still needs to be evaluated very carefully.

The push for financial intermediaries to be active in the metaverse could arise from the need to counter the threat of the emergence of decentralised finance (DeFi) (OECD 2022b) or the possibility of an economic system that operates in the total – or almost total – absence of financial intermediaries, thanks to the affirmation of new technologies such as DLT. As will be explained later in the discussion, for intermediaries, the metaverse could constitute the opportunity to concretely enter a new financial ecosystem that will probably overcome the opposition between traditional finance (TradFi), DeFi, and centralised finance (CeFi) (OECD 2022b). In this sense, the entry of intermediaries into the metaverse would allow them to access the non-fungible token (NFT) segment and to better recover their role in the cryptocurrency segment, especially sector's regulation. On the other hand, the absence of a complete regulation can justify the delay with which the intermediaries are considering this dimension.

Despite this caution, banks are approaching the metaverse in different ways, starting, for instance, with the purchase of land in the metaverse (e.g., HSBC and Standard Chartered on The Sandbox) (England 2022; The Sandbox 2022). This potential slice of the business is tempting, considering the estimates of the economy of the metaverse. For example, according to Bloomberg, by 2025, the metaverse could help increase economic growth by up to US$73 billion (Kanterman and Naidu 2021). However, the contours of emerging business opportunities and the associated risks need to be clarified. By integrating different systems and applications on various platforms, the metaverse could amplify the potential risk of cybercrime in the financial and banking sectors, which are already the object of criminal interest.

In this chapter, we want to explore banks' approaches to the metaverse as a different way to exploit the potential of DLTs. Having noted the essential elements for defining the phenomenon and tracing its recent evolution, we intend to present a summary framework of the development opportunities (and related hazards), mainly for banks.

The Changing Landscape of Metaverse, Analysing Recent Developments

The debate on the metaverse is currently quite heated and involves experts (and non-experts) from multiple disciplinary fields. Despite this attention, there is still no commonly accepted definition of metaverse, possibly due to its multifaceted and multidimensional nature. The absence of an unequivocally recognised definition has compelled every author, every operator, and every company to give their own. Mark Zuckerberg, founder and chief executive officer (CEO) of Meta, formerly known as Facebook, considers the metaverse as *the embodiment of the Internet,* where users can enter and not just see what is inside but also interact directly with others in the virtual world (Tassi 2021).[1] For Tim Sweeney, founder and CEO of Epic Games, the producer of Fortnite, the metaverse is a 3D social media that can be accessed in real time and allows users to create and share content through digital media, with the additional benefit of users having the same opportunity to change the socioeconomic conditions of the virtual world (Park 2021). Another interpretation was provided by the CEO of Newzoo, Peter Warman, who considers the metaverse a place that allows its users to be players, fans, and creators simultaneously, to optimise user engagement and drive potential and digital business opportunities.

The diversity of approaches appears even more straightforward if one refers to the following definitions of metaverse from the online *Encyclopedia Britannica*, the online *Cambridge Dictionary*, and the *Oxford Advanced Learner's Dictionary*:

Proposed network of immersive online worlds experienced typically through virtual reality or augmented reality in which users would interact with each other and purchase goods and services, some of which would exist only in the online world. Builders of metaverse technology consider it the next step in the evolution of the Internet after early 21st-century developments such as smartphone applications and social media. (Gregersen 2022)[2]

The internet considered as an imaginary area without limits where you can meet people in virtual reality (= images and sounds, produced by a

[1] The original definition is as follows: 'It is a virtual environment where you can be present with people in digital spaces. You can think of this as an embodied internet that you are inside of rather than just looking at.'

[2] E. Gregersen 2022. Metaverse. *Encyclopedia Britannica*, www.britannica.com/topic/metaverse.

computer, that seem to represent a real place or situation): The metaverse is a virtual world where humans, as avatars, interact with each other in a three-dimensional space that mimics reality.[3]

A virtual reality space in which users can interact with an environment generated by computer and with other users.'[4]

These definitions thus refer to social interactions and technologies. Considering its etymology, the term metaverse consists of two words:

– *meta* (μετά in Greek): a Greek preposition that means after or beyond) – and often refers to the concept of change and transformation;
– *universe* (*universus* in Latin): the environment in which all existing material bodies and all natural phenomena are located.

The combination of these two terms should refer to a post-reality environment or virtual world that combines physical and digital reality, thus allowing multi-sensory interactions between the virtual environment and the users and digital objects it contains.

The dimensions of the transformations and innovations that take shape today in the metaverse began long ago. The first VR machine (Sensorama) was created in 1962 in Brooklyn by Morton Heilig (Rheingold 1991), combining 3D video with sound, scents, and a vibrating chair to replicate the experience of riding a motorcycle. In 1960, Heilig also patented the first head-mounted display, allowing players to see 3D images and listen to stereo sound. In his science fiction novel *Snow Crash*, Stephenson (1992) first used the term metaverse to identify a virtual place where digital avatars could escape the real world. In the author's imagination, it was a parallel virtual universe created by computer graphics where users worldwide could connect via special glasses and earphones.

A driving force behind the metaverse's evolution and application came from the 2010 creation of the prototype of the Oculus Rift VR headset, which gave new impetus to so-called immersive technologies.[5]

---

[3] *Cambridge Dictionary*, www.dictionary.cambridge.org/dictionary/english/metaverse
[4] *Oxford Advanced Learner's Dictionary*.
[5] Even before the introduction of many headsets, games were released that allowed players to immerse themselves in virtual worlds, earn digital currencies, and interact with growing numbers of players. Soon after, more advanced platforms appeared, giving users an even richer experience, allowing them to interact with even more players in games such as Fortnite, Minecraft, and Roblox.

After Facebook acquired Oculus in 2014, several other big tech companies entered the VR market with their own devices, including Sony, Google, Samsung, and Microsoft. Microsoft was the first to combine VR with augmented reality (AR), integrating the real world with holograms. Many other companies are now engaged in developing the metaverse, including gaming companies (Epic Games, Tencent).

The development of the technological dimension assumes an important role in defining and differentiating the metaverse from other first-generation virtual experiences (e.g., Second Life) (Robinson et al. 2022). Generally, the elements that characterise the various metaverse platforms have, as a minimum, the following common denominators:

– Interactive 3D technologies;
– Mixed reality (MR) and extended reality;
– Computational and storage resources;
– Artificial intelligence (AI) and machine learning;
– Communication protocols and data flow management;
– And, of course, DLT.

To create or operate in the metaverse, one cannot disregard real-world scanning devices and software to create 3D images. The graphic aspect, which must be excellent, is the feature that makes captivating and genuinely immersive experiences possible.

In addition to the use of VR and AR, the other technological element characterising a metaverse concerns MR and XR, that is, the integration of the metaverse component with the devices used by users to fully integrate applications and digital products. The term XR (GSMA 2019a; GSMA 2019b) is used to encompass VR,[6] AR,[7] and MR,[8] the entire spectrum of technologies that combine computer-generated

---

[6] VR is a technology that creates a virtual world, where users can enter and interact with each other as in the real world, with VR glasses and headsets.
[7] AR is a technology that expands the real world of humans by adding layers of digital information so that objects that do not exist in the physical world appear as if they do. An example of the application of AR technology is the game Pokemon Go, for which users only need to use a mobile phone that supports AR functions to experience it.
[8] MR is a combination of VR and AR, where objects, places, and humans that exist in the real world are dynamically integrated into the virtual world to produce new environments and visualisations so that physical and digital objects coexist and interact in real time. In its first implementation, MR also used headsets and consoles to support users in experimenting with the new experiences created by this MR technology.

virtual elements with reality. These technologies, with different levels of sophistication, allow users to enter and interact in all the virtual worlds of the metaverse in a simple, rapid, and seamless way (Mystakidis 2022). Now, experiences in the metaverse are possible with both forms of AV and AR, conditioned by the levels of economic access to the enabling hardware technologies.

In the technological dimension of the metaverse, the aspect concerning computational and archiving resources with high levels of performance, distributed, and guaranteeing high availability, reliability, and scalability cannot be overlooked. We must remember the enormous amount of data and information exchanged and processed, which requires modern computational capabilities such as edge computing or cloud computing, which are the ideal solutions.

Connected with the production and processing of data, AI and ML are less recent innovations and more qualifiers in the metaverse. Their use derives from the fact that the metaverse interacts with people, making it essential to develop AI algorithms (think of Google Now or Apple Siri) to create an immersive experience that fits reality as closely as possible. Furthermore, AI technologies allow for greater security and information protection in the metaverse. These technologies are used for the following:

- The creation of avatars, thanks to the ability of computers to mimic human tasks through learning and automation, is understood as simulating functions in areas such as visual processing, speech processing, and analysis typical of humans (Boyle 2022);
- Language processing and interface optimisation help to improve accessibility to the metaverse, for example, through image recognition for the visually impaired, machine translation, intelligent exoskeletons to interact with the digital world, and brain-computer interfaces for the most vulnerable individuals, or, more simply, to make the data more interactive rather than merely readable;
- Reducing energy consumption and improving the performance of 5G networks (the type of connection generally required to exploit the metaverse's potential fully).

Furthermore, the data generated by users' interactions in the metaverse (be it purely social or linked to an economic transaction) can produce more accurate information with optimised and efficient data processing employed not only to improve positive experiences while in the metaverse of users, but also to be used in company forecasting models.

Another essential and qualifying element concerns the infrastructural level of communication protocols and data flow management. Because the metaverse operates through communication flows with devices (including wearables), such a reality requires fast connections and transmission protocols capable of supporting large amounts of data. We therefore refer to bandwidth, such as 5G, the most advanced Wi-Fi processors, and up-to-date graphics cards. It should be noted that, at present, the best performances are possible only with the latest-generation devices and in metropolitan areas equipped with enhanced connections (optical fibre or the latest generation of mobile connections).

A blockchain-based metaverse consists of digital objects with NFTs and organises them according to their rules and structures to enhance their properties and characteristics. As highlighted in the previous chapter, blockchain can be configured as a decentralised system of immutable data, associated not only with transactions but also with forms and processes which, once processed in the system, are substantially notarised. The notarisation (often accompanied by geolocation, entry timestamping, and data validation) is granted by the consensus of the potentially infinite participants in the chain (the nodes). NFTs originate when blockchain is applied in the validation and verification of the digital ownership of some files, which then become unique and non-replicable. NFTs are non-fungible digital tokens – that is, unique digital files with a single owner – that make digital economies work. Virtual digital assets, such as land and collectables, are represented as NFTs and exchanged for cryptocurrencies, while blockchains provide digital proof of ownership of these assets. In the metaverse, which has the private property as its peculiarity, NFTs are the certificates for recognising and attributing asset ownership.

Finally, a short discussion[9] on Web3 is needed. Web3 is built on a blockchain system, which allows data and accounting records to be stored on multiple and distributed computer systems. In addition, users can collectively operate within this system to control their data and track all their activities on blockchain technology. This framework

---

[9] For a more complete discussion, see S. Marchetti 2022.

of Web3 allows for the creation of advanced technologies and applications that can be used by multiple users simultaneously, including the metaverse. The Web3-enabled metaverse advances new opportunities for creators (to create) and users for engagements and experiences through a new paradigm. Web3 introduces a brand-new decentralised environment in which

– Consumers can transform into prosumers who can own, monetise, and utilise their data for their own benefit;
– Creators can mint their content and capacities in different ways.

This enhancement is possible thanks to the following (McKinsey Company 2022): (1) blockchain offering a universal, public, permanent, and single source of truth; (2) digital assets issued on blockchains, representing value portability, and permanence; and (3) smart contracts containing conditional programming code that create utility by facilitating self-executing applications. Therefore, Web3-based metaverse apps have more outstanding durability, functionality, and interoperability than Web2-based VR experiences.

Since digital assets are a fundamental component of the Web3 technological stack, their accessibility is crucial to the future architecture of the metaverse. Creators may build new digital assets on whichever blockchain they prefer and distribute them through Web3-native marketplaces with far cheaper charge structures than their Web2 counterparts. Moreover, non-custodial wallets enable users to access their digital assets by linking their wallets to each metaverse venue. Such wallets may include cryptocurrencies, digital stocks, stablecoins, and NFTs in the form of skins, tools, and even virtual real estate. Typically, assets are issued on the same blockchain as the metaverse venue (e.g., Ethereum, Polygon), although cross-chain bridges enable digital asset movement across venues.

The Metaverse's Financial System: From TradFi to Metaverse Finance

Today, many organisations, inside and outside the financial industry, are testing *metaverse-related innovations* that leverage blockchain technologies. As previously noted, the metaverse allows for the integration of physical and virtual worlds, creating a whole new virtual community that will enable people who access it to connect, communicate, work, play, socialise, and conduct transactions with each other. Thus understood, the metaverse, overcoming existing technology on the web, can create a composite world with opportunities to devise new business models in the financial sector.

Although the investments needed to be fully present in the metaverse may not be small, the forecasts on the potential market tempt many:

- Bloomberg speaks of the creation of a significant financial ecosystem, valued at up to 800 billion dollars in 2024, with an annual growth rate of more than 15 per cent (Kanterman and Naidu 2021);
- PwC estimates consistent overall market growth of $1.5 trillion in 2030 (PwC 2020);
- Goldman Sachs believes in a $12.5 trillion opportunity, corresponding to approximately 33 per cent of the digital economy transitioning to the metaverse and a 25 per cent market expansion (Sheridan et al. 2021).

Based on the data, the actors in the financial system, particularly the banking system, have also begun to adopt concrete measures to optimise opportunities and increase their competitive advantage in the era of technological disruption.

The development of the metaverse will bring about changes such as the development of a new financial ecosystem different from that of the real world. Citigroup says the metaverse will give rise to a unique financial ecosystem called metaverse finance, defined as a combination of DeFi, CeFi, and TradFi (Boyle 2022). This financial ecosystem could offer space for the formation of unique new financial services different from those developed in the real world, but with possible effects on it.

The concept of DeFi involves a financial ecosystem growing through the significant role of DLTs (blockchain in particular). Financial services, transactions, and economic activities are carried out only by the interested parties, without recourse to intermediaries. In DeFi, an attempt is made to replace the intermediary's role by exploiting the blockchain's potential and, in particular, the functions of smart contracts.[10] The bank's role is ideally replaced by technologies that enable

---

[10] A smart contract is a protocol or program designed to run automatically based on orders prepared by its creators, allowing work to be done without human intervention.

the development of financial services based on smart contracts that replicate the role of intermediaries on the blockchain and are tailored to the type of services or activities transacted by the parties.

TradFi is the traditional financial ecosystem operating in the real world, dominated by banks that enjoy the public's trust and intervene in every financial intermediation (OECD 2022b). Banks play an essential role in the financial markets, collecting savings and allocating funds to units in deficit. One of the characteristics of TradFi is the minimal role of technology and digitisation in the services provided, instead offering, support in the provision of the services.

CeFi refers to the financial ecosystem that is transitioning from TradFi to DeFi (OECD 2022b). The characteristics of CeFi are the waning dominance of banks as the primary source of financial transactions, which technology-based institutions, such as FinTech's or centralised crypto exchanges (OECD 2022a). The growing popularity of e-money, digital wallets, and other technology-based forms of payment is another feature of CeFi. Even in the case of e-currencies, the financial ecosystem still relies on several financial institutions but has moved to ones other than established commercial banks.

The Banking Ecosystem in the Metaverse: Opportunities and First Experiments

Financial systems continue to evolve with greater accelerations thanks to recent disruptive technological innovations. The metaverse could lead to another level of development if the underlying technologies keep their promises. This development refers particularly to essential technologies, that is, those connected with the development of digital assets; the technologies underlying the definition of Web3; and, finally, the widespread use of platforms as part of the daily operations of economic operators.

Beyond this necessary premise, in the Web3-enabled metaverse, however, we are beginning to see more creative models of involvement by financial intermediaries. Banks and financial intermediaries in general are moving along three main lines, which concern different types of investments and involvement:

– The exploitation of the metaverse to implement *marketing strategies*, especially regarding communication channels for customer *engagement* and the creation of supplementary distribution channels;

- the use of the metaverse for the improvement of internal processes; and
- the creation of new *products and services*.

After briefly outlining the operational content of the paths undertaken, the following sections identify some concrete experiences.

Using the Metaverse for Marketing from Branding Strategy to Virtual Branches

The first actions of banks in the metaverse have mainly been directed towards their so-called branding strategy (Bain 2022), aimed at (1) establishing their brand, (2) creating or strengthening credibility with metaverse users, and (3) demonstrating the ability to innovate. To this end, the metaverse is used as an innovative and low-cost communication channel to connect with customers in new ways, establishing a different type of communication with existing and potential customers. Concerning the latter, reference is often made to the willingness of intermediaries to use the metaverse to reach the so-called Generation Z, even if, in more recent times, Generation X and millennials have been shown to be equally (and perhaps more) interested in interacting differently with the world of financial intermediation. The last two cohorts mentioned are already reasonably familiar with digital channels, usually transact online, and have social interactions on social networks, all characteristics that make them a class of potential users of interest and – especially Generation X – with a more significant income than subsequent generations.

The investment required to use the metaverse for branding strategies is still relatively small; it is mainly linked to the purchase of the space (still low cost) and the setup of virtual land to advertise the financial intermediary's presence. In any case, these costs are lower than those estimated for acquiring a new customer (about €300); furthermore, the costs are even lower if no operational activities are scheduled (The European House – Ambrosetti 2022).

An example of a branding strategy adapted to the metaverse is that behind HSBC's investment in land in The Sandbox, which will be developed to engage with fans of sports, e-sports, and games (England 2022). The bank states that its partnership with The Sandbox will allow for the creation of innovative branding experiences for new and existing customers.

The Spanish Bank Caixa opened a virtual café in Decentraland, launched by the subsidiary Imagin, which deals with digital innovation as part of a larger project called ImaginLand.

In April 2022, Standard Chartered Bank (listed in both London and Hong Kong) also became a partner of The Sandbox and has taken its first steps towards establishing the brand in this dimension by purchasing a lot in the Mega City district.

In South Korea, the Industrial Bank of Korea has announced plans to open a branch in Cyworld Z. In contrast, Nonghyup Bank plans to create a replica of Dokdo Island in a metaverse where visitors can play games and buy property.

In Indonesia, Bank Negara Indonesia, Bank Rakyat Indonesia, and Bank Mandiri have announced they are joining the metaverse ecosystem. These three banks (among the four banks with the highest capitalisation in Indonesia) have, for the moment, entered into collaboration agreements with WIR Group, a company that develops AR and metaverse technologies (Sidik 2022).

In Italy, Intesa Sanpaolo stated that it is exploring the possibility of approaching the metaverse as a communication channel and an opportunity for experimentation, waiting for more defined regulation. Compared with Asia, in Europe a more cautious attitude is mainly adopted.

The metaverse creates an opportunity for banks to strengthen their brands further, making it easier to market the financial services they offer, and not necessarily those in the metaverse. In this sense, we are moving from the more straightforward use of the metaverse as a communication channel to its more complex use as a distribution channel. Intermediaries are launching digital branches and/or multi-brand stores in partnership with companies belonging to other sectors, and implementing cross-selling strategies (as well as investment sharing). Metaverse branches are generally considered in addition to digital (which we could now define as traditional) and physical ones. These new virtual banking branches are created to simultaneously integrate existing distribution channels for old and new services in both the metaverse and the real world.

The development of such virtual bank branches is based on a business model that aims to reach a wider community than the reference model does through different interactions, and to deepen relationships with existing customers. Banks can therefore continue to develop and expand their reference markets without being weighed down by an increase in their physical networks of branches (i.e., *branchless banking*, typical of digital banks).

The concept of digital banking declining in the metaverse allows customers to use banking services autonomously with the help of intelligent assistants or tellers on duty at virtual bank branch, employing avatars, to obtain rapid service with unlimited access and maintain the engagement and interactivity of services in the real world. Among the sector pioneers in this realm is the big US player JP Morgan, the first bank to create a lounge in the metaverse. The financial services firm opened Onyx at the Metajuku mall in Decentraland. Other examples of open agencies aimed at customer engagement in Decentraland are the United Arab Emirates' CBI Bank and the Turkish Aktif Bank.

In June 2022, the Japanese SoftBank Group, in cooperation with the mobile phone operator Y!mobile, opened the first virtual mobile operator store in ZEPETO, with avatars serving customers from both industries. Users can thus open or change their mobile phone contracts after receiving explanations from the shop staff avatars and purchase SoftBank SELECTION services after browsing them in the virtual shop. It is worth noting that the Japanese group is also a partner[11] in The Sandbox and Sorare.[12]

Also on the Asian continent, KB Kookmin Bank, one of the largest financial institutions in South Korea, has developed the KB Metaverse VR Branch Testbed, operational since July 2021 (Zelealem 2021), which is a subsidiary consisting of the following:

- A counter where customers can carry out simple transactions (such as remittances);
- a VIP room where an avatar employee helps clients analyse risk–return profiles or design investment portfolios; and
- a main room where customers can consult their personalised financial information.

Finally, the Swiss Sygnum Bank opened its doors to Decentraland's virtual version of Times Square in the fall of 2022. The virtual branch features an NFT gallery, a cryptopunk virtual receptionist, and an event exhibit hall.

---

[11] SoftBank Vision Fund 2.
[12] A Paris-based NFT fantasy football game maker with 30 employees.

Using the Metaverse for Process Optimisation

Financial companies can conveniently use the metaverse to optimise the phases of their main internal management processes, such as the following:

A. customers' onboarding processes;
B. the population (expansion) and management of the information base relating to customers, also with the use of AI and ML;
C. the optimisation of contracts (e.g., smart contracts);
D. the management of employees through diffusion of the so-called *new work culture* (Anggara et al. 2022); and
E. the optimisation of operating costs linked to the rationalisation of operating offices and more efficient use of human resources (The European House – Ambrosetti 2022).

Items (A) and (B) refer to the simplification of customer interactions and the refinement of their knowledge, especially those who increasingly and recurrently use digital tools in the metaverse. The amount of data obtained by digital transactions contributes to the following:

– improving customer segmentation based on preferences, suggesting to the bank the type of product/service to be provided and the most suitable methods for its delivery;
– simplifying customer recognition and the *onboarding process*;
– assessing creditworthiness with models that take advantage of the possibility of managing and processing a much more extensive database (big data) with *machine learning techniques*; and
– profiling more accurately the level of customers' financial literacy and risk appetite.

With specific reference to items (C) and (D), if the metaverse were to stand by its promises, all the subjects involved in operations would be able to benefit from an interactive and more dynamic professional world. According to the Blue Ivy Group (Parker 2022), an employer branding specialist, several things will impact the *employer branding strategy* and the employee experience over the next three to five years, thanks to the metaverse:

(1) The increased tendency to work remotely;
(2) improvement of the quality of meetings;
(3) valuing diversity and increasing the employees' sense of belonging;

(4) the recruitment, training, and development of human resources; and
(5) the greater involvement of human resources in both onboarding and career development.

To date, technology (Web2) has mainly served to promote communication and interaction in the workplace in a practical way by covering physical distances, but it has not managed to fully replicate the experience of being in the presence of other members of a work team, making it complicated to read body language or share spontaneous ideas if individuals are not casually crossing paths, which usually happens when meeting or working in person. In the metaverse, anyone can join *team members* in a virtual workspace as 3D avatars, replicating body language in the most refined cases.

Operating in the metaverse, moreover, requires employees and all interested parties to adapt to new ways of working and interacting, resulting in *an* ad hoc training need. Regarding this area, there are already concrete experiences in the banking sector. For example, *Bank of America* has organised immersive training for 50,000 employees with its project *Bank of America VR Training* (Bank of America 2021). In this branch employee's training, different customer service scenarios were simulated, so the employees could learn to detect emotions and adapt their behaviour accordingly. According to Bank of America, this experiment is halfway between Web2 and Web3, since it is not a fully immersive VR experience. South Korea's *Hana Bank,* which has created a *task force* to develop ventures in the metaverse, recently held an induction ceremony for new employees in ZEPETO (Park 2021). Also in South Korea, *Nonghyup Bank* held a town meeting in the metaverse, during which an awards ceremony was held to celebrate employees' achievements in digitisation. Since March 2022, the asset management group Azimut has regularly held global managers' committees in the Horizon Workrooms, designed by Meta, to allow managers to interact more effectively, eliminating physical distances, and transforming them into a technology collaborative.

The Metaverse for Creating Products and Services

The metaverse seems to promise, in addition to the possibility of distributing traditional products and services, the opportunity to create new services/products to satisfy specific needs of the virtual world (e.g., the need for intermediate exchanges), as well as ride the wave of market products related to the world of digital assets in a broad sense (e.g., digital asset custody services). Banks gain new opportunities to develop their business in both cases with the metaverse.

Considering that the *metaverse ecosystem* is a virtual space where it is possible to conclude transactions for the purchase of goods and services, it is easy to imagine the active involvement of banks in the area of payments. It is worth pointing out that, on the different metaverse platforms, only cryptocurrencies are used today, and not necessarily the same ones on the different platforms (e.g., MANA in Decentraland, SAND in The Sandbox). In addition, a plausible scenario is that central bank digital currencies (CBDCs) could soon be available in the real world and in the metaverse.[13]

In the near future, metaverse digital and traditional tools (e.g., credit cards) could coexist with intermediate exchanges, creating a business opportunity for banks. There are three possible paths for banks to explore, also to be combined with more traditional payment services in virtual branches:

1. Metaverse-ATMs;
2. metaverse-wallets; and
3. ad hoc metaverse payment services.

Item (1) includes the case of Transak, which, in cooperation with Decentraland, opened the first metaverse ATM, allowing avatars in that space to withdraw MANA; the kiosk also allows them to convert currencies (e.g., dollars) into digital currency.

The second case refers to the possibility for intermediaries to offer a metaverse *wallet*, whose basic version allows customers to keep cryptocurrencies (obtain, retain, and negotiate) and possibly real-world currency; in the most advanced version, the wallet can also provide a custody service for all customers' digital assets. The de facto meta-wallet can be interpreted as simultaneously functioning as a deposit account in the metaverse and custody service (if it comes to including the custody of NFTs). The market in this sector is undoubtedly of

---

[13] In Italy, for example, ABI (Italian Banking Association) recently proposed a simulation of the purchase of products with an example of a digital euro, programmable, and capable of native integration with DLTs, instead of the usual cryptocurrencies (potentially less stable and riskier).

interest, considering that the growth of digital *assets under custody* has increased by 600 per cent since 2019 (PwC 2022).

An example of a *metaverse wallet* has been developed by the Swedish digital bank Mercobank, which is interested in offering its custody service for digital assets. The experience of Latvia-based ZELF, which is launching embedded banking for players in the Discord metaverse through its MetaPass. ZELF intends to facilitate the transfer of value from the virtual to the real world by combining meta-wallet with a bank account. This is a card that allows for the storage of dollars and NFTs and operates on the Visa circuit (also associated with credit transactions, see below).

A large part of the transactions needs to be developed on a block-chain infrastructure in the metaverse; therefore, if we ignore limiting banks from offering cryptocurrency exchange services (a service of potential interest for intermediaries) – and in the absence of CBDCs in the metaverse – banks can collaborate with payment system architecture providers to develop blockchain-based systems. This is also the case of the Square, which studied a bridging solution to enable the US companies Citibank and JP Morgan Chase and Co. to process payments in the *metaverse ecosystem* using their existing infrastructure.[14] This mechanism should save the cost of the independent development of a payment infrastructure that must be borne by the bank and ensure the reliability of the current infrastructure capable of processing payments in the metaverse. The London-based fintech Sokin is developing an autonomous infrastructure to process payments, transactions, and investments in the metaverse (Leonards 2022). The position of *American Express* is more to wait and see, and, despite having applied for seven patents[15] relating to NFTs and the metaverse, it has yet to take concrete steps.

If businesses are carried out in the metaverse and digital assets are purchased for even significant amounts, this can lead to a request for credit for the metaverse. First, consider the volatility increase

[14] Cryptocurrency Facts. *Square's cash app.* Available online: www.cryptocurrencyfacts.com/exchanges/squares-cash-app/.

[15] Of the seven, three seem the most interesting: one is for e-commerce software that allows consumers to transact electronic commerce in the metaverse; another is for creating an online marketplace for buyers and sellers of digital media, that is, NFTs; while the third is for assistance in electronic money transfers and banking services in the metaverse.

and overall rise in prices for purchasing property on the various platforms. Nonfinancial but, above all, unregulated companies are responding to this credit request, and not without some concern. This is the case of the North American technological company (and therefore not an intermediary), TerraZero, which disbursed the first mortgages aimed at purchasing virtual properties in the metaverse (Murar 2022). Another example of an exchange of services in the credit sector between the two worlds is that of ZELF, which, based on tokens kept in its offered wallet, allows it to guarantee small loans up to a maximum of $50 a day.[16] Generally, there have been many loans with collateral consisting of fungible tokens and NFTs, also provided by non-intermediaries.

In addition to payments, funding, and lending, an autonomous demand for advisory and investment services can also arise in the metaverse. Recent years have witnessed the development of the issuance of digital assets and subsequent trading on ad hoc platforms/exchanges. The limits to this development at the moment are regulatory constraints that leave room for the growth of such activities by non-regulated entities; in prospective terms, an exciting space can, in any case, be determined for intermediaries in assisting issuers (on the primary market) and investors in trading (on the secondary market). Many intermediaries have invested in NFTs, such as JPMorgan Chase and Co., Hana Bank, Kookmin Bank, NatWest, Mastercard – American Express, Visa, Imagin, and HSBC, to name just a few. However, concrete experiments without a clear regulatory framework are limited. IBK Investment and Securities has partnered with MetaCity Forum to create a virtual space that offers a wide range of services, including entertainment, e-commerce, and tourism. The brokerage firm will provide virtual financial assistance for the metaverse targeting Millennials and Generation Z.

South Korea's NH Investment and Securities is preparing to tentatively launch its metaverse platform, NH Universe. The platform aims to create a vast virtual space where up to 2,000 clients will be able to interact while enjoying various services, such as seminars and investment analysis games. It is specifically targeting the Millennials and Generation Z, which account for 52 per cent of the company's mobile trading intermediation services.

---

[16] This is a reasonable amount, considering the user is sometimes only 17 years old.

One of the slightly more transversal experiences that embraces the different areas of intermediation is that of Shinhan Bank, one of the top four lenders in South Korea by net profit. Shinhan Bank has officially launched its metaverse platform, Shinamon, aimed at financial service providers, and it is not the country's first bank to do so. The bank states it conducted a five-day trial of Shinamon's services in June 2022, attracting around 85,000 visitors. Shinhan Bank's announcement follows a series of the lender's experiments with services related to blockchain and cryptocurrencies. In December 2021, it conducted a trial of sending international remittances in real time via stablecoins to the Standard Bank of South Africa, using the Hedera blockchain network Hashgraph. Shinhan Bank is also an early investor in Korea Digital Asset Custody, an industry consortium offering cryptocurrency custody services. The bank is currently partnering with Korbit, one of the five largest South Korean cryptocurrency exchanges, to provide users with non-anonymous deposit and withdrawal accounts, as required by local regulations, to ensure transaction transparency. Shinhan Bank also intends to be the first bank to offer services in the metaverse to large clients, particularly universities, to address – through them – Millennials and Generation Z, in the belief that these two groups are the key to digital platforms. The completion of Shinhan Bank's metaverse platform is scheduled for mid-2023.

Risks and Challenges Posed by the Metaverse

The challenges and risks conditioning the development of the activity of banking intermediaries in the metaverse are mainly attributable to the following:

1. Interoperability issues;
2. information technology and data security;
3. reduced awareness of use and dissemination;
4. digital divides; and
5. the need for precise regulation.

One of the areas needed for the improvement of the metaverse relates to the inability to create a user profile that allows access to all (or most) *metaverse platforms*. The lack of interoperability does not allow for the effective use of all the functions of the metaverse, *to* offer users a seamless experience between different platforms. This also includes issues of accessibility across various portals, from browsers to mobile applications, and from computers to laptops and tablets. Furthermore, another interoperability challenge involves the integration of various digital objects and services into the metaverse created by different systems and developers.

As pointed out in the preceding pages, the metaverse stands for the use of digital technology that retrieves, stores, and processes all user data and information to match users' needs in the new dimension. Therefore, ensuring the security of systems, data, and applications is challenging for developers and service providers. Some cyber risks, such as *phishing, hacking,* and *malware,* can harm all services, applications, and digital devices in the metaverse, and all users' personal information can easily be stolen. In addition, risks of a different nature are associated with selling NFTs, such as counterfeiting and recourse to this market for money laundering. An integrated system security framework is therefore needed that allows users to conduct secure transactions even in the metaverse.

Although the construction of an infrastructure and digital technological tools is driving many operators to explore this dimension to stimulate users' awareness and desire to adopt or use metaverse services, it is still a challenge. The community's understanding, awareness, and willingness to enter – and stay – in the metaverse condition the achievement of those profitability objectives promised in many consultancy relationships. This, together with the other hazards, explains the hesitation of many intermediaries to take more decisive steps in the new ecosystem.

The COVID-19 pandemic has highlighted how *digital divides still exist* between countries – and within them –with different intensities across geographical areas. Regardless of the opportunities presented, the metaverse could accentuate the emergence of greater digital divides due to the need to access the Internet, suitable devices (from smartphones to enabling accessories such as viewers), and a 5G connection to interact optimally in the metaverse.

One of the challenges faced by policymakers is in formulating a regulatory framework applicable to the metaverse. Rules on access rights and the management of all data generated in the metaverse are needed, such as the regulation of intellectual property rights, including copyright and related infringements, to name just a few. The presence of financial intermediaries raises the problem of a reference regulatory framework for the various areas of operation and the identification of appropriate supervisory agencies for verifying compliance with the platforms' rules. Since the metaverse is a virtual world without a predetermined domicile, two main theories have been developed to establish potential regulatory frameworks (Anggara et al. 2022):

(a) The *data centre location theory*: according to this theory, the reference legal framework could be identified in the metaverse based on the data centre's location, because the latter must necessarily have a legal domicile. By extension, the law that applies to a specific data centre will apply to the metaverse whose data it protects. This theory originates from the legislative provisions for the various geographical areas of the General Data Protection Regulation, which seek to determine the law applied to services or goods based on the law applied in the country of domicile of the company or bank. The advantage of this theory is its apparent simplicity of application, which considers only that the metaverse could comprise multiple data centres and, therefore, numerous jurisdictions.

(b) The *theory of the law of the metaverse*: according to this theory, the jurisdiction is that of the metaverse; therefore, an ad hoc regulatory framework must be provided that is probably different from that of the natural world or real world, if we are talking about different jurisdictions. Given the benefit of having a single corpus applicable to all metaverse platforms, its implementation is complex due to the absence of a subject with the right to regulate and supervise the metaverse as a whole. Even predicting the creation of a subject of this type would be complex. The only feasible path at the moment is linked to the data centre location theory, even if, as anticipated, it is not free from defects.

The presence of a defined regulatory framework will grant supervising authorities the right to supervise activities in the metaverse. In this scenario, there are several solutions under evaluation.

A point of reference in this context, may be represented in Europe by the so-called PISA framework (The Eurosystem oversight framework for electronic payments 2021), which extends the perimeter of oversight to digital payment tokens, including crypto-assets with a payment function, and in particular stablecoins. Emphasising the new concept of 'transfer of value', replacing the traditional and more circumscribed notion of 'transfer of funds', it recognises the crucial role of central banks in the context of DLT initiatives. Other, similar, stimulating ideas derive from the possible use of a CBDC in the metaverse, which could create the opportunity for the issuer (one or more central banks) to assume its role as regulator and supervisor.

In addition, some authors suggest the establishment of Self-Regulatory organisations (SROs), as defined by IOSCO (2000). SROs can respond to regulatory requirements in fast-changing corporate contexts because of their nature. The SRO method also allows market players with extensive knowledge of the market to write laws that meet business and market demands and maximise regulatory advantages (e.g., orderly markets, client protections, and systemic risk reduction). SROs may efficiently supervise metaverse activity. MetaFi is decentralised, so market participants outweigh regulators. Company-implemented industry innovation has also produced the metaverse. Thus, the metaverse is an industry-driven ecosystem that is best controlled via the SRO method, allowing industry to participate in regulation.

The road to the definition of regulators, rules, and supervisors still seems long, creating resistance to entry for operators, such as financial intermediaries, used to moving in a context that guarantees fair play, conditions of stability, and the protection of operators, even if the rules of the game are numerous (or, according to some, too numerous).

Final Considerations

The metaverse offers new growth opportunities for various productive sectors and, consequently, the financial system, which has always been an infrastructure of the real economy. However, can the financial system be the infrastructure of the metaverse? Indeed, the component linked to the regulatory framework and supervisory agencies does not currently have a defined role in the new dimension; however, financial intermediaries, especially banks, have begun – with some prudence – to adopt more or less concrete measures to exploit existing opportunities.

Financial institutions, as briefly seen, are starting to carve out a role for themselves using new technologies to strengthen their brand, for employee training, to create virtual 'financial cities', telework centres, and interaction spaces, and offer virtual advisory services on investments and old and new products for their customers. Although these applications can be described as fully operational in some cases, their impact on the business model in the financial services industry is only modest, as pointed out by McKinsey Company (2022). We still need to achieve the ecosystem defined in the previous pages as metaverse finance.

Since the rates of acceleration in metaverse development are unknown, financial intermediaries will still have to decide between investing and entering this new reality on a large scale, establishing a minimum position for strengthening the brand, or maintaining a wait-and-see position. It is a decision that depends on four factors: a willingness to bet on the future value of the metaverse, the ability to develop a relevant position, the scale of the *metaverse's potential customers* and relevance to existing and prospective customer bases, and the extent to which the *metaverse's vision* fits with the strategy and culture of a company and its employees.

In this still uncertain scenario, banks will need to find a balance between prospects and opportunities in the metaverse. Above all, they need to explore this possibility by following a precise strategy that appropriately considers the possible risks.

The growth of use cases and their complete integration into banking processes and products capable of defining new business models will depend, on the one hand, on the extent to which the *metaverse will be adopted (populated?)* and, on the other, on the possibility that the value and convenience of the financial services therein exceed the current utility of online or physical services.

References

Anggara, M. R. H., Davie, M. R., Margani, M., and Aulia, M. 2022. 'The presence of commercial banks in metaverse's financial ecosystem: Opportunities and risks'. *Journal of Central Banking Law and Institutions* 1(3): 405–430.

Bain, M. 2022. 'How brands are using NFTs to keep customers hooked'. *Business of Fashion*, March 31.

Bank of America 2021. 'Bank of America is first in industry to launch virtual reality training program in nearly 4,300 financial centres'. Posted October 7. Available online: www.newsroom.bankofamerica.com/content/newsroom/press-releases/2021/10/bank-of-america-is-first-in-industry-to-launch-virtual-reality-t.html.

Boyle, K. 2022. 'Metaverse and money: Decrypting the future'. *Citi GPS*, March 30. Available online: www.icg.citi.com/icghome/what-we-think/citigps/insights/metaverse-and-money_20220330.

England, J. 2022. 'Why are banks and Fintechs entering the metaverse?' *Fintech Magazine*, April. Available online: www.fintechmagazine.com/crypto/why-are-banks-and-fintechs-entering-the-metaverse.

GSMA 2019a. 'Cloud AR/VR whitepaper'. *GSMA Future Networks*. Available online: www.gsma.com/futurenetworks/wiki/cloud-ar-vr-whitepaper/.

GSMA 2019b. AI and automation: An overview. *GSMA Future Networks*. Available online: www.gsma.com/futurenetworks/wiki/ai-automation-an-overview/.

International organisation of Securities Commissions – IOSCO 200. 2000. 'Model for Effective Regulation: Report of the SRO Consultative Committee', 3. Available online: www.iosco.org/library/pubdocs/pdf/IOSCOPD110.pdf.

Kanterman, M., and Naidu, N. 2021. 'Metaverse maybe $800 billion market, next tech platform'. *Bloomberg Intelligence*, December 1. Available online: www.bloomberg.com/professional/blog/metaverse-may-be-800-billion-market-next-tech-platform.

Leonards, A. 2022. 'Sokin to launch e-commerce payments in the metaverse'. FStech, posted February 2, 2022. Available online: www.fstech.co.uk/fst/Sokin_To_Launch_Ecommerce_Payments_In_The_Metaverse.php.

McKinsey Company 2022. 'Value creation in the metaverse: The real business of the virtual world'. Available online: www.mckinsey.com/capabilities/growth-marketing-and-sales/our-insights/value-creation-in-the-metaverse.

McKinsey Digital 2022. 'Innovative and practical applications of the metaverse'. At the Edge podcast, March 29. Available online: www.mckinsey.com/capabilities/mckinsey-digital/our-insights/innovative-and-practical-applications-of-the-metaverse.

Murar, K. 2022. 'Tech firm closes first metaverse mortgage for acquisition in Decentraland'. Bisnow. Posted on January 27, 2022. Available online: www.bisnow.com/national/news/technology/tech-firm-closes-first-metaverse-mortgage-for-acquisition-in-decentraland-111659.

Mystakidis, S. 2022. 'Metaverse'. *Encyclopedia* 2(1): 486–497. Available online: www.doi.org/10.3390/encyclopedia2010031.

OECD 2022a. 'Lessons from the crypto winter: DeFi versus CeFi'. OECD Business and Finance Policy Papers. Available online: www.doi.org/10.1787/199edf4f-en.

OECD 2022b. 'Why decentralised finance (DeFi) matters and policy implications'. Available online: www.oecd.org/daf/fin/financial-markets/Why-Decentralised-Finance-DeFi-Matters-and-the-Policy-Implications.pdf.

Park, A. J. 2021. '"Metaverse" becomes new growth engine of financial industry'. *The Korea Times*. Available online: www.koreatimes.co.kr/www/biz/2023/01/602_ 314385.html.

Park, G. 2021. 'Epic Games believes the Internet is broken. This is their blueprint to fix it'. *The Washington Post*, September 28, Available online: www.washingtonpost.com/video-games/2021/09/28/epic-fortnite-metaverse-facebook.

Parker, S. 2022. 'How the metaverse will change your employer brand and workplace culture'. Available online: www.bluivygroup.com/blog/how-the-metaverse-will-change-your-employer-brand-and-workplace-culture.

PwC 2020. 'Virtual and augmented reality could deliver a $1.5 trillion boost to the global economy by 2030'. Press Room. Available online: www.pwc.com/th/en/press-room/press-release/2020/press-release-29-01-20-en.html.

Rheingold, H. 1991. '*Virtual reality*'. Simon and Schuster, New York, NY.

Robinson, J., Whyte, J., and Segura, C. 2022. 'Exploring metaverse and the digital future'. *GSM Association*, February 2022. Available online: www.gsma.com/asia-pacific/wp-content/uploads/2022/02/270222-Exploring-the-metaverse-and-the-digital-future.pdf.

Sheridan, E. Ng, M., Czura, L., Steiger, A., Vegliante, A., Campagna, K. 2021. 'Framing the future of Web 3.0: Metaverse edition'. *Goldman Sachs Equity Research*, December 10. Available online: www.goldmansachs.com/insights/pages/framing-the-future-of-web-3.0-metaverse-edition.html.

Sidik, S. 2022. 'State-owned banks join the metaverse business'. Available online: www.katadata.co.id/syahrizalsidik/finansial/622726c509321/bank-bumn-ramaikan-bisnis-metaverse.

Stephenson, N, 1992. '*Snow crash*'. Bantam Books, New York.

Tassi, P. 2021. 'Mark Zuckerberg is building the wrong metaverse'. *Forbes*, 29 July. Available online: www.forbes.com/sites/paultassi/2021/07/29/mark-zuckerberg-is-building-the-wrong-metaverse/?sh=61c2702d5b74.

The European House – Ambrosetti 2022. 'Metaverse and the financial system: A new opportunity for the business community? September, 41. Available online: https://innotechhub.ambrosetti.eu/en/docs/index#lg=1&slide=0.

The Sandbox 2022. 'HSBC to become the first global financial services provider to enter The Sandbox', March 16. Available online: https://sandboxgame.medium.com/hsbc-to-become-the-first-global-financial-services-provider-to-enter-the-sandbox-c066e4f48163.

Zelealem, F. 2021. 'South Korea's KB Bank enters metaverse space'. Yahoo, November 30.

13 | *The DLT Landscape in Banking*
Key Features of Prominent Use Cases through Strengths and Weaknesses

SABRINA LEO AND IDA CLAUDIA PANETTA

Introduction

Distributed Ledger Technology (DLT) solutions, particularly Blockchain, are experiencing growing interest from policy makers, industry, consumers, and supervisory and regulatory authorities. This trend emerges from different analyses, with DLT projects estimated to reach $19 billion in 2024, compared to only US$1 billion in 2017 (Perrazzelli 2023). In this context, the important role played by the banking and financial sector in investing in Blockchain solutions, accounting for 29.7 per cent (Taylor 2022) of the global total in 2020, must be emphasised.

DLT is widely recognised as a key source of future financial system innovation (Iansiti and Lakhani 2017; Kavuri and Milne 2020; Lewis et al. 2017; McKinsey 2016; Philippon 2016) with the potential to transform business models across many industries, particularly the banking industry (Holotiuk et al. 2017; Nowiński and Kozma 2017; Morkunas et al. 2019; Rajnak and Puschmann 2021). Among analyses of potential use cases, cross-border payments are the most relevant, accounting for around 16 per cent of the total. DLT solutions can enable consumers and companies to transfer money internationally at significantly reduced cost (Taylor 2022). This can be a major boost for payment services and consumers, with benefits for the commercial and manufacturing sectors as well. Market surveys conducted by leading consulting firms (e.g., Deloitte 2021) have shown that financial service providers that have implemented DLT solutions have mainly used them in connection with crypto-assets and the tokenisation of assets, such as the digitisation of real estate and works of art, through the use of so-called non-fungible tokens (NFTs).

In this context, the application of so-called smart contracts appears to be growing, driving further developments in the field of Decentralised

Finance (DeFi). The current relation between banking systems and DLT is challenging, however, since, in addition to the numerous opportunities DLT has to improve conventional banking procedures, it is viewed as a threat to traditional banking business models, and not just to payment systems. Ever since the initial Blockchain craze has subsided, many digital businesses, innovations, and technology decision makers are still waiting to determine if DLT – particularly Blockchain – deployments in the banking industry can deliver sustainable business value. To map the various business models within the scope of this chapter, academics have generally navigated the evolving DLT financial landscape by considering (Mansour et al. 2021) the following:

A. The component of the financial system considered (e.g., IsDB 2021), financial institutions, financial instruments, rules and regulations, and operational mechanisms (including the data infrastructure).
B. The technological standpoint, considering the different layers, such as protocols[1] (e.g., Corda, Hyperledger, Clearmatics, and Quorum), networks[2] (e.g., We.Trade, Verified.Me, and Komgo), and applications[3] (e.g., digital assets, workflow automation, identity and authentication, timestamping, and notarisation).

To date, different use cases in the financial industry have been developed through all different layers and components of the financial system (see Table 13.1), with different levels of implementation, ranging from theoretical ideas to consolidated experiences.

The rise of digital assets, defined as a 'virtual record of value directly held on and transferred across a shared cryptographically secured ledger' (Milne 2022 p. 6), poses challenging questions for the business models of regulated intermediaries in the financial system. Owning

---

[1] The protocol layer consists of the technological building blocks of the back end, at the lowest level. It is the assortment of fundamental protocol frameworks. Shared platforms are introduced as one of the use cases at this level (Rauchs et al. 2019).
[2] The network layer consists of the current peer-to-peer (P2P) networks that bring a DLT system to life by linking members to facilitate data sharing and verification. Networks can be constructed by using a standard core protocol framework or a collection of modular core building blocks from several core protocol frameworks (Rauchs et al. 2019).
[3] The application layer is the principal user interface for DLT networks, where business applications are connected to existing business networks to generate business value (Rauchs et al. 2019).

Table 13.1 *Traditional taxonomy of the DLT financial landscape*

		Technological perspective		
		Protocol layer	Network layer	Application layer
Financial system perspective	Financial infrastructure	☑	☑	☑
	Financial institutions	☑	☑	☑
	Financial instruments	☑	☑	☑
	Financial superstructure	☑	☑	☑

digital assets directly on distributed ledgers rather than indirectly as liabilities of commercial or custodial banks alters ownership transfer: digital assets are no longer controlled by a single intermediary, as is the case with indirect financial assets; instead, ledger operators accept transfers after the automatic authentication of an asset owner's digital signature. In this scenario, the intermediaries' function changes with the direct holding of digital assets and digital signature-validated transactions. This consequently significantly affects business models, even though holders could not notice any difference in managing their money and investments, whether they own digital assets directly or indirectly, as managed through a modern user-friendly interface (online or mobile) or call centre agents. The new business models and ways of interacting between operators in the financial system will therefore be the result of the combination of new products/services and new ways of managing processes among intermediaries.

In light of the above, this chapter aims to provide an essential overview of DLT in banking, highlighting the current challenges for the industry, as well as major changes in the financial industry. With this aim, we navigate the main DLT projects and implementations in banking, grouping them into two main categories identified by the type of need fulfilled: (i) *products and services* created to address financial institutions' customer needs and (ii) *internal processes and operations* to meet financial intermediaries' needs (see Table 13.2). Consequently, in the following subsections, we concentrate on the main characteristics of the use cases in the industry, focusing on aspects not covered in the previous chapters.

Table 13.2 *A new taxonomy of DLTs in the banking*

Categories	Type of DLTs project in the banking
Products and services	Payment instruments and services
	Credit and lending retail
	Corporate and investment banking
	Asset management services
	Metaverse product and service
Internal process and operations	Data management
	Production-based
	Marketing-based
	Risk management
	Regulatory compliance

Products and Services

Payment Instruments and Services

To understand the evolution of payment system, we must first recall the distinction between account-based and token-based payments. According to Bechtel et al. (2022), payments can be made and recorded in either account-based (i.e., bank-based) or token-based systems. As is known, account-based payments involve using credit money that moves credit/debit positions to or from a bank. The transaction's initiation consists of the customer's authentication (in more or less technologically advanced forms), the payment's execution, and the related balance update. In token-based forms of money, on the other hand, the authorisation of a transaction is not based on the customer's authentication, but on the verification of the token's validity, which incorporates all the information necessary to verify its legitimacy and carry out the transaction.

The danger of theft and other losses is minimal when money is placed with a regulated institution, such as a bank, because the account provider is in charge of maintaining records and managing the account. Additionally, account-based systems often have better levels of fungibility and interoperability. Because financial intermediaries have agreed on common (technical) standards, the euro is fungible inside an account-based approach and the systems are interoperable. The same, however, is not always the case for digital euro equivalents that use tokens. Various institutions can issue tokens on diverse technological platforms, resulting in non-fungible and non-interoperable versions of the digital euro. Finally, because accounts are tightly linked to the current regulatory frameworks, account-based money offers regulatory advantages.

Token-based systems, on the other hand, could overcome some of the privacy, resiliency, and efficiency issues that account-based systems face. Since the token holder does not need to be verified by an intermediary, tokens can be transferred between individuals. It is crucial to guarantee that the tokens cannot be copied or faked. DLT is a ground-breaking idea that allows for the creation of decentralised digital token-based forms of money and addresses for the first time the issue of digital double spending. DLT also makes tokenisation possible, such that all tangible assets, products, and rights can be represented by exchangeable digital tokens. P2P transactions using token-based money improve payment efficiency, since they eliminate the need for intermediaries and allow for direct communications between the two counterparties of a transaction. Furthermore, because payments may still be performed, even when an intermediary is unavailable or acting maliciously, this P2P feature improves the robustness of payments. In token-based systems, payment privacy may also be more critical.

Following Bechtel et al. (2022), we show the main characteristics differentiating account-based from token-based payments in Table 13.3.

In light of the above, the next generation of payment systems may use DLT as a platform, improving the integration and reconciliation of settlement accounts with related ledgers. The use of DLT in payments is assisting in automating the whole process, lowering the number of intermediaries often necessary in payment transactions, and improving process efficiency. By eliminating the need for banks to manually settle transactions (Dixon 2021), DLT applications in payments are lowering the cost of these transfers and fostering more trust between parties (Banque de France 2018). Boumlik and Bahaj (2018) developed a P2P monetary system that does not require a third party or cash for worldwide bartering. However, because DLT can provide bankers with immutable data, real-time access, and consensus verification, it is without a doubt the future of banking. Wright et al. (2019) noted that the assurance afforded by Blockchains is sufficient motivation for banks to reconsider the deployment of Blockchain technology. Given that payments represent a substantial portion of banking, the

Table 13.3 Comparison between account-based and token-based payments

	Convenience of storage and transactions	Risk of loss/theft	Interoperability with DLT systems	P2P transactions	Payment resilience	Payment efficiency	Privacy	Regulation embedding
Account-based money	[High]	[High]	[Moderate]	[Not possible]	[High] Possible only online	[High] National payments / [High] Cross border payments	[High]	
Token-based money Cash	[Moderate]	[High]	[High]	[In person]	[High] Possible offline	[High]	[High]	[High]
Crypto assets	[Moderate] [Increasingly]	[High]	[High] On the same DLT	[Global]	[High] Possible offline in a limited context	[High] Large-value payments / [High] Low-value payments	[High] due to the anonymity of most cryptocurrencies	[High] [Increasingly]

Source: Authors' elaboration on Bechtel et al. 2022.

[Low] Low [Moderate] Moderate [High] High **+** Increasingly ⊠ Not possible In person ⊕ Global business is ripe for disruption (Wu and Liang 2017). The banking industry is seeing a shift due mostly to the increased speed and nature of transactions performed via Blockchain technology.

Many central banks have regulatory and operational duties in payment systems and have taken an active interest in DLT trials, allowing them to test prototypes while studying their potential safety and efficiency consequences in the public interest (Shabsigh et al. 2020). In particular, central banks have an interest in cross-border and wholesale payments. Concerning cross-border payments at the moment, central banks provide settlement services exclusively to domestic players. Private banks have therefore established corresponding banking services in which cross-border settlements are carried out through their own accounts. To bolster their corresponding networks and gain access to national central banks and private systems, certain prominent multinational banks have opened subsidiaries in significant markets. If central banks' supposedly permissioned DLT networks prohibit cross-border involvement, this issue may not alter DLT deployments. A fundamental obstacle in supporting the effective interbank cross-border settlement of large-value payments from a technological standpoint is the lack of a unified settlement platform and network with global reach. Central banks have experimented with different ways, whose details are available in Box 13.1.

Regarding wholesale payments, prototypes have demonstrated the viability of employing DLT as a transaction booking technique. The DLT consensus procedures underpinned all the prototypes, which used less processing power and offered more anonymity. This increased the need for faith in the validator nodes, which is not a problem in a system run by a central bank or other reliable institutions.

Although throughput,[4] dependability, and resiliency are essential requirements for operational production, they have not received enough attention in prototypes. They, therefore, are not seen as adequate evidence of production viability.

Privacy and liquidity savings seem to be top priorities for central banks. Prototypes have used central bank deposit receipts or token-based central bank money, and their system structures were derived

---

[4] The term *throughput* is used to describe the time frames in a day within which banks must transmit a fraction of the total value of their day's payments to a payment system.

Box 13.1 Payment instruments and services
use cases

RETAIL PAYMENTS

In April 2018, **Banco Santander** launched the first Blockchain-based international money transfer service, allowing customers to complete international transfers on the same day or by the next day. The service also shows the exact amount that customers will receive in the destination currency before they make the transfer.

The French investment banking firm **BNP Paribas** has been studying the use of Blockchain technology in the market for money market funds and in the processing of purchases.

Bank of Montreal, Commerzbank, Caixa Bank, and **Erst Group** are working diligently on Batavia, a Blockchain-based global industry finance network designed to streamline the transfer of goods and funds with greater transparency and efficiency.

REMITTANCES

In Uganda, Nigeria, and Kenya, **BitPesa** enables Blockchain payments. The platform has processed millions of dollars, with a transaction volume increasing at a rate of 20 per cent per month. BitPesa has helped bridge the remittance gap in Sub-Saharan Africa, which is considered the most expensive region in the world to send money. The presence of cryptocurrency platforms such as BitPesa has resulted in a 90 per cent reduction in transfer fees throughout the region.

WHOLESALE PAYMENTS

More than **60 Japanese banks,** representing 80 per cent of the Japanese banking industry, have joined Ripple, which is attempting to provide alternatives to Society for Worldwide Interbank Financial Telecommunications (SWIFT), to facilitate relatively rapid international financial transactions.

Santander Bank used Ripple's xCurrent protocol in the United Kingdom to enable international payments of US$10 to US$10,000,000.

The **Bank of England** (BOE) has proposed integrating real-time gross settlement devices with Blockchain technology to expedite payments and cash transfers.

Leighton (2018) stated that **Goldman Sachs** also uses its internal funds to swap Blockchain futures for its clients.

CROSS-BORDER PAYMENTS

The potential for using CBDCs and DLT for less expensive and safer cross-border payments and settlements has been demonstrated by a prototype of multiple Central Bank Digital Currencies (mCBDCs) developed by the Bank for International Settlements (BIS) and four central banks. The **BIS Innovation Hub Hong Kong Centre, the Hong Kong Monetary Authority, the Bank of Thailand, the People's Bank of China's Digital Currency Institute, and the Central Bank of the United Arab Emirates** are all partners in the mBridge initiative.

In contrast to the several days typically needed for any transaction to be completed using the existing network of commercial banks and operations on a 24/7 basis, the common prototype platform for mCBDCs settlements is able to complete international transfers and foreign exchange operations in seconds. According to the project's assessment, the cost of such activities to consumers can be decreased by up to half.

Shabsigh et al. (2020) shows that central banks have investigated DLT and its potential for large-value cross-border payments, with the following examples:

- The **Bank of Canada** (BOC) and the **Monetary Authority of Singapore** (MAS) joined their experimental domestic payment networks to allow cross-border and cross-currency payments using CBDCs. The project linked two DLT platforms to enable Payment-versus-Payment (PvP) settlements without the requirement for a trusted third party to function as an intermediary (BOC and MAS 2019).
- In previous research, **BOC, Monetary Authority of Singapore (MAS)**, and **Bank of England (BOE)** investigated various approaches for resolving problems in cross-border payments (BOC, BOE, and MAS 2018).

from those supported by the external DLT software and protocol providers chosen. The pre-funded money injected into the system was what the prototypes relied on in terms of liquidity concerns. Cost–benefit assessments were not conducted in most of the tests. Central banks feel that wholesale digital token design considerations necessitate clarity on the nature of the claims underlying assets or funds, the legal foundations, and institutional and risk evaluation.

Given the above, the following are essential considerations during research and prototype development: (i) the application of DLT-style solutions for automated transaction-level reconciliation, Public Key Infrastructure (PKI)-encrypted transactions, and the security of central bank and Real-Time Gross Settlement systems (RTGS) participants' money transfers; (ii) a Liquidity Saving Mechanism (LSM) based on slitting DLT payment transactions into partial settlements, utilising easily accessible tokens in the proper priority sequence, which is not applicable to the liquidity saving models used in current RTGS systems (since existing liquidity will be exploited as effectively as possible when even small quantities of tokens are moved throughout a network); (iii) analysis of the operational and regulatory adjustments required for activities available 24/7/365 that do not require end-of-day processing and a cost–benefit study of various DLT deployment strategies; (iv) interoperability between various DLT systems; and (v) the advantages and drawbacks of settling international payments with a universal digital asset or basket of assets.

Lending

Lending and credit supply precede the establishment of banks. Since the beginning, banks and lenders have underwritten loans using a credit checking and reporting system, frequently employing specialised credit agencies. When a person requests a loan, the bank must first analyse the likelihood that the person will be unable to repay the amount. To determine whether to grant the loan, the bank considers characteristics such as the person's credit score, debt-to-income ratio, and property ownership status. The bank consults the applicant's credit record to gather the relevant information. Based on this information, banks consider the risk of default in determining the interest and fees they charge for loans. Customers may be intimidated by such a robust system and it may be complicated, time-consuming, and stressful for borrowers who want money quickly.

The distributed ledger provides a new realm of opportunities for digital loans that might be more cost-effective, efficient, and secure. DLT can potentially catalyse a realistic and secure P2P lending system. This technology has distinct advantages when lending involves several parties, and it eliminates gatekeepers in the credit market, making low-interest loans more secure to borrow. Tokenised identities and zero-knowledge proof are examples of innovations that help borrowers gain access to finance. If there is a decentralised, cryptographically protected registry of earlier payments, applicants' creditworthiness can be established using a global credit score. Such a system gives banks a complete picture of an applicant's credit history and increases the likelihood that applicants will qualify for loans.

Distributed ledger lending thus offers a more secure method of distributing personal loans to a larger pool of users. It also reduces expenses while increasing efficiency and security during the lending procedure. It enables P2P lending, sophisticated programmed loans with mortgage-like structures, and a faster and more secure lending procedure.

Even though Blockchain lending operations are still in their early stages, there are a few promising ideas in terms of P2P loans, infrastructure, and credit. Box 13.2 summarises some of these.

Box 13.2 Lending use cases

The **Agricultural Bank of China** has approved mortgages totalling $300,000 using DLT technology.

The **Royal Bank of Scotland, Barclays**, and **NatWest** are involved in a consortium working on a 'decentralised home buying network', including Blockchain mortgages.

SALT Lending uses Blockchain to make cash loans. The SALT Lending platform enables users to borrow money using any cryptocurrency as collateral or a Blockchain asset. The loan is accepted based on the value of the collateral instead of the borrower's credit score. While securitised loans are not a novel concept, collateralising loans with assets such as cryptocurrency allows the lender to optimise liquidity in a 24/7 market, significantly reducing risk.

Dharma Labs' system for tokenised debt is another example of how Blockchain improves lending by allowing new suppliers to enter the market. The protocol provides programmers with the tools and rules to build online lending marketplaces covering the range from consumer and margin lending to municipal bonds.

Bloom employs Blockchain technology to create a system for regulating identification, risk, and credit ratings. This advancement benefits everyone, from consumers, who can rapidly check for credit alerts and identity theft, to businesses, which can easily run background checks.

The major purpose of the **Decentralised Depository System for Mortgage Accounting** project was to lower the cost and time of mortgage accounting, storage, and securitisation. The project's depositories constitute of a cloud system for the distributed storage of electronic mortgages and accounting for depository account activity. The participants' processes are automated using smart contracts that follow Russian law. The project's key participants are DOM.RF, Rosreestr, depositories, and mortgage lenders. The electronic mortgage accounting was developed in a decentralised depository system, and accounting for other securities is part of system development. After Masterchain certification, the financial market's decentralised depository system for mortgage accounting was commissioned on 19 December 2019.

SberBank and specialist depositories were the first to endorse the idea, and by 2019, five other significant Russian banks and depositories were using it. Blockchain infrastructure and a regulatory framework for financial market participants were needed to launch the first such solution. Amendments were made to the federal law On Mortgage, the relevant regulations of the Bank of Russia on depositary operations, digital document formats for electronic mortgage, and structured messaging requirements for depositories. The project will cut storage, accounting, preparation, and securitisation costs, according to the Financial Technology Association. It is also projected to shorten operating times from days to minutes and improve mortgage storage and depositary account transaction data dependability.

Bank Guarantees

A bank guarantee,[5] that is, a bank's unqualified promise to pay one party in the event of another's default, is used to secure contracts in a variety of industries, including the trade of goods and services, financial transactions, industrial projects, the development of real estate, and the leasing of assets. In place of a cash deposit or rental bond, prospective tenants sometimes utilise bank guarantees to obtain commercial real estate leases. As an alternative to cash, bank guarantees provide greater freedom for renters in securing their lease commitments. Commercial landlords can offer the reassurance of a financial institution in the case of tenant default (e.g., failure to pay rent or

---

[5] A bank guarantee is an independent promise by a bank, on behalf of its client, to pay a designated beneficiary if the customer fails to fulfil contractual commitments with that beneficiary. Importantly, the obligation to pay is unconditional and can be triggered by the beneficiary's presentation of a simple claim or demand, regardless of the customer's performance or non-performance of the underlying contract.

Table 13.4 *Characteristics of bank guarantees*

Characteristic	Critical issues
Physical document management	Expenses, hazards, and delays involved with the physical printing, issuance, exchange, and retrieval of guarantee documents
Monitoring and reporting	Difficulties in the tracking, reporting, and general openness of a guarantee's status while it undergoes possibly several handoffs and revisions
Lack of standardisation	Human work is necessary to study and negotiate the terms and conditions of a guarantee, which might differ from bank to bank and landlord to landlord

make good upon departing a property) while eliminating the administrative overhead of monitoring cash deposits and trust accounts. The benefit to landlords is so great that many incorporate the necessity of a bank guarantee in their standard form lease agreements. However, although a helpful financial tool, bank guarantees issued today are paper based, resulting in various inefficiencies (see Table 13.4).

Regarding physical document management, a Blockchain network is established between the renter, the landlord, and the bank to digitalise and securely transmit information on bank guarantees in circulation. Where a paper guarantee would ordinarily be granted (i.e., after the completion of appropriate bank credit checks and approvals), the bank would instead generate a new record on the shared ledger to reflect the newly issued digital guarantee. The existence of this guarantee would be instantly apparent to both the renter and the landlord, who would then commence the procedure typically initiated by the receipt of a paper guarantee (e.g., commencement of the lease). This dematerialisation of the guarantee eliminates the physical handling and transmission of papers during issuance, cancellation, and revision. Although outside the scope of this first Proof of Concept (PoC), this process has paved the way for the complete elimination of physical settlements through digital signatures.

In terms of revisions, dematerialisation would allow the guaranteed amount to be adjusted, subject to landlord approval, without needing to collect and exchange the old and new documents. Regarding requests and cancellations, the procedure would never be slowed down by a missing digital guarantee, since the distributed ledger would offer a trustworthy record of the current status of all guarantees. In addition, the implementation of Blockchain technology would provide a complete and verifiable record of every transaction that led to the present state. The result would be a digital guarantee that eliminates the dangers associated with losing guarantees, delays in retrieving them, the need for issuing duplicates, and the inconvenience of having to surrender a guarantee in person at a branch for a call-up or cancellation.

As for monitoring and reporting, the potential of a Blockchain system to establish a single source of truth across many parties is one of its primary advantages. Traditionally, this is accomplished by entrusting a central authority with the ownership and operation of a registry for the benefit of others. The Blockchain system federates trust and accountability across the network. The rules for updating and maintaining the database – that is, which records may be altered, how they can be altered, who can change them, and who must obtain consent – are defined and incorporated within each network node.

Consensus techniques guarantee that updates coming from various nodes are committed in a manner that ensures all nodes always maintain a consistent and shared view of the database. The encryption of each transaction and record ensures that only participants in the transaction may read its contents, ensuring the secrecy of business transactions in a dispersed environment. This allows for the obligation to produce and update records to be distributed among participants at pertinent moments in the lifespan of a guarantee.

In a distributed ledger, the renter and landlord can request the creation or modification of a guarantee, but only the bank can act on the request. This assures that neither renters nor landlords can improperly modify active assurances to their advantage (e.g., increasing a guaranteed amount before claiming it, terminating a guarantee before an anticipated claim by the landlord).

The ability for the landlord to request a new guarantee on behalf of a tenant is a notable improvement over the current process. It is intended to reduce the effort in the issuance and subsequent rework of incorrect guarantees due to the tenant providing incorrect landlord/beneficiary information to the bank (e.g., beneficiary name).

Finally, regarding the lack of standardisation compared to conventional databases, a distributed ledger supported by Blockchain technology offers both advantages and disadvantages. Storage is an

---

Box 13.3 Bank guarantee use cases

In April 2017, **ANZ** and **Westpac**, two providers of bank guarantees, partnered with **Scentre Group**, the owner and operator of Westfield in Australia and New Zealand, and **IBM**, a leader in Blockchain and DLTs, to demonstrate that a Blockchain solution could be used to replace the current paper-based bank guarantee process, thereby reducing the risk of fraud, driving standardisation, and enhancing efficiency for the three primary parties involved. To demonstrate viability within a short time, the scope of the project was limited to bank guarantees in the context of commercial property leasing in Australia, with the expectation that any proven solution would be applicable to a larger context of guarantees. Given that ANZ and IBM are founding members and ongoing sponsors of Hyperledger, Fabric was chosen as the fundamental Blockchain technology.

The final goal of the **Masterchain** project is to create a Blockchain of digital bank guarantees issued by banks operating in the Russian Federation and to avoid paper guarantees. Its intent is for digital guarantees to be the primary digital documents, to be reproduced on paper only if necessary for information purposes.

---

illustration of this concept. While the cryptographic linkages between transaction blocks produce a complete and auditable history of transactions, the ever-growing nature of this transaction chain necessitates careful consideration of the volume and type of information to be maintained. Blockchains benefit more from discrete, organised data sets than unstructured data or big data. Despite appearing to be a constraint, this trait can also serve as an impetus for simplifying and standardising existing processes and procedures. In sectors with a long and storied past, it is usual for current procedures to be the result of incremental advancements. Quite frequently, these are a blend of simple upgrades and temporary workarounds designed to circumvent the technological restrictions of the past. Without disciplined, continuous improvement efforts, these cumbersome procedures become ingrained routines that are difficult to alter and do not take advantage of technological developments. As a vehicle for exchanging information and facilitating process flows, Blockchains also enable the detection of network participant similarities. Some examples of use cases for bank guarantees are summarized in Box 13.3.

Trade Financing

Trade financing, where financial institutions provide credit facilities to guarantee the exchange of goods, is a centuries-old industry that has not changed significantly despite the expansion of global trade flows. DLT was hailed as a technology capable of reinvigorating trade finance, driving efficiencies, lowering the cost basis, and creating new income opportunities through new credit and funding methods to support trade. Trade financing involves numerous document exchanges between exporters and importers, banks, insurers, transportation and logistics businesses, and government officials. As a result of market friction, obtaining finance and concluding transactions is a time-consuming and intricate procedure that involves lending, providing letters of credit, factoring, and insuring the parties (Lang 2017). Financial institutions are needed to undertake credit evaluations and payments across many parties, sometimes involving the paper-based exchange and confirmation of documents (Financial Stability Board 2022). Generally, a single transaction can take days to weeks to complete.

According to the literature (Cong and He 2019; Yermack 2019), the characteristics of DLT allow it to relieve these trade frictions by lowering the volume and complexity of documentation and document flows. By leveraging Blockchain technology in particular to digitalise and authenticate records (e.g., through smart contracts) and allowing all parties involved in an operation to access the same data, it is possible to save time and costs and reduce operational risk (Buithenek 2016; Guo and Liang 2016). This means that Blockchain may enable participants from different industries (e.g., banking and freight shipping) to interact directly and share information in a way that is more easily verifiable and decentralised, thereby increasing the speed of transactions and reducing the need for paper reconciliation (Financial Stability Board 2022). DLT's capacity to connect numerous parties in a decentralised network and provide a permanent, tamper-proof distributed digital record of transactions make it the ideal technology to make the US$5.2 trillion global trade finance ecosystem more efficient, transparent, and secure.

Consequently, among the first instances of corporate finance products exploiting this technology, we find different projects referring to trade finance. In particular, DLT contributed to enabling the effective digitisation of the process used to track and trace in:

- Supplying clients with DLT-verified records of the processes a particular product went through to reach them.
- Demonstrating the legitimacy of specific products, thereby combatting the trafficking of counterfeit goods.
- Quickly tracking and detecting tainted items, allowing corporations to recognise possible dangers and take swift action.

Since the first experiment in 2016, when Barclays PLC issued the first letter of credit, concluding a 20-day transaction in four hours, trade finance players have supported numerous Blockchain proofs of concept, pilots, and industry consortia. Bank collaborations (e.g., We.Trade, Marco Polo Network, Contour, Komgo, Batavia, and CordaKYC; see also Box 13.4) have sought to build industry-wide platforms, while financial technology (FinTech) companies have used the technology for letters of credit, bills of lading, fraud detection, cross-border payments, asset distribution, and Know Your Customer (KYC) utilities.

Any digital procedure is only as robust as its weakest digital link, calling for the perfect integration of customs in many international trading systems, which is why interoperability and the development of end-to-end solutions are essential to the future of digital trade. This could be considered a weakness for developing projects running on different DLTs. Even though some governments are testing or considering implementing DLT for their customs operations and single windows to overcome these limits, most initiatives are still in the conceptual or pilot stages (Patel and Ganne 2020) or have been abandoned (see Box 13.4). Consequently, it is fair to ask why such a promising technology for this sector is encountering such difficulties getting off the ground.

The reason may not lie in the technology per se. Some (Wass 2022) argue that such projects were developed to solve supply-side issues (especially with banks) instead of firm ones, and they could then not generate a flow of demand to justify their implementation. DLT may not have changed trade finance as predicted, but the technology is still vital to the business, and the past six years of testing have not been wasted. In addition, companies such as c, Enigio, and Contour, to name but a few, are not giving up on Blockchain for their particular applications in the trade finance industry. HSBC, one of the world's largest trade finance banks, continues to see an opportunity for Blockchain technology to accelerate trade digitalisation.

Box 13.4 Trade finance use cases

Among other experiences, we cite the following main ones, balancing between projects that are still ongoing and those that have been terminated.

Contour[6] (previously known as Voltron) is an open industry[7] platform powered by Corda for the creation, trade, approval, and issuance of letters of credit. It employs a point-to-point data broadcast system, allowing the elimination of the notion of a single principal ledger, opting instead for transactional data to be shared only with those entities on the network specifically involved in the transaction. This design ensures a higher level of privacy for all nodes by sharing data strictly on a need-to-know basis. Corda connects all on-chain contracts to a conventionally recognised written legal agreement describing the intended usage of each contract by permitting the inclusion of an object within the code. This helps to eliminate any legal ambiguity around the enforceability of smart contracts. In addition, as a permissioned network, each node must be certified and associated with a registered company, thus adding an additional layer of legal accountability.

In the summer of 2019, Standard Chartered PLC successfully executed the pilot of the first Blockchain-based cross-border letter of credit (Standard Chartered Bank 2019), involving the transfer of an oil product from Thailand to Singapore, achieving a reduction in processing time and cost. In October 2020, R3 announced the acquisition of eTitle to launch Corda eBL. Corda eBL is a legal and technology toolkit that enables companies to embed negotiable title document functionality within their own applications. The toolkit, which is extensible beyond its starting point of electronic bills of lading (eBLs) to other negotiable title documents, will be natively embedded into Corda.

After the production launch at the conclusion of the third quarter of 2020, all participants were allowed to host their own nodes on the enterprise network. The application provides co-drafting applications, issuance, modifications, presentation, connectivity to digital document providers, dispute resolution, and settlements. Additionally, it uses bank-grade security safeguards. It is envisaged that the income model for Contour's permissioned platform is based on monthly subscription

---

[6] See https://contour.network/blog/letters-of-credit-how-they-work-and-the-need-for-change/ and Patel and Ganne (2020).

[7] Bangkok Bank, BNP Paribas, CTBC Bank, Citi, ING, HSBC, SEB, and Standard Chartered are some of the founding banks and major participants.

fees and volume based, instead of value-based transaction fees. Contour intends to roll out a guarantee solutions, which will be expanded to include both standby letters of credit and guarantees at its production launch. Additionally, they seek to provide a solution for document collections that uses digital documents rather than paper.

Skuchain's EC3 (Empowered Collaborative Commerce Cloud) provides end-to-end supply chain and trade finance solutions, with EDIBUS, ICF (Inventory Control and Finance), and Transaction Manager as platform applications. EDIBUS allows organisations to share electronic data interchange papers, Excel spreadsheets, CSV files, and more with their supply chain ecosystem partners while retaining field-level data privacy. ICF allows companies to access supply chain finance via Distributed Ledger Payment Commitment (DLPC), a Blockchain network payment commitment standard. Skuchain's Brackets smart contracts power the Transaction Manager. Brackets digitise and produce Blockchain-accessible trade finance documents such as letters of credit. EC3 users can write their own transaction business flows and interface with bank back offices at crucial points. This flexibility facilitates deep-tier and inventory finance. DLPCs are used instead of letters of credit.

Skuchain works with various significant mining, minerals, electronics, automotive, and fashion companies and their banks throughout Africa, Asia, Europe, South America, and the United States, since these enterprises pay membership and transaction fees to use EC3, although the platform is not geographically limited. EC3, which is based on Hyperledger Fabric, is compatible with the Corda and Ethereum networks.

TradeWaltz is a new platform developed by NTT DATA that will allow all parties[8] in the complex international trade ecosystem to share information and provide value for all users. TradeWaltz aspires to provide an information platform that safeguards international trade by facilitating the exchange of electronic documents of guaranteed authenticity in each transaction and by offering trustworthy information that users may access conveniently and securely when necessary.

---

[8] As of March 2020, the participants in TradeWaltz included MUFG Bank, Ltd., Sumitomo Mitsui Banking Corporation, Mizuho Bank, Ltd., Tokio Marine and Nichido Fire Insurance Co., Ltd., Sompo Japan Nipponkoa Insurance Inc., Mitsui Sumitomo Insurance Company, Limited, Sumitomo Corporation, Mitsubishi Corporation, Sojitz Corporation, Toyota Tsusho Corporation, Marubeni Corporation, ITOCHU Corporation, Kanematsu Corporation, Mitsui and Co., Ltd., Kawasaki Kisen Kaisha, Ltd., Nippon Express Co., Ltd., Nippon Yusen Kabushiki Kaisha, and Ocean Network Express Pte. Ltd.

We.Trade is a trade finance born as a consortium centred in Europe[9] with intentions to expand globally. We.Trade currently has a number of live products involving:

– Auto-settlement, which is the automation of payments based on pre-agreed terms.
– Bank payment undertaking (BPU), which is confirmation that the buyer's bank will make a payment to the seller, and BPU financing, a financing option for the seller based on the BPU.
– Invoice financing, which is a financing option for the seller based on a single sales invoice.

The consortium had planned to foster Resource Planning (ERP) connectivity, Application Programming Interface (API) readiness (for third party and back-office integration), more payment triggers, and the addition of partial payments/multi-payments, enhanced client directory, insurance, and logistical services. We.Trade has attracted a number of investors and member groups by collaborating with IBM to construct a permissioned network on the Hyperledger Fabric technology. In May 2022, however, We.Trade decided to discontinue its activities.

The **People's Bank of China Blockchain Trade Finance Platform** is a collection of four Blockchain applications: account receivables financing, bill rediscounting, tax filing, and international trade information collection. Before expanding its geographical scope, the People's Bank of China Blockchain Trade Finance Platform was initially introduced as the Bay Area Trade Finance Blockchain Platform. Currently, 48 banks engage in the China-centric platform, with the Bank of China, China Construction Bank Corporation, and Industrial and Commercial Bank of China as representative banks. In addition to major banks, Beijing Financial Assets Exchange has joined the network. The Digital Currency Institute of the People's Bank of China independently created the DLT technology underlying the platform. Currently, it is working on a cross-platform initiative with the Hong Kong Monetary Authority's eTradeConnect, a trade finance consortium headquartered in Hong Kong, China. eTradeConnect's link with the We. Trade network has contributed to the expansion of the platform's and its members' global reach. The permissioned platform's non-profit

[9] Member institutions included CaixaBank, Deutsche Bank, Erste Group, HSBC, KBC, Rabobank, Société Générale, UniCredit, Nordea, Santander, UBS, and IBM as shareholders, as well as UniCredit Germany, Eurobank (Greece), ČSOB (Czech Republic), Komerční banka (Czech Republic), Ceska Sporitelna (Czech Republic), and CBC Banque (Belgium).

business model enables it to concentrate on offering the most urgently required features and applications to the organisations that need them. The solution targets Small and Medium-sized Businesses (SMBs) but is not limited to trade finance. It also encompasses supply chain accounts receivables, central bank rediscounting, computerised tax filing, and international trade oversight. Hong Kong Trade Finance Platform Company Limited operates **eTradeConnect**. The DLT-based platform now provides members with products and procedures, such as purchase order and invoice preparation, pre- and post-shipment trade finance on open account trades, duplicate financing checks, and payment status updates. In the near future, eTradeConnect intends to launch cross-chain technologies that will enable interoperability across various DLT trade platforms.[10] eTradeConnect's permissioned network was developed in collaboration with Ping An Technology (Shenzhen) Co., Ltd. and Shanghai OneConnect Financial Technology Co., Ltd. utilising the Hyperledger Fabric framework.

The **Marco Polo Network**, powered by R3's Corda DLT platform, is comprised of over 30 institutions with a global presence. The network's primary objective is to promote working capital finance solutions using a decentralised trade finance platform. Currently, this consists of receivables finance and payment promises, with and without financing, as well as payables finance, with the goal of adding a payment product in the near future. In addition, it offers safe distributed data storage and accounting, identity management, and asset verification. Through the use of APIs and compatibility with legacy systems, banks may simply integrate their corporate clients' ERP systems with the Marco Polo ERP App. This reduces internal disturbances and facilitates contact with enterprise customers.

The first transactions on Marco Polo were performed in March 2019. The German banks Commerzbank and Landesbank Baden-Württemberg (LBBW) supported these transactions between the technology business Voith, the pump and valve maker KSB, and the logistics company Logwin. Over 35 financial institutions and other players, including Accenture, Microsoft, Mastercard, and Pole Star, have

---

[10] Australia and New Zealand Banking Group Limited, Bank of China (Hong Kong) Limited, Bank of East Asia Limited, DBS (Hong Kong) Limited, Hang Seng Bank Limited, Hongkong and Shanghai Banking Corporation Limited, Standard Chartered Bank (Hong Kong) Limited, Agricultural Bank of China Ltd., Hong Kong, China Branch, BNP Paribas, the Hong Kong branch of Industrial and Commercial Bank of China (Asia), and Shanghai Commercial Bank Limi are current platform participants.

joined the network since then. Even so, Marco Polo Network shelved its Blockchain-based payment commitment in 2022.

Komgo is a functional, fully decentralised network[11] for commodity trade financing built on the Quorum Blockchain. Currently, more than 150 businesses use the platform. Komgo offers three primary product categories to its customers. The first is digital trade finance-related products (including letters of credit, standby letters of credit, receivables discounting, and inventory financing), allowing commodity houses and other participants to submit digital trade data and documents to financing institutions and apply for credit directly on the platform. The second product category includes a KYC solution that standardises and simplifies the process while preserving privacy by communicating data on a need-to-know basis: users and non-users benefit from a single source of trust to exchange documents on a secure and private network to conduct KYC activities. The third product category includes a certification function that enables both Komgo users and non-users to authenticate their papers on the network. Specifically, the letter of credit and standby letter of credit product have a six-year track record, with over 20,000 letters of credit issued. As significant corporations and banks sign up, these numbers continue to increase. The permissioned Quorum framework-based Komgo has global operations with offices in Geneva and Singapore and added an office in the United States in 2021. The subscription fees and professional service fees for integration-related activities ensure the participants' profitability. Komgo is currently trying other technologies instead of a Blockchain.

There have also been a number of PoCs and pilot projects involving customs, including the US Customs and Border Protection's North American Free Trade Agreement/Central America Free Trade Agreement PoC (U.S. Customs and Border Protection 2018), the European Union Directorate-General for Taxation and Customs Union ATA Carnet PoC conducted with the International Chamber of Commerce, the Korean export clearance project (Kang 2019), and Shanghai's Single Window project. However, several of these initiatives appear to have made limited progress or have not made any evidence of their success available to the public.

---

[11] The company's investors and shareholders include Citi, ING, Credit Agricole CIB, BNP Paribas, Société Générale, ABN Amro, Macquarie, MUFG, Natixis, Rabobank, Gunvor, Mercuria, Koch, Shell, Total Trading, SGS, ConsenSys, and Jupiter Financial Opportunities Fund.

Syndicated Loans

The global syndicated loan industry relies on antiquated back-office processes, administration, paperwork, tax rules and regulations across borders, transparency and trust concerns, and integration problems between syndicate members. The outcome has been prolonged settlement periods (Fanning and Centers 2016), high overheads between various parties (banks, borrowers, agencies, and regulatory organisations), hefty fees, and high intermediary and documentation costs. The majority of the difficulty stems from the nature of the business. Furthermore, hundreds of borrowers and lenders may be involved in a single project.

The secondary loan market is a great deal more complicated. Lenders buy and sell loans with the help of several agents for different loans, using old-fashioned fax machines. Due to possible operational inefficiencies, borrowers, lenders, and loan agents have difficulty determining where they stand. Furthermore, because of flaws in recordkeeping between agents and their lenders, position breaks emerge. This causes banks to miss out on larger, more lucrative syndicated deals due to the extensive manual work and time required to execute these more sophisticated transactions. While the syndicated loan market has been sluggish to join the technological revolution that has advanced other areas of banking, attitudes throughout the industry are swiftly catching up with current trends. A recent Loan Market Association (LMA 2020) study indicates that more than 60 per cent of questioned members regard fintech as a chance to improve essential aspects of the syndicated loan process, such as document management and overall operations. Due to DLT's characteristics, the syndicated loan sector would achieve the following main benefits (Rutemberg and Wenner 2017):

– Improvement in the transparency of loans payment through smart contracts, allowing syndicate member banks to auto-disburse principal and interest; furthermore, the decentralised database assures the exchange of deal-related information (borrower financial information, KYC criteria, and project specifics) between syndicate members.
– Automation of the underwriting and due diligence process, using smart contracts.
– Better handling of documentation and administrative work, thereby eliminating intermediaries in the deal life cycle, using smart contracts that consent to manage automated event-based workflow, and creating a common automated framework that could contribute to restoring the lack of trust in rating syndicate member banks.

Box 13.5 Syndicated loan use cases

In terms of concrete experience, BBVA were the first to negotiate and sign a syndicated loan on DLT (Karppinen 2018). The transaction was arranged using a private Blockchain network in which six players had the ability to act in an agile manner: the corporation Red Eléctrica Corporación; the funding banks BBVA, as sole bookrunner, BNP Paribas, and MUFG; and the legal advisors Linklaters SLP and Herbert Smith Freehills. Solid collaboration is unquestionably crucial in these types of transactions, particularly for deploying a private network's various nodes. This transaction allowed BBVA and the other participants to share and learn from a real-world experience. All of the advantages afforded by Blockchain technology contributed to an enhanced client experience. Each negotiation step was stored in the DLT network alongside a user code and a timestamp. Then, all the nodes participating in the private Blockchain network (Hyperledger) had access to and shared the same relevant information regarding the negotiation process, ensuring the immutability of the information. Finally, once the contract was signed, a unique document identifier was recorded in Ethereum's public Blockchain network (particularly in its test network, testnet) to ensure immutability and confidentiality.

Finastra's Fusion LenderComm (Finastra 2018) is another DLT-based (R3)[12] solution for syndicated lending, supported by numerous banks, including BNY Mellon, HSBC, ING, State Street NP Paribas, Natixis, and Société Générale. The project, launched in 2017, allows the member banks to specify and publish lender-specific deal information directly from the agent bank loan servicing platforms (i.e., from Finastra's Fusion Loan IQ to Fusion LenderComm) in real time. This data were previously only periodically provided by fax by agents or through lenders' telephone or email queries.

– The use of a consensus protocol to reach agreements among syndicate stakeholders, allowing for more efficient resolutions of possible disagreements between them.

Banco Bilbao Vizcaya Argentaria (BBVA) was the first bank to deliver a syndicated loan (See Box 13.5) using DLT (Blockchain in this case), concluding around €150 million in transactions. BBVA, with its

---

[12] See *Finastra fusion lendercomm.* Available online: www.finastra.com/solutions/lending/syndicated-lending/fusion-lendercomm.

funding partners BNP Paribas and Mitsubishi UFJ Financial Group (MUFG), financed Red Eléctrica, completing the syndicated loan in record time.

Derivatives

Due to their conditional logic-based payments and delivery, derivatives are generally an ideal area for the application of smart contracts and DLTs. However, these technologies are still in development in the derivatives market, and there is no consensus on the nature of smart contracts (ISDA and Linklaters LLP 2017), how they might be used in the market, or how they might conform to legal standards and different national regulations. Most PoCs of novel technology for Over the Counter (OTC) derivative transactions focus on transaction-level events such as payment obligations and collateral transfers.

International Swaps and Derivatives Association (ISDA) has been at the forefront of the standardisation of trade documentation in the OTC derivatives market. To date, the primary emphasis has been on standardising the documentation of derivative transactions to facilitate the automation of contractual terms and the development of smart contracts. Different steps have been completed by ISDA, starting in 2017, to explore issues of legal and regulatory uncertainty as market participants have sought to apply new technologies:

– Between 2019 and 2020, several guidelines[13] were produced with the intention to explain the core principles of ISDA documentation and to raise awareness of important legal terms that should be maintained when a technology solution is applied to derivative trading.
– In 2018, ISDA developed the ISDA Common Domain Model to improve interoperability and eliminate the requirement for reconciliation. This data model provides a single common digital representation of derivative transactions and life cycle events. Adoption of this approach by businesses is anticipated to facilitate their ability to automate procedures, given that they will maintain similar records of all transactions. This model is anticipated to facilitate the creation of smart contracts.

---

[13] For guidelines on the Master Agreement, see ISDA (2019a); on collateral documentation, see ISDA (2019b); on interest rate derivatives, see ISDA (2020a); on equity derivatives, see ISDA (2020b); on credit derivatives, see ISDA (2020c); on foreign exchange, see ISDA (2020d).

- In 2020, ISDA published a clause library that provides standard drafting alternatives for the most frequently negotiated clauses of an ISDA master agreement, as well as a variety of variants for each of these provisions.
- In 2021, the ISDA Interest Rate Derivatives Definitions were written with the explicit intent of making the definitions simpler to code.

Despite these new technologies, ISDA's efforts in helping the industry advance and in providing a common foundational standards layer to support technological change and a future of frictionless (or frictionless-ish) interactions, two main issues remain to permit this sector's development on DLT platforms (Schammo 2022):

- The players must find a solution to the realisation of network effects and the presence of considerable switching costs.
- Central institutions (basically regulators) must be willing to promote the adoption of the Common Domain Model, detailing the terms under which they are willing to do so.

Some examples are summarized in Box 13.6.

Box 13.6 Derivatives use cases

An OTC interest rate derivative in the form of a digital smart derivative contract was traded by **DZ Bank** and **BayernLB** in June 2021, with the resulting payments settled daily at Deutsche Börse. The partners created the digital OTC derivative using DLT and cloud technology. A smart derivative contract digitalised the contract material and processed its conditions autonomously. DZ Bank and BayernLB functioned as trading partners, and Eurex Clearing, which is owned and operated by Deutsche Börse, acted as a neutral account manager for exposures resulting from the non-cleared OTC transaction. According to these companies, using smart derivative contracts not only makes the complicated settlement processes of OTC derivatives simpler and more expedient, but also creates an economic advantage by reducing counterparty risks and procedural uncertainties, which leads to a competitive advantage.

JP Morgan and **Baton Systems**, a specialist in DLT, have formed a partnership to collaborate in the development of a DLT-based platform that assists in the automation of derivatives margin payments. According to the partners, the service makes it possible to orchestrate cash and collateral transfers to numerous clearing houses very close to real time. It thereby promises to resolve the issue of excess funds being tied up across the clearing workflow by combining settlement instructions for custodians and other funding sources with existing optimisation and treasury systems, instead of having to dismantle technology infrastructures. Because the platform incorporates JP Morgan's own proprietary system, it is able to automate and synchronise pre-existing business procedures. Therefore, the coordination of numerous systems, reports, or spreadsheets is no longer required.

The resultant end-to-end automation of the margining and collateral operations provides full visibility of the asset movements between JP Morgan and clearing houses, along with complete audit trails and real-time notifications of any changes. According to JP Morgan and Baton Systems, there will thus be less of a need to pre-fund margin payments under the existing infrastructure of the market that is tied to margin settlements. This system has already been scaled across all of the world's clearing houses and is currently accessible for deployment across all of the major derivatives firms.

Digital Assets

Digital assets in mainstream banking offer many benefits, including the cross-industry standardisation of financial operations, improved security based on public key cryptography, and no settlement requirements when transferring the ownership of digital money or securities. However, these benefits have high adoption costs. In addition, digital assets and client private keys must be managed securely in internal systems.

Digital assets challenge business paradigms as demonstrated by commercial banks.

Consider a consumer moving from indirect bank deposits to a directly distributed ledger, e-money, or CBDC holdings. Commercial banks will still offer consumers access to these new forms of money, either directly or through commercial partners; however, the service's fees will be based on digital assets kept on shared distributed ledgers, rather than fractionally reserved deposit liabilities on their balance sheet. Commercial banks must borrow from money and bond markets to replace core retail deposits. The real-time settlement would disrupt the business models employed in foreign exchange and securities markets, where much of the liquidity for trading is based on delayed settlement and the chance to offset net transactions and save capital and funding.

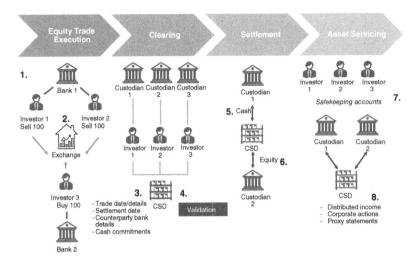

Figure 13.1 Subjects involved in the settlement and clearing of orders when using an exchange
Source: authors' elaboration.

A distributed ledger reduces asset exchange costs, opens up additional global markets, and reduces the volatility of the antiquated securities market by eliminating the intermediary in asset rights transfers. The financial markets rely on a complex network of exchanges, brokers, central security depositories, custodians, and clearinghouses. All parties preserve records based on an old paper ownership structure that is sluggish, prone to human error, and vulnerable to fraudulent conduct. Although technology has dramatically enhanced information storage and transmission, the core of the process remains primarily unchanged and requires numerous intermediaries. Most customers want to avoid self-custody and the day-to-day chores that come with it, such as protecting stock certificates, processing dividends, and bookkeeping. They therefore entrust administrators with the safeguarding of their stocks. To execute and settle trades, these custodians rely on a complicated network of exchanges, brokerages, and clearing firms. This implies that a request to buy or sell an item is routed via a slew of intermediaries. Ownership transfers are complex, because each side keeps its truth in a separate ledger (see Figure 13.1).

This method not only is ineffectual, but also has considerable potential for error and requires continual settlement. Securities transactions

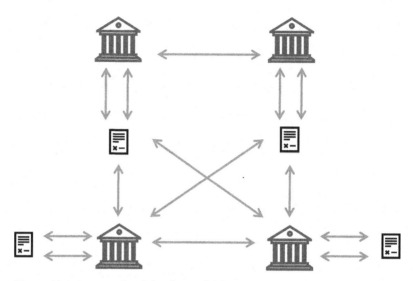

Figure 13.2 Decentralised database of different digital assets
Source: authors' elaboration.

can take three days to complete, since each party's books are separate yet must interact with the others through a sequence of checks and reconciliations. Transactions usually need human confirmation due to the presence of several participants, each one imposing a fee.

Tokenised securities can lower asset exchange costs by using DLT to remove intermediaries such as custodial institutions. DLT can revolutionise financial markets by creating a decentralised database of various digital assets. The rights to an investment asset can be swapped by using cryptographic tokens representing assets 'off chain' via a distributed ledger that operates as a centralised source of truth that each party may access (see Figure 13.2). Tokenised assets can also operate as programmable equity via smart contracts, allowing for the straightforward execution of stock buybacks and dividend payments. Finally, placing actual assets on Blockchain technology can broaden access to financial services, opening up additional global marketplaces.

Financial institutions are not standing still either. Since 2017, the Australian Stock Exchange has been collaborating with Digital Asset Holdings to replace its current accounting, clearing, and settlement system with a Blockchain solution. Following suit, HSBC announced its aim to digitise the US$20 billion records in assets under its

Table 13.5 *Major crypto legislation*

Region	Regulation/Law	Year
European Union	Markets in Crypto Asset Regulation (MiCA)	Approved. It will come into force in 2024
UK	Regulatory package on crypto-assets	April 2022 (forthcoming)
US	Presidential executive order	May 2022
Japan	Stablecoin regulation	June 2022
Canada		
Australia	Updating their crypto laws	Under processing
South Korea		

Source: authors' elaboration from Biancotti (2022).

management in 2020. The bank's Digital Vault system would 'digitise paper-based records of private placements', allowing investors to obtain real-time data on their assets.

Despite being one of the most promising parts of a distributed ledger, the most crucial impediment to tokenisation is a lack of transparent laws. Although some legislators aim to control the notion of tokens themselves, the underlying asset represented by the tokens should be the subject of legislation. Therefore, a far more extensive collection of assets may be tokenised while preserving the necessary control in each case. Digital assets provide significant regulatory concerns. Regulating permissionless distributed ledgers that enable decentralised financial and crypto-asset trade is the most crucial problem. The cypherpunk beginnings of digital assets mean that this exchange happens online, outside existing legal and regulatory borders, with no identifying individuals or institutions to regulate financial operations using digital ledger technologies. Nowadays, major governments are enacting comprehensive crypto legislation (see Table 13.5) to stimulate innovation while protecting consumers, preserving financial stability, and safeguarding monetary sovereignty.

Central banks and market regulators play critical roles in creating and enforcing the regulations, which are called to respond to critical challenges (Biancotti 2022), three in particular: (i) the first is the presence of tokens that have no claim on any entity yet are exchanged as financial assets in crypto marketplaces. This issue has

---

Box 13.7 Digital asset use cases

Fortress' focus is on evolving the NFT and Web 3.0 markets to
use NFTs to form the digital future of global asset holdings. From
in-game items to ticketing, financial instruments, and royalties, almost
everything on the globe is non-fungible. Through tokenisation using
Blockchain applications, platforms can start merging with these assets
to promote utility and transparency and establish clear ownership and
authenticity. By embedding a digital wallet into its existing mobile and
web applications, an enterprise can quickly and seamlessly add NFT
capabilities to its feature set. Doing so allows users to hold and transact
with tokenised assets of all kinds without the need to send users out of
their ecosystem to third-party wallets.

Solana, a decentralised Blockchain that allows for market-ready,
scalable apps, is a key participant in the digital asset field. It is one
of the quickest Blockchains on the market and a rapidly developing
crypto platform. Solana hosts dozens of projects, ranging from DeFi to
NFTs to Web 3.0.

---

no analogue in the old world and is intrinsically difficult to control.
(ii) The second challenge is the ecosystem's persistent dedication to
the ideals of decentralisation, anonymity, and resistance to censor-
ship. These were major aspects of cryptocurrency in the early days,
and they continue to be vital in a number of initiatives that could
bring value to investors and consumers but do not fit well with legal
systems. (iii) The third challenge involves cooperation between regulators and industry, which, although necessary to prevent obsoles-
cence and law breaking, must take on a persuasive and successful
form for all parties involved.

Some examples are summarized in Box 13.7..

Internal Processes and Operations

DLT can enable smart contracts, immutable transaction logs, and
real-time transactions, improving traditional financial institutions'
competitiveness (McKinsey and Company 2016; KPMG 2017).
Thus, if banks can integrate Blockchain DLT into their business
model to provide services, they can use it to reduce operating costs
and time. DLTs can help banks automate inter-organisational

operations, boost transparency, and reset operational benchmarks. This technology has several banking applications (Yermack 2019), derived, in particular, by enabling smart contracts, maintaining immutable transaction logs, and facilitating the real-time execution of transactions. DLT can thus be used to change how banks provide financial services and therefore offer potential benefits (in terms of cost, speed, and data integrity) over conventional methods of proving ownership.

By leveraging the positive side of Blockchain (i.e., the fact that information is disseminated and exchanged only with those who have permission and in an immutable manner, hence ensuring cybersecurity), banks can gain a number of benefits. Numerous academics and market participants (Buitenhek 2016; Guo and Liang 2016; Peters and Panayi 2016) believe that DLT could solve the majority of the issues currently plaguing traditional banking processes, such as efficiency bottlenecks, transaction lags, fraud, and operational risks, by reducing costs, enhancing process efficiency, and enhancing security (Martino 2021). The main applications of DLT to internal processes currently involve compliance and its derivations KYC and Know Your Transaction (KYT). Of course, the design of products and services based on DLT requires reengineering some processes, and DLT could be used as an opportunity to exploit the technology to render the process more convenient and more efficient. Wong and Wong (2020) have provided a notably well-organised discussion of the benefits of Blockchain development in a banking environment. They examined the opportunities and challenges associated with implementing Blockchain technology across the entire banking industry, focusing on cost savings and power efficiency.

An additional advantage of DLT for banks is access to an abundance of data. With a complete and transparent history of all client banks recorded on a distributed ledger, Blockchain may enable banks to gain quick and secure access to updated customer data, resulting in increased operational efficiency and a decrease in the time and cost required to gather and process data. Data are a crucial source for accumulating information that can give a corporation a competitive advantage (Prescott 2016) to better exploit unmet customer needs and develop new products and services. According to Sun et al. (2014), DLT not only generates considerably more data, but also makes big data more secure and valuable by storing a wider set of information in an orderly manner, in preparation for big data analytics. The following sections present some examples of the opportunities linked to the use of DLT.

Compliance

The amount of information that banks and other financial organisations must submit to regulators is growing dramatically. DLT may help in this context, since it allows regulators to efficiently access this data flow. In this respect, by automating portions of banks' business processes, DLT may also drastically lower the expenses associated with such areas as compliance, which are characterised by highly manual and paper-based processes that result in delays, inefficiencies, and heightened risks of errors and fraud (Capgemini Consulting 2016). Providing authorities with ever-increasing volumes of data from around the globe is a time-consuming chore for the financial companies and regulators that must process them, and DLT could drastically lower the costs involved. DLT may also reduce the amount of administrative effort associated with the compliance process, because both Blockchain transactions and compliance database updates are automatic. For instance, Buithenek (2016) suggests that, by enabling smart contracts, DLT could make it possible to enforce compliance upfront rather than verifying it after a transaction, drastically reducing the time and effort that financial institutions spend on regulatory reporting and enhancing the quality, accuracy, and speed of the entire process. Consequently, DLT will also lower the associated costs. This means that compliance can operate in real time with regard to the payment process (and, more generally, any banking activity), hence increasing the speed of operations and decreasing their associated expenses. In addition, Blockchain can be used to keep track of the steps required by regulations: immutably recording transactions on the distributed ledger, which decentralised the information and makes it accessible, provides a comprehensive, secure, and irreversible financial audit trail for regulators to verify compliance, thereby eliminating the need for regulators to collect, store, reconcile, and aggregate information. By allowing regulators and central banks to independently extract transaction data, banks can eliminate administrative work (Auer 2019; Martino 2021) and reduce the need to actively gather, validate, and deliver data (e.g., sending out thousands of reports).

Know Your Customer and Know Your Transaction

Identity management is a crucial component of financial services, because, as system gatekeepers, banks are responsible for preventing financial crime and fraud. KYC forms an essential element of identity management and plays a vital role in fraud prevention and tracking and combatting terrorist financing and money laundering. Although its premise seems simple, KYC is complicated and costly, with success contingent upon streamlined processes that include specific and consistent requirements. KYC procedures require an original identification document (or a copy) to help ensure authenticity; however, this requirement often makes KYC substantiation inefficient and time-consuming. The major disadvantage of traditional KYC systems is that each organisation authenticates individuals independently, and each check takes time and money. This process increases risk, because each attestation requires the transfer of personal data from the client server to an external server (Moyano and Ross 2017), where it may be intercepted and hacked. From the financial organisation's standpoint, this kind of operation is inefficient, time-consuming, and error prone, costing money and hurting clients (Capgemini 2019). Incorrect client information, a lack of visibility over customer activity, and data and privacy concerns further complicate matters. From most bank customers' standpoint, sharing information across different financial entities with different processing standards may result in frustration because of long turnaround times and redundancies that lead to inefficiency.

According to consultants and academics, DLT can speed up the KYC process and make it more secure and efficient, allowing a system to collect information from various service providers within a single cryptographically secure and unchanging database that does not need a third party to verify data authenticity. This means that, after consumers complete the KYC process with one bank, their information can be shared with other banks, eliminating duplication work and reducing the verification KYC procedures. Blockchain may enable the establishment of a chronological, decentralised, and shared data depository in which banks that need to conduct KYC processes for a customer can directly verify the result of a previous KYC process conducted for this consumer, saving time and money.

Efficiency can thus be boosted, since KYC processes are then cheaper and faster and customers can open accounts immediately, unlike in other systems. DLTs can also speed up customer onboarding and eliminate the need to repeat information to financial services providers (KPMG 2018).

All these factors are intriguing for bank profitability. If banks can integrate this technology into their business models and cut expenses, they may lower consumer commissions and increase their margins. Thus, DLT can improve client services, giving banks a competitive edge. Before DLT can deliver all its benefits, several challenges must be overcome to increase efficiency, that is, reduce costs (Martino 2021); resolve privacy concerns, since clients must authorise data exchange across institutions; and achieve interoperability (Casey et al. 2018). To scale into the financial sector, Blockchain solutions must be compatible with other ledgers and linked with existing systems. According to Moody's (2019), standardisation improves interoperability across Blockchains, Blockchain applications, and legacy information technology systems, enabling Blockchain-based ecosystems. Blockchain is beneficial only if all banks utilise the same information transmission technique. To enable Blockchain adoption and reap its benefits, collaboration is needed across industries (i.e., other financial institutions, such as insurance or non-financial enterprises) and along the value chain.

Generally, the KYC management process (Figure 13.3a) using DLT provides the following benefits to all actors involved along the entire ecosystem (Figure 13.3b).

For customers:

– Each customer retains control of his or her own identity and becomes responsible for updating the information.
– End users can quickly manage and update their own sensitive data, as well as grant their own attestations and promptly update personal information (e.g., renewing identity documents, thus improving customer experience).
– The user experience improves markedly compared to the current scenario, in which there are numerous information sources (even conflicting ones), in which the customer must act as an intermediary between the different obligated parties (overcoming the problems related to the need to use reliable and suitable sources).

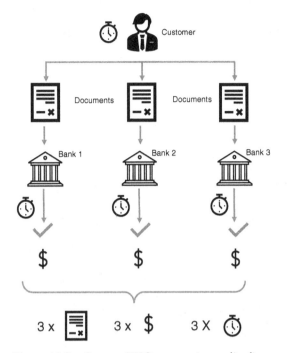

Figure 13.3a Current KYC process (centralised)
Source: authors' elaboration.

For entities:

- Obligated entities participating in the network have direct access to the repository containing verified credentials, without having to exchange information among themselves, as is the case in the current scenario. In this sense, obligated parties assume the role of both verifiers of credentials and users of credentials at the same time (overcoming the problems associated with data repositories).
- Depending on the design of the solution, it is possible to limit access to the shared repository of KYC dossiers to only circuit members, benefiting from the reduction in time and cost in the management and execution of the KYC process, including the exercise of constant control (overcoming the problems related to the need to always have up-to-date data).
- Other entities can be allowed to join the new business network, enabling the disposal of part or all of the information on prospective

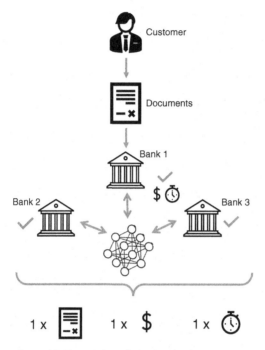

Figure 13.3b KYC with DLT
Source: authors' elaboration.

customers in a more flexible and secure manner to provide some of their services (so-called KYC sharing, which would certainly lead to improved customer experience).

Some examples are summarized in Box 13.8.

Know Your Transaction, or KYT, is a term used in the financial industry to refer to the evaluation of financial transactions for fraudulent or suspicious activities, such as money laundering. As Bitcoin adoption increases, it is crucial for institutions to be able to delve deeply into cryptocurrency transactions in search of proof of financial crimes. Financial institutions must appreciate that financial transactions frequently involve bits of information that are difficult to follow. Examples of financial signals include clearances, bills, and even regulatory paperwork. Such messages must be meticulously maintained with their corresponding record, which is later utilised for auditing, whether for anti-money laundering (AML) or investigative purposes. As reported above, compliance procedures are time-consuming and complicated. Due to increased difficulties in data retrieval, limited due

---

Box 13.8 KYC use cases

From North America to Europe and Asia, governments and banks are paying closer attention to DLT for potential KYC use cases in financial services.

In 2018, 39 organisations (including BNP Paribas, Deutsche Bank, and China Merchants Bank) conducted a global trial of KYC using **R3's Corda Blockchain platform** to run distributed applications on a hybrid architecture of private and public Blockchains (Finextra 2018).

The **Hong Kong Monetary Authority**, for instance, is investigating the use of a decentralised database and functionality to improve paper-based and labour- and time-intensive trade finance operations. Participants in the decentralised database share customer information and transaction histories while protecting privacy and secrecy, as required (Lannquist 2019).

Capgemini's new KYC platform makes KYC transactions immutable, secure, traceable, and efficient, allowing partners to onboard faster and avoid repeating information. R3's Corda protocol powers the platform and Corda gives banks and corporations trusted onboarding. This onboarding technology improves trust, efficiency, and costs for financial institutions. Corporates may onboard faster and avoid repeating information (Sevilla 2019).

At the European level, the European Blockchain Service Infrastructure (EBSI),[14] launched in August 2019, developed a use case for individual identification based on self-sovereign identity logic (Du Seuil 2019), called **EBSI Verifiable Credentials**. EBSI is building data models based on the World Wide Web Consortium's Verifiable Credentials (VC) and Verifiable Presentations (VP). VC define the structure of the data, while VP provide the data model for presenting and exchanging the data. VC and VP represent the standard to which all digital documents conform to improve the efficiency, interoperability, and readability of all documents/certificates.[15]

HSBC, OCBC Bank Singapore, and **Mitsubishi UFJ Financial Group (MUFG)** have partnered with Singapore's Infocomm Media Development Authority to develop a KYC PoC that enables structured information to be recorded, accessed, and shared over a distributed network using advanced cryptography (Mui 2017).

---

[14] EBSI, created in 2018, aims to leverage the power of Blockchain for the public good. EBSI is an initiative of the European Commission and the European Blockchain Partnership.

[15] For further information see *EBSI W3C Verifiable Credentials (VCs) and W3C Verifiable Presentations (VPs)* available online: www.ec.europa.eu/digital-building-blocks/wikis/pages/viewpage.action?pageId=555222155.

diligence methods, and insufficient transaction monitoring systems, financial institutions confront challenging circumstances.

Considering these difficulties, experts have proposed the KYT concept, which entails financial institutions handling more precise, comprehensive, and granular transaction-specific data sets. KYT can be seen as a tool that offers businesses with vital analysis to detect and identify suspicious fraudulent customer transactions based on customer accounts and profiles. An efficient KYT system allows financial institutions to detect suspicious activity by integrating customers' profiles with their personal transactions. As part of the transaction analysis process, the KYT solution supports banks in monitoring and drilling down into transactions to discover suspicious behaviours or fraudulent transactions. This analysis is performed internally on bank data. The findings of the procedure serve as trustworthy evidence, enabling institutions to protect themselves from fraud and regulatory sanctions. The emphasis of cryptocurrencies and Blockchain technology is not on the individual, but, rather, on the entity or transaction, its historical attributions, and its links. Using Blockchain, it is not possible to monitor a client, but it is possible to observe the transfer of funds through an address to assess the transaction's legitimacy and validity. Therefore, as banks and financial institutions become more involved with digital assets, whether directly as a service provider or indirectly as a digital asset account manager, they will need to consider gaining a deeper understanding of transactions and fund flows on the Blockchain, in addition to enhancing KYC due diligence with KYT compliance procedures (Pokrovskaia et al. 2022). Examples of providers of this kind of service are Chainalysis, Scorechain, and Sanction Scanner.

Concluding Thoughts: Is DLT Truly Revolutionising the Industry?

Over the past decade, DLT has attracted considerable attention, surpassing the acclaim of minority cryptocurrency enthusiasts and entering the mainstream discourse of professionals and investors, particularly in the banking and financial services industries. According to a recent analysis by Grand View Research, the worldwide Blockchain technology market size is projected to reach US$1.432 trillion by 2030, expanding at a compound annual growth rate CAGR of 85.9 per cent from 2022 to 2030. As presented in this book, DLT designers have produced exciting and beneficial projects for the financial sector. Based on earlier contributions (Buitenhek 2016; Guo and Liang 2016; Peters and Panayi 2016), applying DLT can solve some of the issues associated with the financial services industry (e.g., rising costs of operations, inefficiency bottlenecks, transaction lags, fraud, and operational risks) and contribute to enlarging or renovating the supply of products and services, even in different dimensions (i.e., the metaverse; see Chapter 12). As stated previously (see Chapter 11), DLTs can enable banks to enter new market segments (i.e., unbanked, and underbanked populations, as well as Millennials and Generation Z) and thus reach large numbers of potential clients and develop additional revenue streams. DLT may increase the efficiency of the procedures underlying the provision of financial services, hence encouraging the provision of higher-quality services, thereby posing new risks to banks' businesses. It may also facilitate the entry of new operators, thus expanding the competitive environment (Zhao et al. 2016).

The benefits of Blockchain technology include accuracy, traceability, transparency, cost savings, and data integrity (Sun et al. 2014). The beginnings of DLT can be traced back to the development of Blockchain in response to the 2008 financial crisis. DLT has the potential to lower costs for banks, as highlighted by Wang et al. (2019), decreasing transaction and processing fees.

After emphasising the potential benefits of DLT application in banking, we note that, despite the benefits presented by academics and operators, this technology faces challenges in achieving what was previously described as a revolution. According to Beck (2018), the banking industry is not entirely prepared to maximise the benefits DLT can offer. This is partly because banks either did not consider DLT to be legitimate or saw it at first as something that could delegitimise their role, leading to DeFi.

DLTs in their declination on the blocks are inherently public due to the existence of public Blockchains such as Bitcoin and Ethereum, which are frequently portrayed as the only type of Blockchain or DLT. This statement is untrue. Other Blockchain types include permissionless, permissioned, consortium, and hybrid Blockchains, which vary in structure, the degree of decentralisation, and other essential Blockchain principles.

New technologies generally expose banks to different models of competition. Competitors are likely to increase their investments in a new technology, given that numerous FinTech firms have emerged and made it cheaper to open bank accounts. The adoption of DLT might, therefore, be a way to influence banking market conditions to improve competitiveness and enable big data to provide recommendations for formulating business strategies.

Any technology, including DLT, that promises seamless industrial interactions depends on how well it is deployed. Thus, more users in a network means greater amount of frictionless data recording, greater administration, and more digital asset transfers. Under these conditions, value cannot be separated from usership, and value propositions that focus only on a technology's alleged ability to enable frictionless interactions are better viewed as referring to an expected value, that is, an anticipated value that depends on wide adoption. DLT, like other network effect-driven technologies, has value beyond its characteristics. Adopters boost network value. New technology adoption may be hindered by network effects. Externalities[16] can also slow technological adoption. Thus, expectations affect outcomes. 'If players expect others to adopt, they too will adopt' (Farrell and Klemperer 2007) is a phrase that determines network product performance in network effect markets. If a critical mass of users joins a network or if more adoption is confidently expected, 'further self-reinforcing adoption follows' (Katz and Shapiro 1994). Thus, 'tippy' markets with large network effects can favour one dominant technology or provider, creating winner-takes-all dynamics.

Switching costs are especially important in the financial/banking sector, which is data intensive and uses hardware and software to capture, process, and communicate data. Regarding these costs, it is important to emphasise that financial firms generally own complicated information technology infrastructures, often including old and new systems that work together. Data processing and recording systems contain multiple data models, since there are no industry standards. Replacing this integrated hardware and software may therefore be quite expensive. Infrastructure modifications may also lead to high learning costs and the disruption of operations. This makes switching to incompatible technologies difficult and locks users into legacy systems and infrastructure.

---

[16] Highlighting this issue in a securities markets context, see Ahdieh (2003).

DLT in banking can be considered both a revolutionary and evolutionary technology. On the one hand, it has the potential to completely disrupt traditional banking practices by changing the way financial transactions are conducted, processed, and recorded. On the other hand, DLT is also building upon existing technologies, such as databases and cryptography, and can be seen as an evolution of these technologies. Implementing DLT in banking is also likely to be an evolutionary process as financial institutions gradually adopt and integrate the technology into their existing systems. This process will likely involve a mix of revolutionary changes, such as the adoption of entirely new business models, and evolutionary changes, such as the gradual integration of DLT into existing systems and processes.

References

Ahdieh, R. 2003. 'Making markets: Network effects and the role of law in the creation of strong securities markets'. *Southern California Law Review* 76, 277–350.

Auer, R. 2019. 'Embedded supervision: How to build regulation into blockchain finance'. *Globalization and Monetary Policy Institute Working Paper*, 371.

Aversa, J., Hernandez, T., and Doherty, S. 2021. 'Incorporating big data within retail organizations: A case study approach'. *Journal of Retailing and Consumer Services*, 60, 102447.

Bank of Canada and Monetary Authority of Singapore (BOC and MAS) 2019. 'Jasper-Ubin Design Paper: Enabling Cross-Border High Value Transfer Using Distributed Ledger Technologies'. *Accenture – J.P. Morgan*. Available online: www.mas.gov.sg/-/media/Jasper-Ubin-Design-Paper.pdf.

Bank of Canada, Bank of England, and Monetary Authority of Singapore (BOC, BOE, and MAS) 2018. 'Cross-border interbank payments and settlements: Emerging opportunities for digital transformation'. Available online: www.mas.gov.sg/-/media/MAS/ProjectUbin/Cross-Border-Interbank-Payments-and-Settlements.pdf.

Banque de France. 2018. 'Payments and market infrastructures in the digital era'. Available online: www.publications.banque-france.fr/sites/default/files/media/2021/01/07/payments_market.pdf.

Bechtel, A., Ferreira, A., Gross, J., and Sandner, P. 2022. 'The future of payments in a DLT-based European economy: A roadmap'. In Springer (ed.), *The Future of Financial Systems in the Digital Age: Perspectives from Europe and Japan* (pp. 89–116). Singapore: Springer Singapore.

BECK, R. 2018. 'Beyond bitcoin: The rise of blockchain world'. *Computer*, 2018, 51.2: 54–58.

Biancotti, C. 2022. 'What's next for crypto?'. Questioni di Economia e Finanza, 711. Bank of Italy. Available online: www.bancaditalia.it/pubblicazioni/qef/2022-0711/QEF_711_22.pdf?language_id=1.

Boumlik, A., and Bahaj, M. 2018. 'Big data and iot: A prime opportunity for banking industry'. In *Advanced Information Technology, Services and Systems: Proceedings of the International Conference on Advanced Information Technology, Services and Systems (AIT2S-17)*. April 2017 (pp. 396–407). Tangier: Springer International Publishing.

Buitenhek, M. 2016. 'Understanding and applying Blockchain technology in banking: Evolution or revolution?'. *Journal of Digital Banking*, 1(2), 111–119.

Capgemini 2019. 'Capgemini Retail Banking Top Trends report, 2019'. *Capgemini Financial Services Analysis*. Available online: www.capgemini.com/wp-content/uploads/2018/11/Top-10-Trends-in-Retail-Banking-2019-Infographic.pdf.

Capgemini Consulting 2016. 'Smart contracts in financial services: Getting from hype to reality'. *Technical Report*. Available online: www.capgemini.com/consulting-de/wp-content/uploads/sites/32/2017/08/smart_contracts_paper_long_0.pdf.

Casey, M., Crane, J., Gensler, G., Johnson, S., and Narula, N. 2018. 'The impact of blockchain technology on finance: A catalyst for change'. *International Center For Monetary and Banking Studies*. Available online: www.cepr.org/system/files/publication-files/60142-geneva_21_the_impact_of_blockchain_technology_on_finance_a_catalyst_for_change.pdf.

Cong, L. W., and He, Z. 2019. 'Blockchain disruption and smart contracts'. *The Review of Financial Studies*, 32(5), 1754–1797.

Deloitte. 2021. 'Deloitte's 2021 Global Blockchain Survey'. Available online: www2.deloitte.com/us/en/insights/topics/understanding-Blockchain-potential/global-Blockchain-survey.html.

Dixon, D. 2021. 'How Blockchain technology is fixing payments and what's next'. *World Economic Forum*. Available online: www.weforum.org/agenda/2021/04/how-Blockchain-technology-is-fixing-payments-today-what-comes-next.

Du Seuil, D. 2019. 'European Self Sovereign identity framework'. Available online: www.eesc.europa.eu/sites/default/files/files/1._panel_-_daniel_du_seuil.pdf.

Fanning, K., and Centers, D. P. 2016. 'Blockchain and its coming impact on financial services'. *Journal of Corporate Accounting and Finance*, 27(5), 53–57.

Farrell, J., and Klemperer, P. 2007. 'Coordination and lock-in: Competition with switching costs and network effects', In Armstrong, M., and Porter, R. (eds.), *Handbook of Industrial Organization Volume 3*, (pp. 2019–20). Oxford, UK: Elsevier.

Finastra 2018. 'A new era for syndicated lending'. Available online: www .finastra.com/solutions/lending/syndicated-lending/fusion-lendercomm.

Finextra. 2018. 'Banks trial KYC on R3 Corda Blockchain platform', June 28. Available online: www.finextra.com/newsarticle/32328/banks-trial-kyc-on-r3-corda-Blockchain-platform.

Financial Stability Board - 2022. 'Assessment of risks to financial stability from crypto-assets'. *Reports to the G20*. Available online: www.fsb.org/2022/02/assessment-of-risks-to-financial-stability-from-crypto-assets/.

Guo, Y., and Liang, C. 2016. 'Blockchain application and outlook in the banking industry'. *Financial Innovation*, 2(1), 1–12.

Holotiuk, F., Pisani, F., and Moormann, J. 2017. 'The impact of blockchain technology on business models in the payments industry, In Leimeister, J.M., Brenner, W. (Hrsg.), (eds.),'. In *Proceedings of 13th International Conference on Wirtschaftsinformatik*, St. Gallen, S. 912–926, Switzerland.

Iansiti, M., and Lakhani, K. 2017. 'The truth about blockchain'. *Harvard Business Review*, 2017, 95(1), 118–127.

ISDA. 2019a. 'Legal guidelines for smart derivatives contracts: The ISDA master agreement'. Available online: www.isda.org/a/23iME/Legal-Guidelines -for-Smart-Derivatives-Contracts-ISDA-Master-Agreement.pdf.

ISDA. 2019b. 'Legal guidelines for smart derivatives contracts: Collateral'. Available online: www.isda.org/a/VTkTE/Legal-Guidelines-for-Smart-Derivatives-Contracts-Collateral.pdf.

ISDA 2020a. 'Legal guidelines for smart derivatives contracts: Interest rate derivatives'. Available online: www.isda.org/a/I7XTE/ISDA-Legal-Guidelines-for-Smart-Derivatives-Contracts-IRDs.pdf.

ISDA. 2020b. 'Legal guidelines for smart derivatives contracts: Equity derivatives'. Available online: www.isda.org/a/CLXTE/ISDA-Legal-Guidelines-for-Smart-Derivatives-Contracts-Equities.pdf.

ISDA. 2020c. 'Legal guidelines for smart derivatives contracts: Credit derivatives'. Available online: www.isda.org/2020/11/03/legal-guidelines-for-smart-derivatives-contracts-cds.

ISDA. 2020d. 'Legal guidelines for smart derivatives contracts: Foreign exchange derivatives'. Available online: www.isda.org/a/bPYTE/ISDA-Legal-Guidelines-for-Smart-Derivatives-Contracts-FX.pdf.

ISDA and Linklaters LLP. 2017. 'Smart contracts and distributed ledger – A legal perspective'. Available online: www.isda.org/a/6EKDE/smart-contractsanddistributed-ledger-a-legal-perspective.pdf.

ISDB 2021. 'Future of finance: Redefining the role of finance in an industry 4.0 world'. *Islamic Development Bank*. Available online: www.isdb .org/sites/default/files/media/documents/2022-03/IsDB_Finance English 22JAN-1.pdf.

Kang, T. I. 2019. 'Korea pilots Blockchain technology as it prepares for the future'. Available online: www.mag.wcoomd.org/magazine/wco-news-88/ korea-pilots-Blockchain-technology-as-it-prepares-for-the-future/.

Karppinen, U. 2018. 'BBVA signs world-first Blockchain-based syndicated loan arrangement with Red Eléctrica Corporación'. *Banco Bilbao Vizcaya Argentaria*. Available online: www.bbva.com/en/bbva-signs-world-first-Blockchain-based-syndicated-loan-arrangement-with-red-electrica-corporacion/.

Katz, M. L., and Shapiro, C. 1994. 'Systems competition and network effects'. *Journal of economic perspectives*, 8(2), 93–115.

Kavuri, A.S, and Milne, A.K.L. 2020. 'Evolution or revolution? Distributed ledger technologies in financial services'. *CAMA Working Paper*, No. 4/2020. Available online: www.ssrn.com/abstract=3527192.

KPMG 2017. 'Blockchain in financial services: A threat or an opportunity'.

KPMG 2018. 'Could blockchain be the foundation of a viable KYC utility?'. KPMG International. Available online: www.assets.kpmg.com/content/ dam/kpmg/xx/pdf/2018/03/kpmg-blockchain-kyc-utility.pdf.

Lang, J. 2017. 'Blockchain in financial services. Three uses for blockchain in banking'. *Blockchain Unleashed: IBM Blockchain Blog*. Available online: www.ibm.com/blogs/blockchain/2017/10/three-uses-for-blockchain-in-banking/.

Lannquist, A. 2019. '10 ways central banks are experimenting with Blockchain', April 3. *World Economic Forum*. Available online: www.weforum .org/agenda/2019/04/Blockchain-distrubuted-ledger-technology-central-banks-10-ways-research.

Lewis, R., McPartland, J., and Ranjan 2017. 'Blockchain and financial market innovation' *Economic Perspectives*, 41(7) 1–17.

Loan Market Association (LMA) 2020. 'Guide to syndicated loans and leveraged finance transactions', July. Available online: www.silo.tips/ download/guide-to-syndicated-leveraged-finance.

Mansour, A., Bedoui, H.E., Pandey, I., Youssef, N., and Roshann, R. 2021. 'Strategies for adopting DLT/ Blockchain technologies in Arab countries'. *Arab Monetary Fund – Arab Regional Fintech Working Group*. Available online: www.amf.org.ae/sites/default/files/publications/2021-12/ strategies-adopting-dlt-blockchain-technologies-arab-countries.pdf.

Martino, P. 2021. 'Blockchain and banking: How technological innovations are shaping the banking industry'. *Springer Nature*.

McKinsey and Company 2016. 'How blockchains could change the world'. Available online: www.mckinsey.com/industries/technology-media-and-telecommunications/our-insights/how-blockchains-could-change-the-world.

Moody's 2019. 'Moody's – Blockchain standardisation will amplify benefits for securitisations'. Available online: www.moodys.com/researchdocu mentcontentpage.aspx?docid=PBS_1180810.

Morkunas, V. J., Paschen, J., and Boon, E. 2019. 'How Blockchain technologies impact your business model'. *Business Horizons*, 62(3), 295–306.

Moyano, J., Omri, P., and Omri, R. 2017. 'KYC optimization using distributed ledger technology'. *Business and Information Systems Engineering*, 59(6), 411–423.

Mui, R. 2017. 'Singapore regulator, OCBC, HSBC, MUFG create 'know your customer' Blockchain prototype'. *The Business Times*. Available online: www.businesstimes.com.sg/banking-finance/singapore-regulator-ocbc-hsbc-mufg-create-know-your-customer-Blockchain-prototype.

Nowiński, W., and Kozma, M. 2017. 'How can blockchain technology disrupt the existing business models?'. *Entrepreneurial Business and Economics Review*, 5(3), 173–188.

Patel, D., and Ganne, E. 2020. 'Blockchain and DLT in trade: Where do we stand'. *Trade Finance Global*, 52.

Perrazzelli, A. 2023. 'Blockchain and Web3: time to build'. *Intervention by Alessandra Perrazzelli, Deputy Director General of the Bank of Italy*. Milan.

Peters, G., and Panayi, E. 2016. 'Understanding modern banking ledgers through Blockchain technologies: Future of transaction processing and smart contracts on the internet of money'. in P. Tasca, T. Aste, L. Pelizzon, N. Perony (Eds.), *Banking beyond banks and money. New economic windows*. Cham: Springer, 239–278.

Philippon, T. 2016. 'The fintech opportunity (No. w22476)'. *National Bureau of Economic Research*.

Pokrovskaia, N. N., Rodionova, E. A., Fomina, I. G., Epshtein, M. Z., and Fedorov, D. A. 2022. 'Blockchain and smart contracting in the context of digital transformation of service', *2022 Conference of Russian Young Researchers in Electrical and Electronic Engineering (ElConRus)*.

Prescott, M. E. 2016. 'Big data: Innovation and competitive advantage in an information media analytics company'. *Journal of Innovation Management*, 4(1), 92–113.

Rauchs, M., Blandin, A., Bear, K., and McKeon, S.B. 2019. '2nd global enterprise blockchain benchmarking study'. Available online: www.ssrn.com/abstract=3461765.

Rutenberg, S.A., and Wenner, R. W. 2017. 'Blockchain technology: A syndicated loan revolution?'. *Financial Technology (FinTech) and Regulation*. Available online: www.sftp.polsinelli.com/ublications/fintech/resources/upd0717fin.pdf.

Schammo, P. 2022. 'Of standards and technology: ISDA and technological change in the OTC derivatives market'. *Law and Financial Markets Review*, 15(1–2), 3–37.

Sevilla, M. 2019. 'A next-generation data exchange platform for KYC and supplier onboarding'. *Capgemini.* Available online: www.capgemini.com/insights/expert-perspectives/a-next-generation-data-exchange-platform-for-kyc-and-supplier-onboarding/.

Shabsigh, M. G., Khiaonarong, M. T., and Leinonen, M. H. 2020. 'Distributed ledger technology experiments in payments and settlements'. *International Monetary Fund.*

Standard Chartered Bank 2019. 'We've completed our first cross-border Letter of Credit Blockchain transaction in the oil industry with PTT Group'. Press release. Available online: www.sc.com/en/media/press-release/weve-completed-our-first-cross-border-letter-of-credit-Blockchain-transaction-in-the-oil-industry-with-ptt-group.

Sun, N., Morris, J. G., Xu, J., Zhu, X., and Xie, M. 2014. 'iCARE: A framework for big data-based banking customer analytics'. *IBM Journal of Research and Development*, 58(5/6), 4–1.

Taylor, P. 2022. 'Worldwide Blockchain market value share 2020, by sector'. *Statista.* Available online: www.statista.com/statistics/804775/worldwide-marketshare-of-Blockchain-by-sector.

U. S. Customs and Border Protection 2018. 'NAFTA/CAFTA proof of concept assessment'. Available online: www.cbp.gov/sites/default/files/assets/documents/2019-Oct/Final-NAFTA-CAFTA-Report.pdf.

Wang, S., Ouyang, L., Yuan, Y., Ni, X., Han, X., and Wang, F. Y. 2019. 'Blockchain-enabled smart contracts: Architecture, applications, and future trends'. *IEEE Transactions on Systems, Man, and Cybernetics: Systems*, 49(11), 2266–2277.

Wass, S. 2022. 'Trade finance industry remains hopeful on Blockchain despite failed projects'. *S&P Global Market Intelligence.* Available online: www.spglobal.com/marketintelligence/en/news-insights/latest-news-headlines/trade-finance-industry-remains-hopeful-on-Blockchain-despite-failed-projects-72557910.

Wong, K.Y., and Wong, R.K., 2020. 'Big data quality prediction on banking applications'. *International Conference on Data Science and Advanced Analytics (DSAA).* 791–792.

Wright, S. A. 2019. 'Privacy in IoT Blockchains: With big data comes big responsibility'. In *2019 IEEE International Conference on Big Data (Big Data)*, pp. 5282–5291.

Wu, T., and Liang, X. 2017. 'Exploration and practice of inter-bank application based on blockchain'. *International conference on computer science and education*. IEEE, 219–224.

Yermack, D., and Fingerhut, A. 2019. 'Blockchain technology's potential in the financial system'. In *Proceedings of the 2019 Financial Market's Conference*.

Zhao, J. L., Fan, S., and Yan, J. 2016. 'Overview of business innovations and research opportunities in Blockchain and introduction to the special issue'. *Financial Innovation*, 2(1), 1–7.

Index

Printed in the United States
by Baker & Taylor Publisher Services